92 Pies

92 Clubs
92 Grounds
92 Games
1 Season
1 Huge Aventure

Tom Dickinson

Blackline|Press

First Published in 2011 by **Blackline Press**
Copyright © 2011 Blackline Press
Copyright in text & photographs © 2011 Tom Dickinson
Cover design by Allium Graphics www.alliumgraphics.co.uk

ISBN 978-0-9563238-4-2

www.blacklinepress.com
Blackline Press,15 Lister Road,IPSWICH IP1 5EQ
info@blacklinepress.com

92 Pies

92 Clubs
92 Grounds
92 Games
1 Season
1 Huge Adventure

Tom Dickinson

92 Pies
Contents

Foreword

by

Brian Blessed

This book is a celebration.

What a fabulous, astonishing achievement! What vision. What imagination. It is decades since I have been so inspired by such an author.

'92 Pies' was an epic mission in which Tom Dickinson successfully watched a game and ate a pie at every one of the 92 football league stadiums in the 2008/2009 season.

It took him 9 months to watch 138 hours of live football spending over £3000 and driving the equivalent mileage of London to Sydney and back.

It is a tour-de-force; one fan's journey in search of football's soul. It is such a gigantic task that one is inclined to conclude it to be beyond the efforts of any mere mortal. Not so!

Dickinson achieves his goal and rivets the attention all the way with a spellbinding story full of courage and tenacity.

His love of football is like the dawn – self evident. The flamboyant author writes with an unrestrained passion and simplicity, building on a natural knack for storytelling. He brings something new and original into the subject matter.

In the vast theatre of soccer he embraces the twin masks of comedy and tragedy.

As a young boy of 10 years I lived in a tiny coal mining village called Goldthorpe, halfway between Barnsley and Doncaster.

In 1948 at Wembley Stadium Manchester United beat Stanley Matthews' Blackpool 4-2 in the FA Cup Final. We heard the match on the radio (there was no television) and saw it later on in the cinema.

As junior infants we had just won the 'totty' cup in the Dearne valley, and days later we could not believe our eyes when we observed Manchester United kicking a ball around on our infant school ground.

They were on their way to play Sheffield Wednesday in their last match of the season. In mad excitement I immediately ran over to the team and asked if we could play them. The captain Johnny Carey smiled and nodded approval.

10 minutes later we were in our school football kit. And after ½ hour of play we beat them 26-0!

I tell you, Manchester United, we beat them! Of course later on nobody believed us. That wonderful sacred experience has remained hidden in my secret place until the moment I read Tom Dickinson's wonderful book.

Due to its magical influence my heart, soul and mind can once again dance the light fantastic.

Brian Blessed.

PROLOGUE

9th February 2008, Harpenden, Hertfordshire.

I was slumped on my sofa. It was 10.28pm. 'If you don't want to know the scores, look away now'. I already knew the scores so I didn't look away. 2 minutes. Weather. It will be overcast tomorrow with showers in North-East England. Hurry up. Here it was. Yesss! The Match of the Day theme tune! The *best* theme tune. Normally a fool-proof method to cheer me up, but not today. I knew Bolton lost 1-0 at home to Portsmouth, leaving us in the almost catastrophic 19th spot with only 11 league games to go. Bolton were depressing me, I was carrying the weight of the underperforming team on my shoulders.

The Bolton highlights were predictably last on the *Match of the Day* running order, even behind Sunderland v Wigan. My friend John, looking particularly scruffy and unshaven, was lying on a beanbag with a beer in his hand, laughing at my distress.

"Look how depressing this is." I moaned as our beanpole right-back Nicky Hunt mis-kicked a shot out for a throw-in.

"It doesn't look *too* bad..." John tried to reason.

"Ugh! Look at the crowd. It's dead. The Reebok looks half empty." I said.

"Or half full..."

"Forever the optimist aren't you?"

The camera panned to a shot of the Bolton manager Gary Megson (AKA the 'Ginger Mourinho') wiping his nose and shouting, before spitting out his chewing gum but getting it half-caught on his chin.

"How uninspiring is this man?!?!" I gesticulated at the TV. "We need Sam Allardyce back pronto."

"Big Sam is the worst manager ever to grace the Premier League." John said, just to rile me. He knows how much I love that man.

"He's an idiot. Remember that season he played Henrik Pedersen at left-back?" I wasn't going to rise to John's attempts to bate me. Diarra scored the only goal of the game for Portsmouth, a scuffed deflected effort. I threw a cushion at the TV. I wasn't in a good mood.

"Well that was crap."

"Stop moaning," said John, "you're still in the Premier League, all's not lost yet! I went to see Luton last week, saw them lose 4-1 at home to Bournemouth. *AND* they've just had the 10-point deduction leaving them bottom of the league, plus all those financial enquiries..."

"And they're based in Luton." I added.

"Exactly! It could be worse for Bolton. Have you been to a lower-league game recently?"

"No. Not for ages." I thought for a moment. "In fact I haven't been to a game of any kind in about a year."

John tutted at me.

"So has it all fizzled out now then? Have Bolton driven you over the edge?!"

I scoffed at John's suggestion. But he was right. What had happened to make me so bloody negative about our beautiful game?

John got up and let rip a world-beating fart.

"Whoops! One for the scrap-book! You should get to more games T. Maybe that will change your outlook," he said leaving the room, before coming back with a copy of *The Sun* from a couple of weeks ago.

"Look at this bloke," pointed John. I started reading Britain's best-selling un-quality daily.

COLIN'S IN A LEAGUE OF HIS OWN!
Passionate Pompey fan Colin Gefferey has made the ultimate football pilgrimage – spending 27 years, over £7,000 and driving 33,000 miles visiting ALL 92 football grounds in the English League. Gas engineer Colin, one of the newest members of the exclusive '92 Club' said: "The addiction is the feeling of walking in the new ground, through the turnstile, looking at the pitch and seeing the players warm up."

"THAT is a football fan. He puts us to shame! How many grounds have you been to? Think I've only done about 10," said John.

I did some quick counting. "13 of the current 92 I think. Plus 4 old demolished grounds and a couple of non-league."

"That's a dismal effort."

I looked at the *Sun* article again.

"Yeah but this bloke Colin took 27 years to see the 92 so that's only three new grounds per season. How does that deserve a half-page spread in the paper?"

My mind started whirring.

"To do all 92 *in one season*. That would be newspaper-worthy!"

John was eating his dinner, a disgusting looking meat and potato pie, straight from the prestigious 'Whoops' reduced-stickered section of ASDA . John and I have a philosophy that a pie and football must always go hand-in-hand, even when you're not at the match.

"Impossible," he said, small chunks of meat flying from his mouth, "but this pie's good. 29p well spent."

I thought for a minute and did some calculations in my head.

"Forget the pie for a sec. A season's about 40 weeks long, so to do it would mean just over 2 games per week. Maybe I should do it to prove you wrong."

"Even if it is possible you're clearly the wrong man to do it!" argued John. "If you haven't been to a single match this season then you hardly have the credentials to do all 92! I would bet you anything you like that you can't do it. I even would get down on my knees and admit to you that Sam Allardyce is a misunderstood tactical genius."

There was a painful truth to what John was saying. I'd always thought of myself as a decent football fan, but maybe I wasn't. Was the impossible becoming a reality? Was I actually falling out of love with the game I adored so much?

Football first entered my radar during Euro '96. There was something very special about that tournament. All my friends at school were going wild in the build up to it at the end of a hot summer term, but I didn't really see what all the fuss was about. I had never really been into football, but once England kicked the tournament off something changed.

It was all so exciting. Three Lions on a shirt! For the first time I could see what every other boy loved about football. Shearer and Sheringham destroying the Dutch, Seaman's heroics from the penalty spot. And then it all got so cruelly destroyed. Gazza missing that ball by an inch against Germany still makes me wince thinking about it today. And of course I felt the required passionate hatred towards the pantomime villains of the piece in Southgate and the German Kuntz.

Despite the tournament ending in heartbreak for England, I made a conscious decision to become a football fanatic. The main problem being that I didn't have a club to support. With my parents not really following any particular team I turned to my Bolton born-and-bred Godfather Chris for advice.

Chris is a passionate white-haired Lancastrian, a supremely intelligent man who could possibly have conquered the world if it were not for his one terrible vice (football). After Chris flirted with the idea of maybe attending the 1986 World Cup in Mexico, his stunning girlfriend, the love of his life, gave him the ultimatum of staying in England and marrying her or going to Mexico but she would finish with him.

He chose the World Cup.

Of course.

"There's only one team to follow young Tom," Chris wisely said to the young me in his softly reassuring Lancashire accent, "and that's Bolton Wanderers."

I nodded in enthusiastic agreement. Wow! Bolton Wanderers. They sounded so *exotic*. I made an oath that day to follow Bolton through thick and thin, but in retrospect perhaps I should have made a couple of checks first. Like the fact that Bolton is over 200 miles away from my home in Hertfordshire. Or that the team had just finished bottom of the Premiership with a record low points total.

Chris took me to see Bolton away at Oxford for my first ever match. This was the day I inexplicably fell truly and utterly head over heels in love with football. It was Tuesday 19th November 1996 and I was 10 years old.

Oxford United 0-0 Bolton Wanderers. It was a school night in November. The Manor Ground. A creaky, dilapidated old terraced barnyard. Doesn't exist anymore, it got demolished. There's a hospital there now I think. I was only 10. What can I remember?

Think. Think. Nothing. Think harder! I can't remember what happened last week, let alone what happened 12 years ago.

I remember... the cold. It was cold. On my feet especially. Why the feet? I was wearing two pairs of socks as well.

I remember it wasn't what I had expected a football match to be like. The ground was smaller, much smaller. It was less glamorous. It was gloomy. It was grey and ugly.

I remember... Scott Sellars running up to take a corner, catching my eye, and winking at me. It was cool at the time. Seems a bit creepy now thinking back about it.

I remember... the swearing. Lots of swearing. Mainly at the ref, poor bloke. He wasn't that bad.

I remember the chants. "We're the one and only Wanderers!" We weren't of course. There was Wolves. And one more, Wycombe was it? I even knew that and I was only 10. "Super, Super John! Super, Super John! Super, Super John! Super John McGinlay!" That was a good one. He _was_ pretty super.

I remember the frustration towards the manager Colin Todd. Why was he taking Johansen off? He's been our best player! I could be a better manager than him. And I was only 10.

I remember longing for a goal. Please. Just one! 0-0 was the scoreline I dreaded. It's worse than a defeat in some ways. My prayers weren't answered. I didn't get a goal.

I remember having a pie. It was nicely steaming in my hands, heating my frosty fingers and promising to warm my stomach. But it was cold on the inside. Not cooked enough. That pissed me off. I remember that clearly. Poor me. I was only 10.

No goals. Freezing cold night. Crap pie. Crap ground. Crap match.

I remember absolutely loving it, but I don't remember why.

I had obviously been worlds away in my wistful nostalgia trip for a while, because John had fallen asleep in the beanbag, his beer can still in his hand but slightly spilling towards his groin.

What on earth was it that made me fall in love with football on that disappointing night in Oxford 12 years ago?

Going to all 92 grounds would be a sure-fire way of rediscovering it. I thought about whether I should actually take up John on the bet. No, I couldn't. It was preposterous. I dismissed the idea as I left John sleeping in the beanbag and went up to bed.

92 games in one season?

It would mean I would spend the best part of a year driving around the whole country, racking up over 20,000 miles (which is about once round the entire world), watching frequently low-quality football. It would cost thousands of pounds that I certainly didn't have, it would render my hard-earned degree pointless, it would probably ruin my relationship with my girlfriend and quite possible be mentally and physically demanding enough to lead to a nervous breakdown.

No. It was ridiculous. There was no way in hell I would do it.

GAME 1
CHARLTON ATHLETIC v Swansea City
The Championship
Saturday 9th August 2008, 3pm, The Valley, Charlton, South-East London

The Millennium Dome came into sight as my younger brother Greg and I stepped out of Charlton station into the pissing rain.

"The Dome was a load of old rubbish wasn't it." I grumbled.

Greg looked at me with his huge dark bush-baby eyes. "I dunno, I can't remember."

"Yeah you can, the whole family went when it opened!"

"No recollection."

My shoes were acting like a sponge to all the rain. Every step I made sounded like a comedy 'squelch' sound you get in a cartoon.

It was the first day of the season. What a day this was! If you discount the FA Cup 3rd-round weekend and the play-offs, this day is as good as it gets in the football calendar! Normally about now I would be moulded into the sofa, slippers on, kettle boiled, waiting for Jeff Stelling to kick-off the new season. Watching intently for the first goal of the season, the first red card of the season, the first opportunity of the season to hear Chris Kamara scream 'unbelievable!' It was always a glorious day of armchair viewing.

Yet here was I doing battling a monsoon at Charlton Athletic, about to watch them play Swansea City in a match I would normally have very little interest in.

I had, against my better judgement, taken John up on his bet. I was going to do it, however ridiculous it was. An epic 42-week mission in which I, Tom Dickinson, would attempt to watch a football match at all of the 92 League football grounds during the 2008-2009 season. And eat a pie at each one.

92 clubs.

92 grounds.

92 games.

92 pies.

One season.

Let me break this down a bit.

That would mean at least 2 or 3 games a week, every week, for the entire season. Every club from Man United to Morecambe must be visited; every ground in the 4 main leagues, trekking through the outer-reaches of England in the freezing winter to watch the likes of Accrington Stanley and Grimsby Town, and spending a small-fortune in the process. I had worked for the entire wet summer gardening by day and guitar teaching by night to save enough money to finance this ridiculous venture. I hadn't spent any cash for about 3 months; I was on a proper shoe-string budget.

Regardless of any stupid half-arsed bet, why oh why on earth would anyone want to do this?

To put it simply, I wanted to find the heart of English football.

I wanted to get to grips with why hundreds of thousands of people across England spend their hard-earned wages watching 22 men kick a ball around, and where the tribal passion of the terraces comes from.

I wanted to discover differences and similarities between clubs and leagues, find out about folklore, superstition and legends.

I wanted to visit new towns, new stadiums, meet new people, discover new things about places I know nothing about, find out what role football has in English culture.

I wanted to do something I would enjoy for a year, and to put off getting a serious human-being job after graduating from university.

I wanted John to admit that Sam Allardyce is a tactical genius.

And most importantly, I wanted to become one of the first, if not *the* first, to achieve the thoroughly tricky task of attending all 92 League grounds in one season. And in doing so, I wanted to rekindle my dwindling love of the beautiful game.

Whatever it was that made me fall in love with football at Oxford's Manor Ground in 1996, I wanted to find it again. It would take me to every ground in the country, but I was going to find it.

I'd had the idea for a while, but now it was actually happening my head began to fill with doubts. As we reached the Valley I felt a sudden sinking feeling in my stomach. I was nervous about this project, was it really feasibly going to happen?

As we went through the turnstiles I felt a huge commitment to the cause. This was it. I *had* to do it now otherwise I had just paid £20 to watch Charlton for no reason at all. Greg could sense my nervous apprehension.

"Okay Tom? Excited?"

"Yeah I think so, I'm a little bit confused about what I'm actually doing here."

"Let's get you the first pie, that'll sooth your nerves."

This was when I made my first disastrous discovery about my mission to eat a pie at all 92 League grounds.

Charlton Athletic don't sell pies.

I couldn't believe it. Balls. *Big* balls.

"What am I going to do?" I panicked to Greg. Greg browsed the alternatives.

"Steak slice is a pie of sort definitely," he reasoned. "It's a gloopy meaty sauce within a pastry isn't it?!"

"Yes, definitely," I convinced myself, "Steak slice is just a pie that's a bit more flat."

"It's like steak slice is the younger flatter brother of the pie."

"Exactly! It's not cheating is it? No. Definitely not. One steak slice please."

My logic was flawless.

I bit into my steak slice and a dollop of brown splodge fell on my shoe, my stupid spongy shoe, which was wet enough to begin absorbing the brown blob into my sock. This wasn't getting off to the best of starts.

Greg and I got to our seats and I tucked in to my pastry goodie that was most definitely a pie of sorts. The impending doom of *Carmina Burana* was playing on the PA system, suggesting that either the apocalypse was nigh or the new football season was about to begin. The rain had calmed down and my mood had improved. The players had lined up and it was time for kick-off. The first kick of a ball of a season that would last 42 weeks, during which fans across the country would experience every range of emotion as their team battles their way towards championship contention, relegation or mid-table mediocrity. And I was going to be there to witness every ground and every set of fans, the good, the bad and the ugly.

Looking around at the Charlton fans, they were firmly positioned in the latter.

Three minutes into the match Mark Hudson scored for Charlton, a powerful header from a corner. Fantastic! Even better was that Hudson was making his debut for Charlton, *as captain*! This was a Roy-of-the-Rovers style fairytale happening right here, right now in front of my eyes. The steak slice/pie catastrophe was long forgotten; I was back in the football zone.

Even though the match wasn't a classic, I was having a blast. Greg and I were enjoying the rather questionable banter between the Charlton and Swansea fans, with a huge amount of anti-English or anti-Welsh sentiments. Can you be xenophobic against the Welsh? I'm not sure if it *technically* counts as racism, but Charlton fans definitely made their opinions well known about what gentlemen from Wales get up to with sheep in the cold lonely valleys.

"So what was actually in the Dome then?" Greg asked me as the terrifically named JonJo Shelvey received some treatment for a knock. "It was dancers and trapeze artists, and side attractions about science being fun and stuff." I said trying to remember anything of note. "You remember you got your picture taken with E.T.?"

"What was E.T. doing there?"

I racked my brains for a minute. "Probably watching the dancers and trapeze artists."

The Charlton fans had been quiet in general, regardless of the excitement of the new season, or that their team had been leading since the third minute. There were muted cheers when Swansea captain Garry Monk got sent off and Andy Gray scored Charlton's second goal to seal the victory, but it was generally rather subdued at The Valley.

The rowdiest section of the Charlton support was two boys sitting directly in front of me, who spent almost the entire 90 minutes chanting "Alan Pardew's eating salami!" which was as confusing as it was inaccurate. I was almost certain that there was no salami consumption occurring in the Charlton dugout.

I left the Valley feeling relieved I had successfully started the mission, and both nervous and excited about what would lie ahead in the coming weeks and months.

"This is it G. I'm going to do it! I'm going to bloody well do it!"
92 Pies (or pastry-based pie substitutes) here I come
1 down, 91 to go.   Eeek.

CHARLTON ATHLETIC 2 (Hudson 3, Gray 85)
SWANSEA CITY   0
Attendance 21,675

GAME 2
MILTON KEYNES DONS v Norwich City
Carling Cup First Round
Tuesday 12th August 2008, 7.45pm, stadium:mk, Milton Keynes

Okay. I was really going to do this. I couldn't justify spending £20 on watching a shoddy Charlton v Swansea match if I wasn't going to follow it with the remaining 91 League clubs. That would be both foolish and ridiculous.

I checked my emails to find one from my Mum listing a number of potential job application forms. After a moment of personal reflection I pressed the delete button, found my car keys, put on my scarf and set off to see MK Dons v Norwich in the first-round of the Carling Cup.

Milton Keynes is a town I am fairly familiar with as I live just a few stops down the M1, but I have very little affection for the place. A bland, flat, character-free urban jungle of roundabouts, Milton Keynes has the personality of a stodgy pancake, and I was intrigued to see whether the football team reflected this.

As a club, I have mixed feelings about MK Dons. On one hand, I think it's great that the decline of Wimbledon led to a successful relocation, hitting a peak last season with two trophy wins under Paul Ince. On the other, more cynical hand however, I can't escape the feeling that the creation of a new club in such a formulated way is a bit soulless.

After negotiating about 100 roundabouts I reached the ground too modern for capital letters, 'stadium:mk' (undoubtedly the second crappest-named stadium in England after York City's 'Kit Kat Crescent') in the nick of time.

I grabbed my seat just as the match kicked off. The stadium was impressive; a huge, bowl-shaped arena fitting for a stage beyond the lower-leagues. With the spaceship electric ticket-turnstiles and (relatively) luxury toilets, I suspected that this may not be a fair representation of League One. Would Yeovil Town have similar facilities?

Steak and kidney pie in hand, I looked around to see what kind of company I was in, and quickly noticed that there was certainly a family-friendly atmosphere at MK Dons. There were plenty of kids at the game, which made it even more inappropriate that I smelt quite strongly of beer. The previous day I had been on an all-day pub crawl and spilled at least one pint of ale (possibly several more) on my jacket which I had then thrown on unwashed in haste whilst running late on the way to Milton Keynes.

I felt a bit apprehensive being there anyway with it being the first time I had ever been to a match on my own. I now was a lonely unshaven man, smelling of ale sitting alone amongst the innocent children of Milton Keynes.

I looked around at the fans surrounding me and noticed that sitting three seats away from me was a lad of about 9 or 10 in a replica MK Dons shirt, cheering on his team by himself, without a parent in sight. "COME ON DONNNNS!!!!" he screeched in encouragement as they won a corner. This peculiar case of a lone child at a football match was perplexing me. Had he turned up on his own? Maybe he had run away from home in hope of achieving his (as-yet-limited) lifetime goal of attending all 92 League grounds in one season?! Perhaps this child could be a younger version of me, my spiritual football brother! Maybe I could take him to the rest of the matches with me and have a laugh about whatever 10 year-old boys like to do nowadays, playing with Action Man and watching *Playdays* or whatever. The whimsical adventures we could have at Accrington Stanley!

'Stop planning to kidnap this poor boy Tom,' a voice in my head was suggesting, 'you'll only end up on the sex-offenders register and never be a welcome face at social gatherings.'

I focused back on match, which wasn't inspiring the crowd, even though the Dons were playing pretty well in their new manager's first home game in charge. What an inspired appointment by MK Dons. Here he was, one of the most elegant players the Premiership saw in the 1990s; Roberto Di Matteo, now making his managerial debut in the 'Milan of England', Milton Keynes.

Di Matteo's MK Dons played some really good football today against a Norwich side in the division above, and deservedly won the match 1-0 through a superbly taken goal from the young striker Sam Baldock.

The crowd clapped politely throughout the match, showing limited enthusiasm despite their team's eye-catching display. A couple sitting behind me were discussing car insurance for the majority of the first half, and the fact that you could see the moon moving in between the pillars of the ground if you looked every few minutes. Most of the crowd, it seemed to me, were new football fans of a new club. I found it pretty hard to swallow that fans could be distracted by car insurance when their team are causing a cup upset. The only thing that could distract me from the terrific team performance was Di Matteo's immense grey suit, probably hand-sewn by Giorgio Armani himself. I couldn't imagine Paul Ince in one of those bad-boys.

Shortly before the end of the match a tannoy announcement came on the PA; 'Could George Saunders please report to the nearest steward. That's George Saunders, to the nearest steward.' The young lone lad sitting by me meekly arose whispering "Excuse me" and indeed reported himself to the nearest steward. Rather than a being a maverick 10-year-old football renegade, he was most probably indeed just a lost boy. I sighed, rather let down by the fact George and I would not be partaking on a wild footballing adventure together, and I would most likely be attending Accrington Stanley by myself after all.

When looking at the club from the outside, everything about MK Dons is extremely impressive; a newly promoted family-friendly club with a tight squad and exciting young manager, playing good passing football in an attractive (albeit criminally craply-named) new stadium with the most comfortable cushioned seats outside the Premiership. Given all these factors I should have liked MK Dons a lot more than I did. I just couldn't escape the viewpoint that MK Dons is a club that perfectly suits the roundabout metropolis of Milton Keynes. Both are new, nice-looking, clean and pleasant, but ultimately lacking in much soul or character.

MILTON KEYNES DONS 1 (Baldock 34)
NORWICH CITY   0
Attendance 6,261

GAME 3
SOUTHEND UNITED v Brighton & Hove Albion
League One
Friday 22nd August 2008, 7.45pm, Roots Hall, Southend-On-Sea

I was feeling great! This was what it was all about. I defied the Friday Bank Holiday traffic warnings and made it to Southend for the seaside derby against Brighton. As the sun began to set I eventually located the humble Roots Hall, almost invisibly integrated into a row of houses, somehow fitting in 8,000 people from nowhere. Much like the Narnia wardrobe. A magical, witch and lion-filled League One wardrobe.

There was a definite Bank Holiday buzz around the town that transferred into the stadium. Both sets of fans were bustling with optimism for the season ahead, and probably eagerly anticipating a weekend eating soggy chips at the seaside. I was in a great mood whilst purchasing my pre-match pie, even the unholy trinity of Bryan Adams, Chumbawumba and M People on the loudspeakers didn't dampen my spirits.

The first thing I noticed about Southend was that there were plenty of elderly gents at the match; wholesome fellows who looked a bit like David Attenborough. They probably watch matches with their old chums, take their grandchildren to the beach, share Werther's Originals and build sandcastles, live in cottages with big chimneys and play Scrabble. If it wasn't for the smoking ban I'm sure they'd have their pipes out, the cuddly old rascals.

I squeezed between various old people to take my seat, noticing the confusing Southend mascot roaming the pitch. It looked like a slightly phallic triangle with legs, but was probably just a shrimp. Not quite as traditional as a bear or a lion.

There was a great atmosphere around the stadium. It was absolutely packed, every single tiny seat around me filled despite the views being seriously restricted by a big pillar with a ladder leaning against it. Due to how cramped the seats were I cursed my luck I was sitting next to a somewhat overweight gentleman (or 'fat bastard' in football-fan language) who was suspiciously vibrating around the bottom region at frequent intervals. His legs were rubbing against mine in a manner that would be homo-erotic if it wasn't so overwhelmingly un-erotic.

I decided to strike up a conversation with this man. I wasn't used to going to matches on my own, I needed some interaction! What should I talk to him about? A good ice-breaker...Hmmm... The linesman had made a couple of dodgy decisions.

"Phhhh." I said to the fat man. "The linesman's having a nightmare." For some reason I was putting on what I thought might be a Southend accent, but ended up sounding Cornish.

"Ah he's rubbish isn't he," the fat man replied.

Yes! I had crossed the boundary. Idle chit-chat for the remainder of the match here we come! Maybe he would stop rubbing against my leg?

"OI LINEO! DO YOU TELL YOUR MISSUS YOU'RE A TRAFFIC WARDEN?!" he shouted at the linesman. This was great, I was feeling a lot of warmth from the cramped stands and the match was decent, although the first half ended goalless. The man was still rubbing against my leg but I would let it slide, we can't have everything in life.

"Harding's working his magic down the left today isn't he mate," fat man said as the halftime cheerleaders got rousingly applauded off and the players re-emerged for the second half.

"Yeah! Outstanding." I replied, pretending to know who he was talking about.

Now, I would normally be reluctant to use the phrase 'game of two halves' a mere three matches into my season-long journey. But given the circumstances, and my lack of a better alternative, I now state that Southend v Brighton was very much, for me at least, a game of two halves. I will save the likes of 'over the moon' and 'sick as a parrot' for later in the season.

The reason that it was a game of two halves for me was not so much concerning which team was on top, but rather the atmosphere, which abruptly and awkwardly turned sour during the second half. The turning point was a fight between the Brighton goalkeeper and a Southend forward, which raised the heat both off and on the pitch.

Every decision by the referee was greeted with massive vocal disgust from the Southend fans. Tackles came flying in and the bookings began tallying up, and the fury shown to the ref Jarnail Singh reached a pinnacle when Southend midfielder Franck Moussa was shown a red card for a wild tackle in the 63rd minute.

Fat man was absolutely dripping with fury, quite literally.

"THE REFEREE'S A WANKER!" he began chanting, which I stood up and chanted along with, despite secretly thinking the referee was in fact not a wanker, but doing a sound job in a difficult match under ferocious pressure from the home crowd. But that would have been a less catchy chant I suppose.

Now I have wished the odd bubonic plague on a referee whilst watching Bolton before, but the venom in the hatred of the Southend fans was pretty strong. Once down to 10 men, Southend conceded twice in the last 20 minutes to lose 2-0, with the ref needing a police escort to leave the field at the final whistle.

I wanted to make a swift exit. I said a fleeting "See you," to the fat man.

He shook my hand. "If I saw the ref now, I'd rip his turban off and twat him," he said with complete aggressive sincerity. Time to go I think!

I escaped the fat man and his racial slurs and quickly nipped to the Gents before my long drive home. I stood at a urinal sandwiched between two silver-haired red-nosed old men swearing vulgarly about poor Mr Singh. Looking up I noticed an advert featuring a topless lady. *KATZ STRIP CLUB IN BASILDON!!!* it proclaimed boldly. *BRING YOUR SOUTHEND MATCH PROGRAMME AND GET HALF PRICE ENTRY!!!*

"Wouldn't mind them in your face hey son?" the elderly gentleman said to me, nodding at the lady's breasts. He shook himself, spat on the floor of the toilets as he was walking out, and continued to call the referee the c-word to his friend with a walking stick.

Walking back to the car I came to the conclusion that perhaps my initial prognosis on the old men of Southend was wrong, and they were more into swearing and Basildon strip clubs than sandcastles and Werther's Originals.

As I turned the keys to open my car door, parked in one of the roads behind Roots Hall, a topless ratty-faced man leaned out of the upstairs window of the house I parked outside;

"Oi mate, you want any weed? No? Any coke?" I politely declined and quickly drove away from Southend, wondering whether that mascot was in fact a giant walking phallus after all.

SOUTHEND UNITED   0
BRIGHTON & HOVE ALBION 2 (Murray 74, Forster 89)
Attendance 7,976

GAME 4
BARNET v Brentford
Saturday 23rd August 2008, 3pm, Underhill Stadium, Barnet, North London

I found myself swearing profusely at my *TomTom* as it inconsiderately told me to take a right turn where there was just a massive brick wall. The little bastard.

Parking in Barnet is not easy. I had been circling the stadium in sweaty stressy vain for about 40 minutes, and kick-off had already passed. Bollocks! I nearly crashed into a truck. This was seriously stressing me out, why didn't I leave my house earlier?! Was the classic 4th tier encounter of Barnet v Brentford worth me abandoning my car in a nearby field and allowing it to get towed?

I finally found somewhere and reached Underhill a mere 10 minutes late, which could be construed as a mini-victory considering the lack of parking. But the moment I went through the turnstiles I heard a huge cheer and missed a goal, which inevitably turned out to be the only goal of the game.

Barnet FC and me definitely got off on the wrong foot. Before leaving for Barnet I was fairly excited about the game, I would be losing my 4th-tier-football virginity which was thrilling enough by itself, but I would also be losing my 'standing-on-the-terraces' virginity too! All in one afternoon! *At least* two forms of virginities being lost!

But something about Barnet just didn't sit well with me. I think it all comes down to the colour orange. I found the glowing orange of the stadium and the terraces a bit too much to handle. All kinds of negative orange connotations came swarming into my mind; *Cheesy Wotsits*, molten lava, Mick Hucknall, *Sunny Delight*, sick. I think there was too much anger in the orange terraces for me to calm down after my parking fiasco.

Barnet, in their disgusting kit (also orange) were not playing very good football. The supporters were carrying the burden of the team; any poor touch or pass from the players was greeted with a world-weary sigh or swear from the fans. It made it worse that the cheerful noise coming from the Brentford end was relentless.

The Barnet fans were discouraged by their team, and let their frustrations show. Was League Two always this dismal? The pitch at Underhill was on an incredible slope, which didn't help the quality of the passing. At half-time, there was an announcement from a Ladbrokes official that there would be a sizeable charity donation from the local betting shop if Barnet were promoted this season, which was greeted by a rousing round of sarcastic laughter from the home fans.

I noticed that for many of the fans surrounding me Barnet seemed to be a secondary thought to a bigger Premier League team. There was a fan a few feet away from me on the terraces with a tattoo of the Man Utd club crest on his forearm. Standing directly behind me was a young bloke in an Aston Villa training top. And most thorough of all, the club itself gave the impression of being in awe of their highflying North London neighbours Arsenal.

I quote from the official Barnet F.C. website on the 'directions to ground by train' section:

Clearly visible to your right is the amazing site that is the new Emirates Stadium and a little further are the wonderful listed buildings that are the East and West stands that once was Highbury.

It was all a bit arse(nal)-kissing from Barnet. To further my theory there were two announcements at half-time, both involving the Gunners. One was advertising the ticket sales for the next couple of Arsenal reserve matches, which take place at Underhill, and the other promoting a drinks deal for that evening's 5.15pm kick-off Arsenal v Fulham at the local pub.

Like most Barnet fans I wasn't enjoying the match, but for me it was mainly because of the wasps. It was a warm summer day and the wasps were out in their masses for the Bees vs. the Bees. With the action on the pitch being pretty horrendous, I focused all my efforts into keeping the pesky wasps from eating my chicken and mushroom pie. I have a profound dislike for wasps, unlike my mate Jack who in the summer months warmly invites them to roam his food and drink, and lovingly strokes them. He's Welsh. As my wasp-fending continued, the tannoy announced that the Barnet number 9 Cliff Akurang was being substituted, which was cruelly cheered.

"You've been crap Akurang you waste of space!"

I felt sorry for poor (but wonderfully named) Cliff Akurang. True, he missed an open goal, but he was only as shite as the rest of the Barnet team. The dismal match was essentially a tale of two penalties. Whilst Brentford's Glenn Poole scored his with great confidence (or so I heard) Barnet's Albert Adomah predictably scuffed his shot wide.

The overwhelming highlight of the game, and the only thing which kept me from having a miserable afternoon, was when he ball was kicked over the ground midway through the second half. A replacement ball was thrown to the Brentford goalkeeper who, upon bouncing it, quickly realised it was flat.

The game was paused for about 7 or 8 minutes whilst the players looked for someone to either fetch the lost ball or pump up the flat one. This hugely bizarre but entertaining farce highlighted Barnet's ineptitude. "Shit club, one ball!" bellowed the Brentford supporters. Which I think most of the Barnet fans would have grudgingly accepted as a fair assessment, before heading to the pub to watch Arsenal.

BARNET   0
BRENTFORD 1 (Poole 10 pen)
Attendance 2,815

GAME 5
WIGAN ATHLETIC v Notts County
Carling Cup Second Round
Tuesday 26th August 2008, 7.45pm, JJB Stadium, Wigan

"Alreet la!" my good friend Collo greeted me with a warm bear-like embrace at his front door in Wigan. Collo, an old uni pal, is Wigan personified, only perhaps a bit more lovable. At 6 foot 3 and with a well-rounded and notably hairy body he is every bit the gentle Northern giant, with a particular fondness for dodgy earrings, early 1990s Slavic-style jackets and drinking lots and lots of beer.

"How was the journey up?" Collo enquired, handing me a can. "Beerski?"

"Cheers mate. Yeah it was fine, all the better for knowing I have a high quality chunk of football goodness coming up later."

"Don't hold your breath. At least you get to eat a proper pie at last though."

It was true, the Southern pie efforts had been mediocre at best. Perhaps a true slice of Wigan in pastry form would be worth the trip alone. A few more 'beerskis' later we set off for the JJB, with Collo's remarkably square-headed boxer friend Kingy in tow. Collo had warned me that the biggest problem with the JJB was that it was essentially built on marshland, which was the reason behind the consistently shoddy state of the pitch. On the walk to the stadium this was duly noted as my holey shoes began to get grimy water seeping through. We took a shortcut to the ground, walking briskly through an underpass full of young Wiganers who looked suspiciously like they were sniffing glue.

"I didn't think people actually sniffed glue in real life," I said quietly.

"Aye it's massive up here," Collo replied nonchalantly.

"I'll look twice now if I ever see you near some Pritt-stick."

We had been betting about how low the attendance would be for this Carling Cup tie against unglamorous opposition. I speculated it would be around the 8,000 mark, but Collo thought it would be half that, and on entering the stadium it became clear that my prediction was a gross overestimate. The town of Wigan has struggled to fall in love with football, even with the fantasy rise of the team under chairman Dave Whelan from the depths of the 4th tier to the Premier League. There is still such little glamour or excitement surrounding Wigan Athletic F.C., even when playing the likes of Man Utd and Chelsea week-in week-out. To quote a recent *Daily Mirror* interview with Whelan; *"When you play Chelsea and we only have 15,000 of our own there you have to ask, 'Does Wigan deserve a football team?' We have built this club up bit by bit from the old Fourth Division, but it's just not a football town."*

On the way to the match there had been no signs suggesting there was a football match happening, we didn't see any fans in the town centre or even on the walk to the ground. The biggest problem is that Wigan is, and always has been, a rugby league town. Egg-chasing is the be-all and end-all for any Wiganer worth their salt. Football is a secondary thought to most, and with the bigger clubs in Manchester and Liverpool in close vicinity for potential supporters, Wigan Athletic just doesn't have the fan-base to grow any further.

The match kicked off with barely 4,000 in attendance, but the fans present did their best to cheer their team on. The first half was dull and my eyes began to get a bit heavy after those afternoon beers. The few fans inside the JJB Stadium were eventually treated to a confident performance against vastly inferior opposition on a pitch that consistently cut up just as Collo had predicted. With names like Heskey, Zaki and Valencia turning out for Wigan they were always going to make light work of Notts County.

Wigan won 4-0 without really breaking sweat and even with a couple of rotten performances, notably from the infamous Titus Bramble and Kevin 'Zinedine' Kilbane, they rolled Notts County over. The fans, though few and far between, made a decent effort at making a bit of noise, although the level of humour was often pretty shoddy. "You're so gay it's unbelievable!" intelligently chorused the Wiganers to a County fan waving at them. "Oi Nash! Nash! Nash! Yeah Nash! You! Nash! I shagged your mum!!" a loan County fan bellowed at the Wigan goalkeeper as he lined up a goal kick.

One of the Wigan fans got bored and did something to piss off a steward, resulting in a very amusing chase between the overweight official and the young Wiganer, zigzagging in between the empty seats to get away from his pursuer for at least 5 minutes.

With Wigan being the home of pies I was eagerly anticipating the chunky steak *Pooles Pie* that was about to enter my gullet. It didn't disappoint. It was a dreamy pie, a sensual pie which massaged all my erogenous zones with its chunky steak goodness. People tend to associate Wigan with either pies or its pier. Whilst the pies tend not to disappoint, the pier really does. It was about as unimpressive as it could have possibly been.

"That's it." Collo pointed at a bit of wood next to some graffiti over the canal earlier that evening.

"We went on a school trip there when I was a kid, just to look at that piece of wood. Next to that nightclub where the gangs from Liverpool and Manchester meet up to bash the shit out of each other. It's pointless la." George Orwell would have echoed those sentiments I'm sure.

"Up for a Tuesday night out in Wigan then?!" Collo grinned, to which Kingy suddenly perked up and started rubbing his massive, massive hands together.

"That's an offer a boy can't refuse," I replied, a tad apprehensively, prepared for whatever Wigan nightlife had to hit me. Figuratively speaking.

Walking out of the stadium on the way to the town centre we were behind a bloke with his son looking fairly happy from the match. I eavesdropped their conversation to see if I could gain an insight into the match; perhaps the renaissance of Camara as an attacking threat or the exciting signing of Zaki, but instead heard them talking enthusiastically about the upcoming rugby league derby between Wigan and St Helens. Which summed it all up really.

WIGAN ATHLETIC 4 (Camara 32, 62, Zaki 60, Kupisz 90)
NOTTS COUNTY   0
Attendance 4,100

GAME 6
PETERBOROUGH UNITED v Bristol Rovers
League One
Saturday 6th September 2008, 12.15pm, London Road, Peterborough

I came to Peterborough with low expectations. I have a friend who grew up in the city and describes it fondly as 'a horrible shit-hole'. The grey and gloomy weather as I was driving through the outskirts of the town did not present Peterborough in the most glamorous of lights. London Road Stadium also looked pretty grim; a small shaky ground that has seen better days, set aside from the busy road and overlooking the banks of the canal. This could theoretically have been quite an idyllic setting, but the sideways-rain, grey skies and rubbish-filled canal didn't equate to a postcard scene.

It turns out that the Posh are not in fact very posh. I admit to being fairly ignorant about Peterborough United; everything I knew about the football team came from one of my all-time favourite TV programmes, the majestic 'Big Ron Manager' on Sky One, broadcast in 2006. For those of you unfamiliar with 'Big Ron Manager', it followed Peterborough United's fortunes during the latter part of the 2005-2006 season in which they were battling for promotion from League Two.

They were comfortably in the play-offs under caretaker manager Steve Bleasdale until Ron Atkinson (thick in his post-Desailly shame and subsequent attempted redemption) and Sky TV cameras arrived to 'oversee' the club which resulted in Bleasdale furiously resigning an hour before kick-off in a crucial match and the players brawling in the dressing room. Peterborough missed the play-offs that season. Tremendous telly.

The star of the show was not Big Ron or indeed the fuming Bleasdale, but the Dark Lord of Peterborough himself Mr. Barry Fry. Barry Fry's aura looms over Peterborough like an omnipotent demon. No longer manager or chairman Fry is now 'director of football', and feels to me like a ghost trapped inside Peterborough United's cupboard, destined never to leave.

33

It is certain that Fry, famed for his attacking football philosophy at the expense of a solid defence, would have approved of Peterborough's remarkable 5-4 win against Bristol Rovers this afternoon. The defending by both teams was *unbelievably* lacklustre, especially the comedy own goal scored by Peterborough defender Shane Blackett. I was in my element as a neutral, loving the crap defending by both teams, but Peterborough fans did not enjoy the match nearly as much as I did, and were frequently heckling their own players.

I stood next to a red-nosed cloth-capped OAP who had a newly purchased ASDA 'Smart Price' deep fat fryer by his feet. He was a sole renegade Peterborough superhero, defending his team by telling off the boo-boys.

"Be quiet! They're doing their best! Get behind the team, don't abuse them." His stern tickings off tended to work, especially on the younger fans.

This happened on frequent occasions during the first half, with the boo-boys reacting like naughty school kids each time. Despite the occasional inter-fan bickering the terrace had a lively and exciting atmosphere. The supporters, in the most part, were real life, hard-edged, haggard-faced, working-class men, smoking and drinking like troopers at half-time. My mediocre pie ended up tasting of fags.

Both teams looked really up for it in the second half. Everything good about Darren Ferguson's Peterborough team came through their Jimmy Bullard lookalike striker Craig Mackail-Smith, who scored three goals and was involved in setting up the other two.

The low point of the match for me came in the second half when a Bristol Rovers striker hit a wild shot which came flying at me. Being the mature man in his twenties that I am, I had injured my thumb earlier that week on a bouncy castle at an extended family gathering. A few champagnes had been consumed, and I can safely conclude that alcohol + bouncy castles + added water = an accident waiting to happen.

My thumb was still in agony, and rather than catching the ball with macho dignity I poncily shielded my hand with my other arm and let the ball smack me in the ear. This obviously was hilarious to everyone around me, except me.

"No! Don't let the Peterborough fans think you're a jessie!" I thought to myself, and attempted to make up for it by throwing the ball back with a manly, forceful throw, only for my left handed lob to feebly trickle back on to the pitch. Various cat-calls from the younger members of the crowd followed.

"Hahaha! Poofter!"

"Ponce!"

The man in the cloth cap next to me looked at me with disgust. ME. I was worse than the boo-boys to him. I was a *ponce*. He would go back home, deep fry some items, and remember me as 'that ponce'. It was a low moment of the day for me, 9 goals or not that was hard to recover from.

Fortunately more interesting things were happening on the pitch. The crazy finale to the game was as exhilarating as you can imagine; real end-to-end stuff. After seeing their team surrender a two goal lead an incredible 4 times during the match, the Peterborough fans breathed epic sighs of relief at the final whistle. I felt knackered just watching it but it was enthralling stuff.

As I walked out the rain had become relentless and once more I was unwisely wearing my shoes with holes in them. I needed new shoes. Mental note – buy new shoes. Despite my soggy socks, aching thumb and public humiliation, I was hugely satisfied with my time in Peterborough, if only for the 9 goals gifted to me. If only all defences in the Football League could be this bad...

PETERBOROUGH UNITED 5 (Mackail Smith 16, 51, 65, McClean 23, Rendell 83)
BRISTOL ROVERS   **4** (Elliot 30, Blackett o.g. 54, Hughes 74, Lambert 85)
Attendance 4,876

GAME 7
LEICESTER CITY v Millwall
League One
Saturday 13th September 2008, 1.00pm, Walkers Stadium, Leicester

I don't envy football fans in the East Midlands. As the 2008/2009 season had started, the region was not exactly brimming with football positivity.

With Leicester City getting relegated to League One for the first time, and Derby County finishing bottom of the Premiership with the lowest ever points total, last season was not a high point in the history of these two clubs. In fact, being a Derby or Leicester fan must be about as depressing as can be.

So what better than to see both these fallen giants play *in the same day!!!*

Looking at the fixture list I was intrigued to see that the Leicester game would kick-off at 1pm and Derby at 5.20pm, making it perfectly possible to watch the match at the Walkers and then pop on up the M1 to Derby.

Brilliant!

Two struggling squads of dilapidated relegation fodder in the same day! I would experience all the woe and misery the East Midlands has to offer on one sunny Saturday afternoon. What more could you want?

For a wholesome day of family fun I took my Dad along for the ride. Dad struggles keeping up to date with football. He grew up a Watford fan but stopped following the Hornets as his other interests, namely documentary filmmaking (which took him to the summit of Mount Everest in 1996) took priority.

Even though he knows little about the current state of the game he is an enthusiastic companion for a day's worth of football, which is exactly what was needed for a gruelling lower-league double whammy.

"You up for some misery today then?" I said, greeting my stick-thin, floppy haired father, his skinny jeans and leather jacket confirming his mid-life crisis. He's one step away from an earring and a motorbike.

"I certainly am! As long as one of the two win I'll be happy," said Dad, clearly entering the day with ill-advised optimism towards the East Midlands.

A surprisingly quick morning drive up to Leicestershire later we reached the Walkers Stadium. It seemed much like your typical, slightly dull, out-of-town new ground located next to a monstrously ugly electric power station. The neat stadium did however look crisp (boom boom), and I was quite excited as we entered, buzzing slightly off Dad's football-novice excitement.

I had never been to the Walkers before, but I did once attend a very memorable match at Leicester's old ground Filbert Street. In 2001, Bolton's first year back in the Premiership, we played our first game of the season away at Leicester, and won 5-0. That was seven years ago, and the one remaining relic from that day, Filbert the Fox, began dancing in front of the Leicester fans.

"Hahaha, Filbert? That's the worst name for a mascot I've ever heard," said Dad.

"At least he looks fairly normal," I said, "Southend have a shrimp that looks like a penis."

It's pretty shocking that Leicester are in the third tier of English football. When clubs suffer a humbling relegation it is a test of club's strength to bounce back, and a huge factor in this happening is the role of the supporters.

The Walkers Stadium was filling up nicely as kick-off approached, and the crowd of almost 20,000 was extremely credible for League One. Many familiar faces from yesteryear were warming up for Leicester; the likes of Matt Oakley, Paul Dickov and, most surprisingly of all, Chris Powell!

"God Chris Powell!" I said to Dad. "He's *ancient!* He must be nearly as old as you!"

"Thanks son."

I thought that Leicester, with a good mix of these experienced players and young loanees would surely be aiming to win League One this season. At half-time I had a different outlook however, because they were *terrible* in the first half, letting Millwall take the lead after 20 minutes.

Despite their dismal display, the fans clapped the team off at half-time in a generous show of encouragement which I was very impressed with. Most teams would have heard deafening jeers after playing that badly.

Half-time was fairly entertaining though. A marriage proposal came up on the big screen, saying 'will you be at the church on the Saturday instead of watching Leicester?' which was greeted with a huge chorus of boos. Podgy former Foxes legend Ian Marshall came out to wave at the crowd and take a penalty against the mascot Filbert, which he hilariously scuffed wide and blamed on his shoes. They *were* quite pointy I suppose.

The team didn't pick up the pace in the second half and the brilliant supporters were not rewarded for their efforts. Leicester basically couldn't use their strikers and were crap at the back, which is not a very helpful combination. The highlight of the match was when Millwall's Tresor Kandol was sent off for a ridiculous assault on a Leicester defender for no good reason. Footballers can be quite thick sometimes.

"What did you think of the match then?" I asked my previously optimistic father.

"You have to go to 92 games like that??? It'll kill you. It'll actually <u>kill</u> you," he said, with an unnerving sincerity to his tone.

"Well the next one's only two hours away so let's get going," I said, speeding away past the depressing and menacing looking electric power station, worrying if Dad might be right...

LEICESTER CITY   **0**
MILLWALL   **1** (Alexander 20)
Attendance 19,591

GAME 8
DERBY COUNTY v Sheffield United
The Championship

Saturday 13th September 2008, 5.20pm, Pride Park, Derby

With half of 'East Midlands misery' day completed, I was feeling apprehensive about the second half. Watching Leicester was pretty uninspiring, and as Dad and I headed up to Derby we were blissfully unaware that something brilliant would later happen at Pride Park. I was intrigued about going to watch Derby. They were in the midst of setting various records for awfulness, including last season's worst ever Premiership points tally of 11. The most alarming statistic was that if they failed to win today against Sheffield United they would have gone a year without a league win. A *year*! 36 torturous league matches. Oh to be a Derby supporter. Would the full year be surpassed today? You would have imagined it would be.

Driving up the stretch of the A52 between Nottingham and Derby renamed 'Brian Clough way' I wondered what old big-head himself would have made of the plight of football in the East Midlands. He definitely wouldn't have let Derby, a team he made League Champions in 1972, become the embarrassment they were last season. A few whiskies before a match and a clip round the ear-holes for the underperformers would have sorted the team out (if David Peace's terrific book *The Damned Utd* is to be believed anyway).

"Where's my copy of *The Damned Utd* by the way?" I asked Dad, "You borrowed it ages ago."

"Oh yeah sorry. I gave it to Brian Blessed."

"You gave it to Brian Blessed?"

"Yes. When we were climbing that mountain in Borneo last month." I decided not to question this fact further and just let it go.

Pride Park is plonked in a vast industrial estate; a fairly typically bland modern stadium complex. It was a smart ground though, complete with a built-in Starbucks. Slightly soulless perhaps, but it certainly beats the typical tea and coffee 'dish-water in a beaker' that you normally get at the football.

The queue for the ticket office had Sky Sports News on in the background, putting up the scores from earlier in the day. Two blokes in front of us began laughing when the Leicester v Millwall score came up.

"Hahaha, shocker for Leicester that isn't it!"

"Yeah nightmare."

Dad turned round.

"We were at that match earlier!" he boldly stated with a proud grin on his face.

The two guys seemed interested.

"Oh are you Leicester fans?" they asked.

"Nope!"

"You're Derby fans then?"

"Nope!"

They looked at us as if we were lunatics.

"So, you just *really* like football then?"

"That's right!"

There was an awkward silence of a few seconds where they weighed up whether we were dangerous lunatics or commendably eccentric lunatics.

"Phew, two matches in a day, that's some going!" they said jollily, concluding that we were the latter.

Try 92 in a season mate.

Chatting to the guys about Derby, I was astonished at how chirpy and optimistic they were. There was a great atmosphere in the ticket office with people laughing and smiling; a stark contrast to how Derby fans should naturally be feeling.

"It's got to happen one day hasn't it?!" one of the guys said. "And when it does, the roof is going to come off the stadium. Maybe you two can be the lucky mascots hey? No wins in a year until you come along? You never know..."

Now here is the astonishing thing about Derby County. For this match against Sheffield United over 28,000 fans turned up. That is incredible. Especially when considering;

      a)   The team hasn't won in a year.

      b)   The team just got relegated with the worst Premiership points total *ever.*

c) The match is televised.
d) The cheapest adult ticket for this Championship encounter is £33!

Only three of the nine Premier League matches this same weekend had a higher attendance, and I doubt any had support as loud and passionate as the Derby faithful.

The mood was set perfectly by the sun setting, and as the match approached kick-off the noise was deafening; the crowd was being spurred on further by the sole drummer at a corner flag and the rather ropey ram they call a mascot. The Derby mascot made Dad laugh even more than Filbert the fox. I think he has a slight obsession with the furry creatures.

'Rammie' was the first *ever* mascot in British football. He is also the only one who has his own DVD; surely a must have item for any Christmas stocking in the Derby postcode. He is definitely showing his age though, with a crinkly head that looks like it could disintegrate if you blew on it softly (the ram, not my Dad).

Derby didn't play very well, and were lucky to be drawing 1-1 at half-time. There was massive controversy in the second half, when referee Chris Foy awarded Derby a penalty, only to change his mind after consulting his assistant.

It didn't matter though, because Rob Hulse scored in the 71st minute with a scruffy goal, sending the Derby faithful wild. It was a tense finale; the fans were biting their nails and pulling their hair out as Derby hit the crossbar twice, and Sheffield United came mightily close as well.

As Foy blew the whistle to end the match, Pride Park became a cauldron of ecstasy.

Derby had won a match.

Strangers were hugging each other as the weight was lifted off the shoulders of every single fan, player and staff member associated with Derby County. It was glorious.

Putting the plight of Derby in perspective, I thought about how gloomy most football fans get, myself included, when their team loses two or three games on the trot. I even heard Peterborough fans bitch about their team winning 5-4! But Derby fans, on the back of defeats to Barnsley and Doncaster were belting out encouragement for their team and not moaning when players made mistakes. You can see why the club's official player of the year last season was awarded not to any player, but to 'Derby County supporters'.

"How about that then hey?" I shouted to Dad amidst the 'We love you Derby' chants.

"Fantastic! Are there any night games on we can rush to?" he asked with a grin on his face.

It was a disappointing display at Leicester earlier in the day, but the fantastic support shown by both sets of fans hinted that maybe football in the East Midlands can once again become great. What is certain however is that the Pride is back in the Park...and I was there to see it! Tremendous stuff.

DERBY COUNTY   **2** (Green 24, Hulse 71)
SHEFFIELD UNITED   **1** (Henderson 26)
Attendance 28,473

GAME 9
QUEENS PARK RANGERS v Southampton
The Championship

Sunday 14th September 2008, 4pm, Loftus Road, West London

I was dreading lunch with my Grandparents. It happened infrequently enough for the inevitable 'so what are you doing with your life Tom?' question to pop up, to which I would have to explain that what I am in fact doing is trawling the country watching football. But as I ate my second portion of roast beef they greeted the news with more enthusiasm than I expected.

"Make sure you reserve the Watford date for when I'm available," said Grandpa. Excellent response. Maybe this project *is* a brilliant, career-furthering idea after all! Anyway, to sour this positive reply slightly, Dad (oddly gasping for more football after two matches yesterday) and I left lunch early to head to Loftus Road on a beautiful afternoon to watch Queens Park Rangers, or as they are now known, the richest club in the universe.

I was, and still am, confused about what the deal is with QPR's finances. With Formula One moguls Ecclestone and Briatore now owning the club, and further investment from the world's 5th richest man Lakshmi Mittal, there is a *lot* of money existing behind the scenes, but with little evidence of this elsewhere. The stadium isn't in great nick and there have been no high-profile signings, despite ridiculous tabloid reports linking either Luis Figo or Zinedine Zidane to join Gavin Mahon in the heart of the QPR midfield.

On entering crumbly old Loftus Road it was immediately striking how QPR do not cater for the larger gentleman. The turnstiles were a massive squeeze, even my pie-defyingly narrow frame struggled to fit.

"Honestly, how would a fat person fit through that?" Dad asked me. "I was just thinking that, it must be impossible! Or they have some kind of fork lift to help them through."

Right on cue, a man who must have been approaching 25 stone walked past us eating a burger. This was impeccable timing.

"See! That's incredible! Without being cruel, there is no way that bloke could physically fit through the turnstiles!" I was befuddled. How on earth did it happen?

"Take it up with the owners."

"Yeah I will! It can be where all the money goes, on new turnstiles."

On reaching our seats the trend continued, with there being extremely limited leg room. Dad, who is 6 foot 1, had his bony knees up by his chin for the whole match. It was pretty funny actually. He looked like one of those tall people who squeeze into a mini to get in the Guinness Book of Records.

"The owners can sort out these seats while they're at it!" Dad said, with me laughing at him.

"Why?" I said. "Bernie Ecclestone's about 4 foot tall anyway. He can stretch out his legs in these no problem."

It was rather cramped. My leg was rubbing against the person next to me by accident. I looked at him and he was staring back at me. Shiiiiit. He looked *exactly* like Harold Shipman. It almost definitely wasn't Harold Shipman I suppose, but it was still a bit unnerving. Why was he staring at me so intensely? I quickly stopped looking him in the eye and stared at the ground. He was wearing socks and sandals. That's *so* Shipman.

I thought it was best to try to avoid stroking Shipman's leg any further so I shifted my legs the other way as the match was kicking off. Within 40 seconds Dexter Blackstock scored against his former club to put QPR ahead, and from then on it was fairly comfortable, especially with Southampton debutant Ollie Lancashire getting sent off in the first half.

"Half-time pie then Tom?" said Dad, almost as an order, leading me to the food kiosk. This was going to be a painful one. I had eaten two helpings of a roast meal after being egged on by my grandparents, and now the last thing I wanted was a pastry filled with sloppy meat. I took a begrudging, unwilling bite into the offending pie. It was gruelling, but I managed it, although I felt rather queasy once I'd finished.

With my stomach making odd noises, I admired the half-time show which was very curious indeed. About 30 Arabic gentlemen from Gulf Air, QPR's latest sponsor, wandered around the pitch waving while a mascot, dressed as an *aeroplane* (I shit you not) zoomed around them. I'm not sure what the QPR fans made of all this pomp going on in their shabby old stadium.

The second half started and it was a bit of a scrappy game in parts. Dani Parejo, the on-loan Real Madrid youngster, was flopping his long hair around and enthusiastically falling over a lot. At one point he got tapped on the shin, writhed in pain for a bit, and pulled down his socks and shin-pads to show the ref how badly he had been studded, only for the ref to shake his head and walk away.

The 10 men of Southampton, to be fair to them, were battling away at QPR and equalised early in the second half. QPR's man advantage became more useful as the game went on though, and they scored three goals in the second half to win by a 4-1 margin which was harsh on the talented young Saints team.

We walked past the turnstiles as we headed towards the exits after a thoroughly satisfactory afternoon of football. These ones looked even smaller than the ones we went through earlier.

"Well in five years time the turnstiles at QPR will be electronic, gold plated and with enough room to fit an elephant through." I said to Dad.

At which point the same fat man we saw earlier walked past, this time eating a Mars Bar. It was an unfortunate coincidence.

QUEENS PARK RANGERS 4 (Blackstock 1, 77, Stewart 63, Agyemang 90)
SOUTHAMPTON   **1** (Lallana 53)
Attendance 13,770

GAME 10
LEYTON ORIENT v Leicester City
League One
Saturday 20th September 2008, 3.00pm, Brisbane Road, Leyton, East London

It was the day after my birthday and I was feeling groggy. *Very* groggy. I didn't want to wake up, not for anyone. In fact, if the Queen had suddenly decided to make a Royal visit to the corner shop down the road (if she fancied some out-of-date ice-lollies then I would have thoroughly recommended it) I still would not have risen to see her.

I prised my eyes open and looked around, finding that for some reason I was sleeping on the couch in my living room, surrounded by empty beer cans with my friends Duffy and Robbie on the floor. "Duff. Rob. Leyton Orient. Come on," I said in my best enthusiastic, 'let's get excited about League One' tone. I received no reply. I kicked them both gently, yet with intent, in their ribs.

"Come on, you said you'd come."

"Grummmmmph. Fuck off," Duffy groaned.

"Look, *Football Focus* is on!" protested Robbie, pointing at an unnervingly close-up image of Mark Lawrenson's face on the TV.

I conceded that my task would be unsuccessful, so I put some trousers on, left my lazy friends watching Lawro and skulked my way to the train station. For today was Leyton Orient Saturday. And regardless of how rotten I felt, it couldn't stand in the way of my trip to Brisbane Road.

It was a sweltering day in London, and the drippy armpits on the Central Line were not soothing my nerves at being potentially very late for kick-off. Arriving at Leyton station with just minutes to spare I pathetically jogged around the multi-cultural high street searching for the ground, regularly hunching over, panting with wretched unfitness and reaching in my bag for my inhaler. The beaming sun was not aiding my sweat from jogging, particularly considering the depth and sincerity of my hangover.

This was a bad one. Frantically running around muggy, sweaty East London was far from the ideal way of spending a day hungover (of course the correct answer would be sitting in my pants swearing at Noel Edmonds on *Deal Or No Deal*, whilst completing the best part of a season on *Football Manager* and eating Jammie Dodgers).

I passed a pub as I approached the ground, the unwelcome stench of dried lager spillages wafted through the open doors of the warm watering hole into my nostrils. As I finally entered the pleasant looking stadium and purchased my pie, the hangover had kicked into what I call a 'phase three'. The patented Tom Dickinson hangover phase chart (of which I spent years perfecting) goes:

Phase one – Nausea and confusion. Consider hair-of-the-dog.

Phase two – Rule out hair-of-the-dog. Self-loathing, severe shaking and full body illness.

Phase three – Reluctance to be alive.

Phase four – Death.

As I bit into the *Pukka* meat and potato pie I had reached phase three. I looked into the sky for help from God, Vishnu, Allah or Joseph Smith[1]. Please relieve me of my pain O Lords! None came to my aid. I felt low. The unwanted gloopy pie didn't say 'Happy Birthday' quite as effectively as a cake with candles.

The match kicked off, Orient were playing Leicester, whose fall from grace I had witnessed only a week earlier. Whilst Leicester were finishing in the top half of the Premiership and winning League Cups only 9 years ago, Orient have been in the bottom two League divisions since the 1970s.

The fans seem quite content with this, especially considering how close they came to liquidation in 1995 when then-chairman Tony Wood's Rwandan coffee business was destroyed during the civil war, leading to current owner Barry Hearn buying the club for £5. I did a module on the Rwandan genocide at university and I certainly never thought that I would be able to write about it in relation to Leyton Orient FC.

I took my mind off the Rwandan genocide and instead concentrated on an overweight Paul Terry (destined forever to be known with the

---

[1] The Mormon Prophet of course.

prefix 'brother of John' attached) run around the pitch aimlessly. Two chirpy cockney blokes in front of me were getting increasingly pissed off with him.

"What the 'ell are you doing Terry?"

"Tell you what Jim, he's had a shocker."

"He's about as agile as the QE2."

Orient were awful for the first 40 minutes but managed to hold Leicester to 1-1 at half-time. The atmosphere had been great, and my mood was quickly improving.

My hangover had knocked down a couple of notches with the fresh air and the footy, so I headed to the bar at half-time for a cheeky hair-of-the-dog, defying my own hangover chart. I got chatting to the two blokes who had been sitting in front of me, Kieran and Jim, who turned out to be father and son, even though they both looked about 40. Either Kieran looked remarkably good for his age or Jim looked way too old. I didn't like to pry. Either way, they definitely start pro-creating young around Leyton. I asked what makes them go to a club like Leyton Orient every week, destined to remain solidly in either League One or League Two without much hope for bigger or better things.

"Well someone's got to haven't they!" Kieran laughed, "I mean we aren't exactly glamorous but it's a good honest club with a decent manager and a small but dedicated fan base. You look at Leicester, getting 20,000 every week in League One. That'll always be the case 'cause they're the only team in Leicester. There isn't any alternative is there? With London you've got Arsenal, Spurs, Chelsea all on your doorstep so the lower-league clubs like us need to work hard to attract the fans in. It's a great club, got a t'riffic family atmosphere and the fans love coming here."

I looked around the bar area and I had to agree. It was more of an indoor social club, complete with carpet, chairs and a 'no glasses on the dancefloor' sign. There was a definite charm to Leyton Orient, especially with the flats at the corner of the pitch where families can step out on to their balconies and watch the match whilst having their lunch.

"The main problem's the bloody team though," said Jim. "What I'd give for a pacy winger or a striker."

"Paul 'QE2' Terry's about as good as we get." Kieran agreed.

A multi-tattooed gentleman came up to us in the bar.

"'Ello Kier! 'Ello Jimbo!"

"'Ello Dave! This is Tom, he's writing a book about all the football clubs in England."

"Awight curls!" Dave said to me, to which I gave a nervous laugh. I suppose my hair *was* quite curly. Dave had no hair whatsoever. Maybe he was jealous of my curls?

"Only joking son," he said, patting me emphatically on the back, causing me to spill about half my pint down myself.

We made our way back to the seats for the second half, with Dave in tow who certainly livened up the experience with his constant swearing at the players.

"Is that Chris faaaahking Powell at left back Jimbo? It only bleeding is! Faaaahking hell! HOW BLOODY OLD ARE YOU POWELL? 102? JESUS! YOU GOT A FAAAAHKING BUS PASS YET POWELL OR WHAT?!" Dave bellowed at an unbothered Chris Powell.

Despite Dave's best efforts to put off Leicester, they showed their class in the second half and won the match 3-1 with two late goals. I walked out of the stadium looking at the families clapping from their balconies overlooking the pitch.

I could see why you would be an Orient fan ahead of the more glamorous London clubs. You can buy quality on the pitch, but you can't buy charm, which Orient have buckets of. Even sweaty, sweary Dave had a certain element of cockney chimney-sweep likeability about him.

I was hungry. That birthday pie did not fill me up whatsoever.

"See you later mate, good luck with the season!" Jim and Kieran said farewell as I anticipated the cake that I had been promised would be waiting for me at home.

LEYTON ORIENT **1** (Chambers 44)

LEICESTER CITY **3** (Dyer 11, Fryatt 87, A.King 90)

Attendance 6,448

GAME 11
ASTON VILLA v Queens Park Rangers
Carling Cup Third Round
Wednesday 24th September 2008, 7.45pm, Villa Park, Aston, Birmingham

A young boy was running up the steps in the Holte End of Villa Park with a smile stretching from cheek to cheek. He ran with such ferocity that every row of fans he passed turned to watch him go. Finally he breathlessly reached his parents, sitting two rows behind me. This kid was in absolute ecstasy. Something big had happened, but I didn't know what.

"MUM!!!!! DAD!!!!!!"
The kid paused for breath.
"GUESS WHAT?! YOU WON'T BELIEVE IT!!!!"
I was literally on the edge of my seat.
"GO ON GUESS!"
Come on! I can't wait any longer.
"OH MY GOD IT WAS SO COOL!"
This is the most tense I've ever been in my life. Please put me out of my misery.
"I...." The kid's eyes brightened up with the reflection of the floodlights in them. His smile almost stretched off his face.
"I..."
I'm going to wallop this kid if he doesn't say what happened in the next 2 seconds.
"I MET NIGEL REO-COKER!!!!!"
I threw my programme to the floor in irritation. Kids from Birmingham are easily pleased I guess.

It was time for the Villa. I had reached Birmingham with plenty of time to spare, and despite the match only being a Carling Cup tie I was excited. I drove into a school car park and paid the old fella on the gate £5 for the privilege. As I got out my car he came up to me and put his hand on my shoulder.

"You know son, you should always reverse into parking spaces rather than going head on," he advised me.

"Oh?"

"Something my father told me when I was young."

Something his father told him when he was young?! About reversing what, horse and cart?

"You could *kill* someone if you have to reverse back out of the parking space."

"I see..." I said, slightly concerned about how bad he thought I could be at driving.

"Anyway, you here for Q.P.R.?" he asked, picking up on my Southern accent.

"Errr no, I'm here as part of a book I'm writing. I'm trying to go to all 92 League stadiums this season."

"WOW!" the man perked up. "That sounds *fantastic*!"

This was by far the most enthusiastic anyone had been about 92 Pies. I liked this guy all of a sudden! I had forgiven him for accusing me of potentially killing someone.

"Who do you support then?!"

"Erm...Bolton," I said, confusing matters even further.

"That's fabulous son. That's fabulous." I don't know why that was fabulous, but it definitely was. The man turned his head and looked both ways suspiciously, before unzipping his coat. Was he going to flash me? I really hoped not. Thankfully, all he revealed from under the coat was a Birmingham City scarf.

"I'm a blue nose you see. Don't go telling anyone. Just work around Villa for a bit more cash. I'm from Wrexham, and they're my main team, but round here it's all about the Blues."

This was getting complicated. Here was a Birmingham City fan from Wrexham talking to a Bolton fan from Hertfordshire outside an Aston Villa v Q.P.R. match. About the hazardous danger of parking nose first. I said an overblown farewell to the gentleman and made my way to the ground.

Walking to the ground, it's hard to ignore the deprived area surrounding Villa Park. There are high crime rates and apparent tension between different ethnicities in Aston, which seems like a different world away from the beautiful Victorian stadium which suddenly appears from nowhere around a corner.

There were fans selling sandwiches out of their living room windows, and the moody dusk which had settled over the stadium created a fantastic ethereal atmosphere in which I could sense the historic importance of Villa Park.

On my first trip to the West Midlands I was delighted to purchase my first chicken balti pie. The balti pie! A Brummie institution. The company who first made the balti pies were *Shire,* whose logo looks like 'shite' but the pies are anything but. The tasty and spicy pie works perfectly on a nippy night like this one.

Delicious pie in hand, I entered the beautiful Villa Park arena, and was delighted to find out that Villa were putting out a pretty strong team, despite it being a Carling Cup match. I thought that Villa would come out against Q.P.R. all guns blazing, but they were unfortunately uncharacteristically poor. I was annoyed to have caught them on such a bad day. A couple of the squad players had stinkers, in particular Marlon 'Goomba'[1] Harewood who, at the age of 29, still doesn't understand the offside rule. Even Gareth Barry, captaining the side for the first time since the Liverpool transfer debacle, ended up missing an open goal.

Half-time arrived, with a silver-haired Villa fan called Colin popping up on the big screen.

"Here, have you seen this?" the bloke next to me said excitedly, pointing at the screen, "this guy's great! He's written his own song about John Carew! An ode to the giant Norwegian!"

"Oh really..." I said, slightly apprehensively.

As Colin started singing the embarrassment was too much for me to bear as lyrics such as 'His name is John Carew, he's bigger than two of you, he'll score a goal or two or three or four' were delivered in a fake transatlantic accent with a shake of his hips and no sense of irony. Cringey. To make matters worse, the Q.P.R. fans started loudly booing poor Colin's video during his moment of fame. I could

---

[1] Goomba is a character from the Mario Brothers games who looks remarkably like poor Marlon.

barely look. Only the bloke next to me was clapping along, enjoying the cutting-edge Birmingham entertainment.

The second half carried on much as the first, with Q.P.R. actually taking the lead. The Villa players just looked half-arsed, whilst the two managers were kicking every ball. O'Neill and Dowie were dancing around the touchline like manic gophers. O'Neill knew that the Carling Cup was a good possibility for potential silverware, but they lost 1-0 without putting up much of a fight.

The 21,000 Villa fans were quiet for the match with the occasional exception of a burst from the Holte End. My biggest gripe though was that the fans started leaving the match from the 82nd minute! WHY? Especially considering that just *one* goal would have brought the tie into extra time.

Everything about my trip to Villa Park was slightly frustrating for me, but it didn't change my opinion about Villa being a fantastic club. They certainly deserve some success under Martin O'Neill, and I have decided that I will have to come back for a league match sometime in the near future.

ASTON VILLA   **0**
QUEENS PARK RANGERS   **1** (Stewart 58)
Attendance 21,541

GAME 12
FULHAM v West Ham United
Premier League
Saturday 27th September 2008, 3.00pm, Craven Cottage, Fulham, West London

I left Putney Bridge tube station feeling fresh, happy, and ready for a wholesome slice of the Premier League. It was a gorgeous sun-kissed Saturday afternoon at the tail-end of summer, and Craven Cottage is the perfect place to spend such an afternoon.

Stepping out of the station I was greeted by two glorious sights for any football fan, immediately heralding that match-day beckons. Firstly there was the tout; the small, mumbling Del Boy figure offering seats for double the price who, despite breaking the law, works seamlessly next to the police without either bothering the other.

Which brings me to the second glorious sight; horse shit. More than replica shirts, chanting, pies, corner flags or floodlights, horse shit is the one thing I associate most with being at the footy. As time goes on I hope police horses are *always* used for football matches, they add an old-fashioned sense of excitement to the match-day experience.

Walking to Craven Cottage is about as pleasant as you could wish for; passing through beautiful gardens on the picturesque bank of the Thames. In a bygone-era you could imagine the training schedules of the Fulham players consisting of jogging through the park, or rowing sessions on the Thames. Possibly not anymore.

Craven Cottage itself is a great old stadium full of character, looking similar to how I imagine it did 100 years ago, despite improvement work over the years. The Johnny Haynes Stand, which is a listed building, is stunning to look at, and the Pavilion area known as the 'cottage' is brilliantly unique. This small raised seating area looks more like a cricket pavilion rather than a part of a football stadium, and certainly adds to the charm of the place.

Fulham supporters are a lovely bunch too, and kept their upper-lips firmly stiff at any West Ham fans showing any form of lairy behaviour. If I ever end up in some kind of Kensington tofu-munching, frappe-sipping existence (which is pretty unlikely) I would *definitely* bring up my children Tarquin and Cecil as Fulham fans.

The atmosphere was family friendly and very non-threatening. I sensed that I was not alone in being a neutral at Craven Cottage; Fulham is a club that attracts tourists, particularly from the Far East. "WE LOVE THE FULHAM!!!!" a smiley Chinese couple next to me were shouting as the game kicked off, banging their free clappers.

Despite the great atmosphere Fulham were off-key; particularly after Andy Johnson was stupidly sent off for two bookings in the first half. West Ham had a host of chances to score more than the two they managed; Craig Bellamy even missed an open goal.

"Come on Fulham! Come on Fulham!" the crowd were enthusiastically cheering, to the inevitable reply of "Fuck off Fulham! Fuck off Fulham!" from the away end. The contrast between the two sets of fans was crystal clear throughout the match. When West Ham scored their first goal, a sole Hammers fan in the Fulham end near me jumped up and started cheering.

"Yessss! Come on the 'ammers! I'M FOREVER BLOWING BUBBLES!!!" I gulped. A lone West Ham fan cheering amongst several thousand Fulham supporters? I looked at the bulky fool. Was it all about to kick-off?

Rather than resort to violent actions towards the rather brave (but idiotic) bloke the Fulham fans sat there quietly, with one tall bespectacled man subtly alerting a steward;

"Excuse me sir, there's a West Ham fan sitting with us. I think you should escort him out before he causes any more trouble."

The Fulham elite. Surely the world's most polite and reasonable football fans. I don't think this would have been the reaction if it were the other way round at Upton Park, with a Fulham fan celebrating in the West Ham end....

At half-time I ate my quite delicious steak pie with a renewed sense of fondness for the Premier League. Fulham were 2-0 down, but the vibe was still brilliant, and more of a sense of *occasion* than I had witnessed in the lower-leagues. It was a treat to be watching the Premiership for the first time this season, and I felt guilty for preferring it to a League Two slog. By this logic, was 92 Pies really for me?

I decided not to dwell on the matter and just enjoy the second half as Danny Murphy pulled one back from the spot. Throughout the match the West Ham fans were gesticulating wildly in both pleasure and disgust at what was happening on the pitch, whilst the Fulham fans remained seated and used their free clapper boards to generate noise. I'm not saying either way is the right or wrong way, but for two London clubs of similar size the differences between the two sets of supporters was huge.

As the match ended the home fans were mildly irritated by the 1-2 scoreline, but it was a quality afternoon of Premiership football for all concerned. Well *almost* all concerned. Jimmy Bullard walked off towards the tunnel past where I was sitting.

"Unlucky Jim," a fan said, clapping Bullard.

"Sorry folks," Jimmy said into the crowd, shrugging his shoulders and looking disappointed at the defeat.

"It's okay Jimmy Bullard! We love you!" the Chinese man next to me said in broken English. Jimmy cracked a cheeky grin.

London is a big place full of many very different football teams, but I do think I am (so-far) most fond of Fulham. I like Fulham's fans, I like Fulham's manager, I like at least one of Fulham's players, I like Fulham's style, I will forgive their owner for any wrongdoings on the grounds of possible insanity, and I definitely like the area of Fulham itself.

Most of all I like the ground; a beautifully designed old-fashioned stadium, one of the most welcoming in the country and certainly one of the most 'homely'. Fulham are a great club. True, they lack a bit of the good honest jellied eel grit and grime that their East End neighbours have, but the Tarquins and Cecils of this world need a club to support as well don't they?!

FULHAM **1** (Murphy pen 59)
WEST HAM UNITED **2** (Cole 43, Etherington 45)
Attendance 23,946

GAME 13
SOUTHAMPTON v Norwich City
The Championship
Tuesday 30th September 2008, 7.45pm, St. Mary's Stadium, Southampton

Forget a romantic meal at a restaurant or any of that mumbo jumbo. For a good date all you need is a Championship relegation clash between Southampton and Norwich, which is the delight that was in store for my girlfriend on a Tuesday night.

That's right, I (the work-shy idiot travelling the football grounds of England for a year), have a girlfriend. Annabel is in the final year of her degree at Oxford (Brookes) University, and whilst not disliking football per se I think her enthusiasm for what I am doing is somewhat limited. Still, she was fairly excited about our jaunt to the south coast.

"Will I know any of the Southampton players?" she asked.

I presumed not. "Bradley Wright-Phillips?" I queried.

"Oh yeah I know him he plays for England."

"No that's his less-of-a-twat and better-at-football brother Shaun."

"Oh."

"Matt Le Tissier used to play for them."

"Who?"

"That fat lazy bloke who scored all those great goals? Never mind." Chopping down the A34 Annabel asked me if Southampton was a nice place, which I immediately answered "Yeah, it's really posh." I then thought about my answer and wondered what I was basing that on. I knew a fairly posh bloke from Southampton at uni. That must be it.

Reaching Southampton, within the first 5 minutes of driving through the city we saw an abandoned burnt-out car and someone projectile vomiting at a bus stop.

"Looks posh," said Annabel.

"It is!" I defended my opinion of Southampton, "every city has its rough parts."

What certainly isn't rough at all is St. Mary's stadium, a shining new ground which is rather attractive but obviously lacking the character of the now demolished Dell. St. Mary's was built at a tremendous cost that you sense is still affecting the club greatly. The vast majority of Southampton's struggling team are made up of recently promoted youth team players, or other youngsters on loan from Premier League clubs. 9 players that featured today were between the ages of 18-20.

"Let's put a bet on!" Annabel said excitedly. Annabel says she's against gambling and always criticises me for doing so, but whenever she watches football she always gets lured in by the excitement of the big red Ladbrokes sign. Settling on Chris Perry to score first at 50-1, we went in to find our seats.

Today Southampton were superb, the youngsters really stepping up, especially the on-loan Jordan Robertson who opened the scoring with the most beautiful curling strike from the edge of the penalty area. The likes of Surman and Lallana bossed the game against the more experienced Norwich players, and Southampton certainly weren't performing like a team struggling against relegation.

Not one to normally attend football matches, Annabel found everything around us very amusing, in particular the old lady behind us who referred to Wright-Phillips as a 'lazy toad' every time he touched the ball. She scored points for an original insult I guess! Better than the 'You'd be better off in prison Bradley!' which also frequently echoed from the home end at every poor touch.

The biggest support was for goalkeeper Kelvin Davis, who produced about 4 world-class saves to keep Southampton in the game. 'England's number one!' sang the fans, only half ironically.

The Southampton faithful were in absolutely fantastic voice, which genuinely made a difference in spurring their young team on to victory. As well as being incredibly loud (and unusually tuneful), they were rather witty with their chants. I had to do a fair bit of super-sleuthing to figure out what they were singing in a derogatory way about Portsmouth. 'Snake' bastards? Was it that? 'Slate' bastards? I was confused so I asked the people sitting behind me. "*Skate* bastards of course," they said.

"Ah yes." I pretended I understood perfectly before turning my head back round.

It turns out that Southampton fans refer to Pompey fans as 'skates'. The reason behind it is simultaneously complicated, historic, disgusting and hilarious. Back in the olden days Navy sailors from Portsmouth used to go out to sea for months on end, and have many a long lonely night without any female company.

According to popular local myth the sailors, using the full force of human initiative, in their fit of sexual frustration often used the mouth of a skate fish to 'help them out'. Yep, that's right. This fishy frolicking was apparently common practise for Portsmouth sailors, with the women back on mainland fending off their advances with the phrase 'I ain't no skate-bait.'

So Southampton fans call Pompey fans 'skates'. That's your history lesson children.

Dejan Stefanovic, Norwich's former Portsmouth defender was feeling the brunt of the skate chants from the home fans, and it certainly affected his performance. I'm not sure if the Serbian Stefanovic will have ever spent any time in the company of fish off the south coast of England though. The 'skate' himself got sent off in the 63rd minute and conceded a penalty which David McGoldrick coolly slotted home to seal the win.

I have new fond feelings for Southampton but I fear for their future, especially considering their dire financial situation. Looking at how beautifully preserved the pitch is, the big screen match coverage complete with their own presenter, and the giveaway of numerous Xboxes at half-time, I could see why the club has no money for players. I have no idea what lies in store for the Saints, but I hope it involves a march back up to the Premiership sooner rather than later.

SOUTHAMPTON 2 (Robertson 29, McGoldrick pen 64)
NORWICH CITY 0
Attendance 14,480

GAME 14
MANCHESTER CITY v Omonia Nicosia
UEFA Cup First Round, Second Leg
Thursday 2nd October 2008, 7.45pm, City of Manchester Stadium, Manchester

I was falling behind already. This was not acceptable. It was time to start sleeping on some floors up north. A few phone calls and route plans later I was off up the M6 to see my brother Greg who had just started at Manchester University.

Man City were playing a UEFA Cup match against Cyprus's Omonia Nicosia, and this would be the start of six games in six days for me! How exciting! I managed to rope my Wiganer chum Collo along for a night of glorious UEFA cup footy followed by drinking snakebite and sambuca and putting traffic cones on heads, dressing up as Hitler and shitting in ponds, or whatever it is that uni freshers do these days.

Greg and two of his mates, Fred and Haz, met us in town as we soaked in a bit of Manchester before the match. The Cypriots were out in their masses around Piccadilly Gardens which was an awesome sight to behold. They were jovially booming out the same song over and over again which was startling the Mancunian businessmen finishing work, but startled me for a different reason.

"I recognise that tune..." I said to Collo.

"I do too..." Collo pondered, deep in thought.

"It's The Offspring isn't it?!" Greg said, "*Why Don't You Get a Job!*"

Greg was right, it was what sounded like a Greek language version of the 1999 number 2 hit by American punk-rock band The Offspring. Which was just plain weird. 'Why Don't You Get a Job?' It was almost like the Cypriots were taunting me.

I was excited about going to see Man City. They had only just been taken over by the Arab billionaires and Robinho, if picked, would be playing only his third game for the club. The enormous investment has made it a hugely exciting time to be a City supporter, and considering it was a Thursday night UEFA Cup first-round match, there were a good number of fans around as we pottered our way to the stadium.

"How much are tickets Tom?" Greg asked as the magnificent City of Manchester Stadium came into sight for the first time.

"Fifteen quid I think. Unless you want to pretend you're under 16 in which case they're a fiver." I said.

Greg and his two mates, all aged 19, looked at each other thoughtfully.

"Three under 16 tickets please." Greg asked the lady at the ticket office. Greg had wetted his hair into a centre parting and was speaking with an awkward squeak in his voice. Fred and Haz stood meekly behind him with their hoods up and hands in their pockets. The lady raised one eyebrow at Greg before shrugging her shoulders and printing out three £5 under-16 tickets.

"Wow!" I said to Collo. "Maybe *we* could have got in as under 16!"

"Your full beard suggests probably not mate." Collo replied.

"True. And your eyes give you away. They've experienced too much debauchery for a 16-year-old."

Collo *does* experience quite a lot of debauchery.

The match kicked off and there was good news and bad news. The good news was that City had a full-strength line up on the field, which meant we were treated to the likes of Elano, the returning Shaun Wright-Phillips and yes, Robinho himself. The bad news was that because this was a European fixture, UEFA guidelines meant that there was no booze on sale. Drat! Those pre-match snakebites at the student union and gin on the bus would be wearing off soon! My dream of re-living a student lifestyle was fading in front of my very eyes!

A goalless first half didn't help matters much, and the City fans were very very quiet. In contrast, the Omonia supporters were belting out their chants (predominately Offspring-based), bouncing around and waving their shirts over their heads. Which was brave considering I doubt it's this bollock-freezing in Cyprus in October.

It picked up in the second half, and City put in a decent performance, particularly from Robinho, who set up Elano's goal. By far the man-of-the-match however was everyone's favourite cheeky Irish weirdo Stephen Ireland. Amongst all the star-studded Brazilians

Ireland was inspirational in the middle of the park, and seemed to be playing with new-found gusto.

I thought the gin was playing tricks on me as number 77 for Omonia was getting replaced by number 99, which must be the most ridiculous substitution in the history of football numbers!

"Nah I see it too." Greg reassured me I wasn't imagining things.

City edged the win 2-1, but I was secretly egging on Omonia in my head for most of the match. City fans will tell you that they're the real club in Manchester, but the crowd barely made a whisper throughout the whole match, or seemed to show much enthusiasm for the new era of Robinho et al.

I will give Manchester City the benefit of the doubt however, because having been to UEFA Cup matches at Bolton, I know the atmosphere at the games can be severely underwhelming, especially in the early stages. Going to the tremendous former Commonwealth Games stadium of Eastlands is undoubtedly a far more atmospheric experience for a Saturday afternoon league fixture.

What on earth the future will hold for Man City I can only speculate. Whether they end up signing Kaka, Messi and the likes remains to be seen, but if so what will that do for Manchester as a footballing city? Will City soon overtake United as the dominant force of English football? Is it fair to become a truly massive club overnight due to an Arab takeover?

So many questions, and only one answer; 'I don't know'. Going back to the student union for some more snakebite would get my mind off it.

MANCHESTER CITY 2 (Elano 48, Wright-Phillips 55)
OMONIA NICOSIA 1 (Alabi 78)
(Man City win 4-2 on aggregate)
Attendance 25,304

GAME 15
STOCKPORT COUNTY v Oldham Athletic
League One
Friday 3rd October 2008, 7.45pm, Edgeley Park, Stockport

I was in my own little dream-world fantasising about a roast dinner until I snapped out of it, suddenly realising that I was sitting in the freezing cold in Stockport on a Friday night, by myself, watching a six-foot owl named Chaddy wiping his arse with a Stockport County scarf. This isn't normal.

Stockport 3-1 Oldham was the first instance in which I didn't really enjoy being at a match at all. The scoreline flattered the very poor game, and the hostile atmosphere spilled over into the first case of actual violence I have ever witnessed at a football match.

Things were different when I first got to Stockport. I was struggling after last night out in Manchester. I forgot how much horrible crap fresher students like to drink, and how an old man like me can struggle to keep up (I say old man, I really mean someone who can't still pass for 16 just from a simple bit of hair wetting).

I had slept on Greg's floor without a cover or a pillow, remnants of a kebab to the right of my head and Collo's feet to the left. I was a tad weary, but my first impressions of Stockport led me to believe I was going to enjoy the evening. The Oldham fans travelling to the match were in great spirits, singing "Oh Chrissy Taylor, you are the love of my life! Oh Chrissy Taylor, I'd let you shag my wife! Oh Chrissy Taylor, I want ginger hair too!" to the tune of *I Can't Take My Eyes Off You*.

Edgeley Park seemed a good honest League One ground, placed nicely in the middle of residential roads, and there was a great atmosphere for the Friday night match. The fans all seemed excited about a good old-fashioned derby.

I was speaking to an old gent in the ticket queue and told him I was there as a neutral.

"You may struggle to get a ticket mate," he said to me, "there might be some trouble because it's a derby, and they don't want any

Oldham fans getting tickets for the Stockport end. So unless you've got a Stockport postcode you might not get in."

I thought that was a bit strong for a Friday night League One match in which the ground was likely to be half full. Fortunately for me I was right, and I got let in without any problems, but the old gent did have a certain Mystic Meg quality with his predictions. More about that in a minute.

I liked Stockport fans but without question, and I mean this in the most respectful way possible (though I don't think this can really be taken respectfully), Stockport fans are the ugliest and weirdest looking fans I have ever seen. Every other person looked like they were a character from Little Britain or the League of Gentleman, or some freak from the Guinness Book of Records (world's hairiest earlobes or something like that). Chins, noses, eyebrows, mouths, nipples, arses, were all in the wrong places, and the wrong shapes. But I liked them. People were cheering their team brilliantly and I was clapping along in the Cheadle End enjoying myself. But it all went a bit wrong when Oldham scored the opener in the 24th minute. About thirty Oldham fans were sitting together amongst the Stockport supporters, the opposite side of the Cheadle End to where I was sitting. They celebrated wildly when Oldham scored, and a big fight broke out between them and many Stockport fans, not only sitting around them, but also those who piled in to the troubled area to get involved.

It was quite shocking, there was a massive police involvement, and the game was stopped for about 7 or 8 minutes while the fight was broken up and the fans were led out by the police and stewards. The fight had spilled onto the pitch by the corner flag, and fans, some with blood all over their faces, were being escorted out across the width of the actual pitch past the bemused Oldham goalkeeper.

The most unpleasant element for me was delivered by a man sitting directly in front of me. He was a small bloke, completely toothless on the upper front-row, and was watching the game with his wife. They were a proper Jeremy Kyle case couple.

The man was a bit edgy for the first 23 minutes, eyeing up Oldham fans, and running towards the side of the pitch to swear at the Oldham players when they got close. When the fight broke out he absolutely stormed over to the area to throw some punches. His wife began crying sitting in front of me. Did I tell her it was OK and try and console her or pretend I couldn't see her crying? I could see the other people around me weighing up the moral dilemma, until her husband came back with a cut on his cheek.

"For God's sake Shaun!" the wife screamed at him, hitting him on the arm. "You haven't got any sense! Think of me and the babies! What will happen to me and the babies if you go to prison again?!"

It was awkward to say the least, especially when the bloke turned round to see me and the rest of my row staring at them. I quickly averted my eyes and pretended that my shoes were the most interesting thing I had ever seen. They weren't. They had holes in them and were soggy, but that was about it.

The other slightly unnerving thing was the amount of kids that were getting involved in the fighting. The early-teen lads piled into the fight area as soon as it kicked off. There were a large amount of hormone-fuelled youths there for the footy at the end of a school week, and I think the lads were mainly getting involved to impress the girls. Which is romantic I suppose.

The atmosphere calmed down a bit and play resumed, and for the rest of the match there were no problems. In fact, it gee'd up Stockport fans and the team for the second half with Stockport scoring three goals and turning over Oldham with relative ease after all that.

Looking back on it, the fighting wasn't *so* bad, but it did shock me to see bleeding faces being led across the pitch by police in an English League match. And I think that's because I'm so used to friendly and harmless atmospheres at grounds across the country.

I will try to remember Stockport by my first impressions of it being a club with a great fan base and a warm community spirit rather than the punches being thrown. It sure was exciting though. If I was brave enough I would try and go to the return leg at Oldham later in the season.

STOCKPORT COUNTY 3 (Turnbull 47, Thompson 68, Raynes 82)
OLDHAM ATHLETIC   1 (Liddell 24)
Attendance 8,360

GAME 16
CHESTER CITY v Lincoln City
League Two
Saturday 4ᵗʰ October 2008, 3.00pm, Deva Stadium, Chester

After a turbulent Friday night in Stockport I headed back to Liverpool, my university city, to the warmth and (relative) comfort of Collo's sofa. Collo, being a foreign language student (a Wiganer speaking an Austrian dialect of German... there's an accent to behold) still has a year left of his degree, and lives with Paul, my other dearest friend from uni. This sofa was glorious. There was something very wet and sticky down the side of one of the cushions, but I chose to ignore it and reminded myself to be thankful that I wasn't on the floor again. I was delighted to be back in Liverpool, where I had a fantastic scattering of extended friends including Jamie and Duffy, two of my oldest and best mates from school.

Chester City was quite a difficult sell for potential game buddies, but I speculatively asked Jamie and Duffy to take the glamorous trip to the Deva Stadium, and with great shock found them both to be well up for it. I suppose they had experienced less lower-league football than me in recent weeks, so there may be some novelty value.
"I've never been to Chester," said Jamie as I was driving under the Mersey.
"Me neither! Is it going to be all nice and old and Hollyoaksish?" Duffy asked me, creating a word in the process.
"I don't know, it's meant to be a lovely place. The town I mean. The ground is situated half in Wales and half in England apparently. There's a fact for you!" I said, trying and failing to impress my friends with some top trivia. The car began swerving in the wind.
"Is the ground not in the town?"
"Errr...no. I think it's in an industrial park outside the centre."
This was a bit of a letdown for Jamie and Duffy, who were expecting the stadium to be placed sweetly in between the cathedral and the historic city walls, with flocks of birds tweeting from the green tree

tops hanging over the sun-drenched terraces as the female cast from Hollyoaks hand out free fudge in bikinis.

We reached the grey and ugly industrial park and it smelt of shit. Really really smelly. I don't know what on earth the smell was. It might have been near some farmland? Or an open sewer? Did it always smell of shit or had we just caught it on a bad day?
The ground wasn't particularly awe-inspiring but we passed some time in the club shop. Well, about 5 seconds. I think I was becoming slowly obsessed with club shops across the country, and the differences between the 'superstores'. We walked in for a browse and saw about 4 shirts on sale and a couple of scarves in a tiny room. The bloke behind the counter looked at us oddly as we entered, and we swiftly exited straight away.
"Just a flying visit then lads?"
"Errrr yeah. " I replied sheepishly.

We got our tickets, (which were made out of paper, and looked a bit like the kind of ticket you would get at a raffle) and sat right behind the dugouts. This was the cause of much amusement between myself and my two pals, mostly at the expense of the lovable wally Lincoln manager Peter Jackson. We were also sitting a few seats away from Frank Sinclair. That's right! THE Frank Sinclair, of former Chelsea, Leicester, and hilarious own-goal specialist fame! Who now plays for Lincoln! What a cause for lots of exclamation marks!
"Look at old Franky boy! Doesn't he look good?! I should get a photo with him?" I said. Sinclair was wearing a matching multicoloured hat/scarf combo. Very dashing.

Jackson and Sinclair were our main form of amusement because the match was, to put it as politely as I can, *absolute bollocks*. Chester were very bad. The crowd of less than 2000 were fairly vocal about their displeasure in being at the match, similar to what I experienced in Barnet in August. One player in particular, one of the two Vaughans that were on the pitch (sons of the chairman), was feeling the brunt of the disgruntlement.

"You're USELESS Vaughan!" a shrill voice creakily shouted from a few rows behind us. I looked round to see that it was a lady who was quite possibly over 100 years old.

"You're too slow Vaughan!"

Vaughan carried on running back, taking no notice of the lady.

"VAUGHAN!! VAUGHAN!!" she continued.

Vaughan turned his head and looked at the crowd.

"You're too slow! You're <u>absolutely</u> useless!"

Vaughan's shoulders dropped and he looked deflated. To be generally slagged off by the crowd is fine, but to be slagged off by a single old lady in such a personal manner must be hard to recover from. Poor Vaughan. Although to be fair to the old lady he *was* pants.

Lincoln scored on the brink of half-time, and then got another early in the second half. Peter Jackson ran to the side of the pitch in celebration and struck a sort of weird Elvis Presley type pose. The wind was getting silly now. The ball was moving in the air, and at one point a McCoys crisp packet got stuck in one of the Chester defenders' hair.

I had a very funny day out with my two old pals, but I find myself not being very complimentary about poor Chester City. The tiny club shop, the paper tickets, the "are they Welsh, are they English" confusion, the horrendous smell surrounding the ground. Chester *almost* have enough quirky charm to make me like them. But not quite enough. I am a sucker for old stadiums built in the hub of a town centre, positioned amongst residential areas and a focal point for a community. Which the Deva Stadium is most certainly not.

The grey day summed up the grey mood of the Chester fans as the final whistle went and the 2-0 defeat was confirmed.

But my mood was terrific!

I only bloody got a photo with Frank Sinclair!

"Wow! Frank! You're my hero." I lied to him.

"Errr right cheers." Frank lovingly replied, pondering whether or not I was a weirdo.

"Can I have a photo?"

"Even though I've got this stupid hat on? Yeah sure."

"I'm writing a book!" I told a fascinated Frank. "I'm going to all 92 League grounds and telling the world about my experiences." "Errr...Ok." Frank affectionately retorted. "I'll look out for that." Yes you will Frank. Yes you will.

CHESTER CITY 0
LINCOLN CITY 2 (Kovacs 45, Patulea 57)
Attendance 1,962

EVERTON v Newcastle United
Premier League
Sunday 5th October 2008, 4.00pm, Goodison Park, Liverpool

To me, Liverpool is a second home. After three fantastic years at university in the city I feel an incredible amount of warmth and familiarity towards both the place and the people. I don't know why I had never managed to get to see Everton before, but my trip to see their match with Newcastle was my first trip to Goodison Park. I was excited. I left Paul and Collo's house with a spring in my step. I got chatting to a lost-looking Chinese guy on the way to the match who was very concerned about being on the wrong bus.

"This for Goodison football?" he asked me in very broken English.

"Yeah mate it is."

"Everton FC?"

"Yep, that's right."

"Everton Goodison Park?"

"You've got it!"

"This bus yes?"

"Yep!"

"Thank you. Thank you."

The very grateful young man I found out was called Woody[1], was from Hong Kong and in England for a few months. The allure of the Premier League had obviously temporarily sucked Woody away from the deep cultural goings on in Liverpool (Capital of Culture 2008 of course).

I moved to Merseyside without any preference between Everton or Liverpool, and came out three years later with a real soft spot for the blues, and a severe lack of fondness for the reds. I could rant

---

[1] I *say* the man's name was Woody, but his English was really rather difficult to understand. After asking him to repeat his name 3 times I decided it sounded most like Woody. Although as far as I know, Woody is not a particularly common Chinese name.

about the intricate reasons behind this, but I might save that for when I visit Anfield. Although to sum it up, I found when living in the city that 90% of Everton fans I met were funny, self-deprecating and charming, whereas 90% of Liverpool fans I met were quite the opposite. There ain't no delusion like the delusion of a bloody Liverpool supporter.

Despite their differences both Liverpool and Everton have huge support around the country, and are two of the most successful clubs of all time in the English top flight. The best thing about this however, is that they haven't lost what makes them inherently *scouse*. The area around Stanley Park is very working-class and full of passionate local fans. Everton call themselves the 'peoples club', and there is a definite element of truth to this.

Goodison is a wonderful old stadium that manages to possess the brilliant mixture of the grandeur of the Premier League with the scruffy, rustic charm of the best of the lower-leagues. The ground is not modernised by any stretch of the imagination, with limited seat room, pillars restricting views and a curiously cramped design for the food and toilet area. Yet somehow this manages to be integral to the charmingly dishevelled nature of Goodison compared to many smarter and more modern grounds.

I entered the stadium and went to find my seat, bumping into a fantastic old gent in the entrance who went out of his way to help me find it.

"Don't worry lad, follow me," he said in a thick and gruff scouse accent (I think I probably could have managed to find it myself, but to be personally led to you seat by an old season-ticket holder is rather nice).

Everton had started the season poorly after a summer of little transfer activity, but went two goals ahead today through the spectacularly-afroed Fellaini and an Arteta penalty. Despite being 2-0 up there was still the sense amongst the fans that the team was probably not going to win, even against a Newcastle side in a state of crisis under interim manager Joe 'volcano' Kinnear. Indeed the negativity around the ground was reflected on the pitch when Newcastle pegged Everton back in the second half, allowing a fair result of 2-2.

I think the poor start to the season had affected the atmosphere. The Everton fans were very nice, but not very loud. The Newcastle fans on the other hand were very loud, but not particularly nice. Predictable anti-scouse chants of 'You stole my stereo!' and 'Sign on, sign on, with hope in your hearts, and you'll never get a job!' chorused the away end.

The fans weren't happy, but I had a great day out at Goodison. I left the stadium and found a most peculiar sight. It was Woody! My old mate. Old buddy old pal Woody. And he was crouching on the floor with a couple of action-figure toys in front of him. This was a bit odd. Woody was carefully lining up the toys in front of the stadium to get a perfect picture.

"Woody!" I went up to him and shook his hand. "What on earth are you doing?"

"I take picture of Goodison."

"With your toys?"

"Yes."

I decided I wasn't going to get much information out of Woody so I decided to probe harder, Newsnight-style.

"Are you taking pictures like this around England?"

"Yes. At football."

I stepped it up a gear. I was Paxman. I was Humphreys. I was Dimbleby. I was Garth bloody Crooks.

"Have you been to other football grounds taking pictures like this?"

"Yes!" Woody looked happy. "I been Manchester, Arsenal, Chelsea."

Oh my word. Woody was my spiritual brother. My doppelganger from Hong Kong. He had it right! Maybe he was writing a book about this! 92 Kung-Po Shrimp! OR maybe he could be my *official photographer!* Tom and Woody! I could change my name to Buzz Lightyear!

I excitedly told him I'd just been to Chester and Stockport the previous two days. After a good few minutes of explaining, I was shocked to find out that Woody had absolutely no idea what a Chester or a Stockport was.

I think Woody was more of a mainstream fellow. He was in it for the big guns. I was sad to realise it, but we were not on the same wavelength after all. I wished Woody the best with his quest, and

I'm sure that if he knew what I was going on about, he would have wished me success with mine. Woody could stick to the likes of Everton. I had Tranmere in the Johnstone's Paint Trophy the next day, and I don't think that competition is broadcast in Hong Kong. *YET....*

EVERTON   **2** (Arteta pen 17, Fellaini 35)
NEWCASTLE UNITED   **2** (Taylor 45, Duff 47)
Attendance 33,805

GAME 18
TRANMERE ROVERS v Crewe Alexandra
Johnstone's Paint Trophy Northern Section, Second Round
Monday 6th October 2008, 7.45pm, Prenton Park, Birkenhead, Wirral

If you look deep enough into my soul you will find a special corner reserved for my everlasting resentment of Tranmere Rovers Football Club. Normally in life I do not hold a grudge; but the pain of Tranmere knocking Bolton out of the League Cup semi-finals in the 1999-2000 season, and John Aldridge's smug victory dance in front of the Bolton fans... Aaargh! My face goes red with anger just thinking about it. The same year we lost the FA Cup semi-final to Aston Villa, *and* the Play-Off semi-final to Ipswich. 3 semi-final defeats in one season. Dark times.

But now I had decided to follow a new, more placid outlook to life in which I do not see John Aldridge's moustachioed grin staring at me whenever I close my eyes. So I made the short trip to the Wirral to watch the mighty Rovers with no pre-judgements or lingering bitterness whatsoever. Nope. None at all.

I roped along Collo and Paul to witness the spectacular near-derby match between Rovers and Crewe, which would incidentally be my first ever Johnstone's Paint Trophy encounter. On the train I found out that both Pauls[1] had been to Prenton Park before, *and* for a JPT match, the 2006-2007 classic of Tranmere 0-1 Darlington.

"Brilliant it was too." Paul over-enthusiastically stated. Paul is a Darlington fan from Loughborough. Probably the *only* Darlington fan from Loughborough, just as I am probably the only Bolton fan in Harpenden. Kindred spirits you see.

"Giallanza penalty, bottom left corner. Perfect." Paul dreamily recalled in his unbelievably low bassy East-Midlands drawl. His voice is so deep, that when I lived with him, if he spoke quietly whilst

---

[1] Collo's real human name is actually Paul Collins. His creative moniker of 'Collo' was born to save the undignified name of 'Paul 2' we threatened to forever refer to him as, on the basis that we knew the other Paul first.

downstairs, the upstairs floor would vibrate. Skinny, with long flowing blondey-brown locks suiting his grungy style, Paul has an incredible memory and is an extreme geek about the two things that excite him the most; lower-league football and the geography of England. In fact, he should really be doing 92 Pies instead of me. Why didn't he think of it first?

"It's not really a derby though." Paul said to me after I commented that Crewe v Tranmere might have been.

"They're pretty close though aren't they?"

"Hmmm. 40 miles or so."

I looked it up later that night. They are *exactly* 40 miles apart. Honestly, you can give Paul the name of any two towns in England and he will give you an accurate distance between the two. Matlock to Uckfield Paul? Why that would be 207 miles, providing you took the M1 for most of the way.

What with all my prejudices and inhibitions about Tranmere being discarded, I am delighted to report that I quite liked Prenton Park (secretly said through gritted teeth). In a pleasant part of Birkenhead, the stadium suddenly pops up from behind some houses, and seemed much bigger that I thought it would be. You have to applaud the fans for keeping their allegiances on their side of the river, and not being tempted by either of the slightly more appealing Merseyside clubs.

It was a very poor match, and we were clinging on to the potential that it could go to penalties, with there being no extra-time in JPT ties.

"I've never seen a penalty shoot-out I don't think," said Collo.

"Me neither!" replied Paul. They looked at me and I floated into my dark place again.

"I have once. Bolton against Villa in the 2000 FA Cup semi-final. A few weeks after we'd lost to Tranmere in the League Cup semi-final actually..."

The pang of hatred for John Aldridge had come back momentarily, but I snapped out of it as the fans around me began laughing at the referee getting the ball smashed into his testicles. Right bang smack in them. Crunched them up. It was quite funny.

Half-time provided much amusement as well, with the Tranmere substitutes getting bored with warming up, and booting the balls to people in the crowd. I caught the eye of one of the subs and gestured to him to place the ball on my head. He saw me and teed the ball up. This was great! I even took my glasses off in preparation. And then the kick went woefully wide of my head into an area of empty seats. With that kind of accuracy I can see why he was a Tranmere substitute rather than playing in the Champions League I suppose.

With slamming disappointment, Tranmere scored four minutes from time, ensuring that the potential penalty shoot-out would be cruelly snatched away from our outstretched arms.

"Ah crap. Another 1-0 at Tranmere. That's the last time I go to Prenton Park with either of you," Collo moaned.

On the way home, tuning out whilst Paul was telling an enthralling story about how Darlington signed Liechtenstein full-back Franz Burgmeier, I decided I would for once and for all make my peace with Tranmere. John Aldridge is probably more associated with Liverpool than Tranmere anyway. Let bygones be bygones and focus my hatred on Liverpool instead. Yep, that'll do.

TRANMERE ROVERS 1 (Shuker 86)
CREWE ALEXANDRA 0
Attendance 2,626

GAME 19
ROCHDALE v Carlisle United
Johnstone's Paint Trophy Northern Section, Second-Round
Tuesday 7th October 2008, 7.45pm, Spotland Stadium, Rochdale

With the fate of my evening in the balance, I held a rusty 2p between my fingers and flipped. Heads I would go to Rochdale, tails I would go to Bury. With the Queen's handsome profile staring back at me the coin had spoken, and I left a stormy Liverpool and ventured forth to Rochdale.

I was very weary after six days full of football, fun, and the occasional frolic. Driving to Rochdale, my car wasn't behaving very well. The brakes were rumbling an awful lot. I decided that Rochdale v Carlisle was worth me potentially risking my life and I carried on driving through the relentless rain, choosing to ignore the violent shaking of the car every time I stroked the brakes.

Driving very slowly, I got to Spotland Stadium a minute late and rushed to the nearest turnstile. I was drenched, but happy I had reached the ground safe and sound as I sat down with the Rochdale fans. Almost as soon as I sat down, Rochdale scored! Brilliant! Michael Bridges! Legend. My brain was fizzing. I thought Rochdale played in Blue, not Red? I must be knackered.

I stood up and cheered along with the Rochdale fans.

"One nil! To the Cumbrians, One nil! To the Cumbrians!" they sang. Hold on.

Something wasn't right.

Rochdale isn't in Cumbria.

And they don't play in Red.

And Michael Bridges doesn't play for them.

I took a lot longer to come to the conclusion than I should have.

....

....

....

Still thinking...

....

....

....

Oh shit!

I was in the Carlisle end accidently!

What a nincompoop! This was cheating the objective of my task! I was in the away end, meaning that my encounter of visiting Rochdale would be tainted by these bloody Carlisle fans surrounding me!

I decided to take immediate action, and went to find a steward and explain my situation.

"So you accidently went in the Carlisle end?" the unimpressed female steward said.

"That's right."

"And you want to go into the Rochdale end?"

"That's right."

"And you're a Rochdale fan?"

My mouth answered before my brain could consider the consequences.

"Yes."

"But you've got a Southern accent?"

Why did I lie? She would definitely be more understanding if I admitted to being a poor young Southern writer just seeking to discover the essence of Rochdale by being amongst the blood sweat and tears of her good fellow-Rochdalian folk.

"Yes I do. I live in London but my dad is from Rochdale so I'm a Rochdale fan." My web of lies continued.

"And you've come up for this match?" she asked, the tone in her voice suggesting that the second-round of the Johnstone's Paint Trophy was not worth a 450-mile round trip.

"Yes."

"You've been Spotland before?" the interrogation continued. Is this in her job description? Come on Tom, get all Keyser Soze on her arse.

"Yes, of course."

"Then why did you go into the away end?"

"Because..." I looked outside for inspiration. "Because it was raining." I incomprehensively replied.

"It was raining?"

"Yes."

She looked at me with utter contempt.

"Come on." She sighed with a bored resignation, and led me through the cordoned off area towards the home end. I was brilliant. I should lie more often.

Once amongst my own people, (what with my new found Rochdale heritage) I relaxed into what was a thoroughly enjoyable match. As soon as I sat down in the correct end, Rochdale scored, and then got another five minutes later. I was a lucky charm to whichever end I was sitting in!

The most interesting thing to note about Rochdale is that they have been in the 4th tier of English football since 1974, which is really quite remarkable. In fact, League Two has often been referred to as the 'Rochdale division' in honour of the perennial mid-tablers. No promotions or relegations in 34 years means life as a Rochdale fan must be fairly dull.

There is little about the club to shout about, but the official website goes to some length to wax lyrical about the ground;

"You are always guaranteed a warm welcome at Spotland. Rochdale AFC offers one of the best match-day experiences in the division. The facilities and hospitality are second to none, as voted by various publications and football ground guides....The only problem with Rochdale is that, unless you are a home fan, you get to go there only once a season."

High praise indeed, although I saw little evidence to support these self-complimentary statistics. Perhaps it was the rain, but there was a fairly dismal atmosphere surrounding the ground, the fans being pretty glum about their team, and the facilities and hospitality certainly being second to many.

In the second half lightning began to strike, and the ball-boy in front of us took the little blue stool he was sitting on and put it over his head.

The conditions led to a match that was enjoyable but shambolic. There were absolutely heaps of chances for both teams and the 2-2 final scoreline could, and probably should, have been doubled. Which meant that, with no extra time in the mighty JPT, my reward for braving the gruelling driving conditions would be a penalty shootout! Oh yes. After the false alarm at Tranmere the day before, I would finally get my penalties.

There was something glorious about watching a penalty shootout knowing it can't end with England getting knocked out. As Carlisle's first penalty taker Simon Hackney stood up to take the kick, a very young Rochdale fan screamed "You earn too much money!" at him. Which is an odd insult to aim at a Carlisle substitute. It worked to put him off though because he missed! Seven successful spot-kicks later, Carlisle missed their crucial one, which meant a triumph for Rochdale. Maybe this could be their season after all! Perhaps not for promotion, but for the Johnstone's Paint Trophy! It is the new FA Cup don't you know...

ROCHDALE   **2** (Thorpe 10, Dagnall 16)
CARLISLE UNITED   **2** (Bridges 4, Madine 71)
(Rochdale win 4-2 on penalties)
Attendance 1,608

DAGENHAM AND REDBRIDGE v Barnet

League Two

Friday 10th October 2008, 7.45pm, Victoria Road, Dagenham, East London

I like to think that one of my best (or worst) character traits is that I have a talent for convincing friends to do things they don't particularly want to do. However, even by my standards, convincing John to spend his Friday night watching Dagenham and Redbridge was impressive. Wow I'm good.

Being partly the reason I am doing this ridiculous adventure, John is a special person (a backhanded compliment which can be interpreted in many different ways). His blonde hair, blue eyes and effortless charm make him a hit with mums across the country, but those who know him better see John escape his mother-friendly facade to become his alter-ego 'Johnny B', a party-loving, reckless and carefree man with the most irritating ability to fall on his feet in any given situation.

Example:

John, although an intelligent fellow, does next to no-work at university over three years, instead spending his time drinking, smoking and seducing. Approaching his final exams, John is struggling to consolidate his overall 2:2 grade. It is statistically impossible for John to get a 2:1. The day before his exams begin, John goes cycling in a forest and falls off his bike attempting a jump. John gets a painful hernia. John's genitals turn blue. John decides to attend his final exams, but sits them in writhing agony. John does, however, take a photograph of his blue genitals and show them to his tutor to prove his pain. John's tutors take pity on John. John ends up with the 2:1 degree, that was statistically impossible to achieve. The day after John's hernia operation, John sleeps with his nurse. John is happy.

We were queuing at the turnstiles to see Dagenham and Redbridge v Barnet (by my reckoning probably the 17th most prestigious of the 17 London derbies that the Football League would be hosting this season), and I was getting angsty, we had already missed kick-off. It was John's fault, he had been late to meet me at the station. He had to go back home because he forgot his wallet. And phone.

"Relax!" said John, taking a guzzle of his hipflask.

"Yeah, I just don't want a repeat of last time I watched Barnet. I arrived 10 minutes late and missed the only goal of the game."

"Nah we'll be fine! Look we're nearly at the front."

The queue was moving very slowly. People obviously weren't in a hurry to see the Daggers play. Finally we reached the turnstiles, and as I handed over my criminally extortionate £17 there was a huge cheer from inside the stadium, just a few dozen feet away. Dagenham and Redbridge had scored. For the love of God! I gave John my disapproving stare.

"Arggh! I am destined to never see a goal in a Barnet game. I guarantee you this will end up 1-0!"

I was initially irritated with the long queue, expensive ticket and punctual goal scorers at Dagenham, but I quickly forgave the club for all this when I realised how brilliantly shabby the stadium is from the inside. The terraces were packed with all different types of football fan, with many families choosing to spend their Friday night together watching some good honest lower-league football.

The terraces at Dagenham are perfect. They ensure that you are so close to the pitch that if you reached out your arm you could touch the players (if for some reason that felt like a good idea). I love watching football from that close; you appreciate much more of the physical side of the game. Knowing that the players can hear every word you say makes you more involved in the match at a personal level; you become a *supporter* in the literal sense of the word.

The terraces felt full even though at 2,629 the ground was less than half of capacity, so to get 6,000 in must be a tight squeeze. Whilst Victoria Road seems full and vibrant with less than 3,000 people in, other huge all-seater League Two stadiums such as the Darlington Arena and Valley Parade would feel massively empty with the same amount of fans.

As I have done at every ground, I got my camera out and took a couple of photos to mark the occasion. John wanted one of him holding his hip-flask in the air with the action in the background. I went to get my pie at a stall just behind the goal and realised you could actually watch the game while in the queue! And at only £2 a pie it made up for the pricey ticket entry.

"The game isn't that good really. Is League Two normally this bad?" I thought about all my League Two escapades so far.

"Yeah it is. Barnet at home were actually worse than they are today."

"Jesus. Number 25's had a good game though." John said looking at Solomon Taiwo as he lunged in for a crunching tackle. "He's a horrible bastard. I like him."

Thankfully, Dagenham got their second goal, meaning that I finally got to see a goal in a Barnet game. In the midst of celebration I noticed that two stewards were walking towards John and I in the terraces. I didn't think much of it until they came closer and closer, eventually arriving at us. Shit! Did they see John drinking his booze? "Is this him?" one steward said to the other as they squeezed past John and stood either side of me. ME?! What have I bloody done? It was John illegally drinking whisky! If I go down I'm bringing that pillock down with me.

"Yep that's him," the other one said.

"Sir..." the bigger one said to me dramatically. "Have you been taking photographs of this game?"

"Errrrr... yes?!" I replied; baffled with what he had just said to me.

"I'm afraid you are not allowed to do that. Please refrain from taking any more photos."

"Okay," I said politely, "but just out of interest...*why* are you not allowed to?"

The steward thought for about 5 seconds.

"Copyright."

"Copyright?"

"That's correct."

What on earth is copyrighted?!?! The players faces? I decided not to argue my point any further and put my camera in the bottom of my bag as the stewards walked away.

John laughed at me.

"That was a close one!" he said with an irritating grin, taking out his hipflask and having a big swig. "You shouldn't be taking photos now Tom. You know better than that."

Full-time came, and I decided that despite a couple of problems I had thoroughly enjoyed my unusual Friday night match in Dagenham.

One of the best things about the Football League is what different experiences it can offer from club to club. The Dagenham and Redbridge experience is a brilliant one, mainly due to the cramped terraces full of happy football fans. It may have been an odd choice of a night out for me and John, but for nearly 3000 people in East London it was perfectly normal.

"What now?" John said we left Victoria Road and wandered back to the tube station.

"Well there's a late night showing of The Dark Knight at the IMAX in about an hour..." I pondered.

"Let's do it!" John grinned.

Dagenham and the Dark Knight. What more could you want from a Friday night out in London?

DAGENHAM AND REDBRIDGE   2 (Ritchie 9, Strevens 62)
BARNET   0
Attendance 2,629

GAME 21
NOTTS COUNTY v Brentford
League Two
Monday 13th October 2008, 7.45pm, Meadow Lane, Nottingham

Notts County's former manager Jimmy Sirrell said upon taking the job in 1969 "*Ask any kid what he knows about Notts County and he'll tell you they're the oldest football team in the world. By the time I've finished he'll know a lot more.*"

The legendary Sirrell, who passed away two weeks prior to my visit to Meadow Lane, would be disappointed to find out that this particular kid only really knows that Notts County are the oldest football team in the world. And not a lot more.

In poor form down in League Two, County's recent dismal fortunes are not the stuff that Sirrell dreamt of. I drove up to Nottingham and the 'stadium area', with Meadow Lane, Forest's City Ground and the Trent Bridge, the cricket stadium all within a short walk of each other. Meadow Lane is an impressive 20,000 capacity ground, but I doubt County have had that many spectators in since 1862 when they were the only football club in the world (there wasn't as much competition back then you see.)

County fans have a fair quarrel to be given the unofficial title of the most 'long-suffering' fans in the country on the basis that no other club has been promoted and relegated more than they have. Personally however, I would take promotions and relegations over becoming a Rochdale-style single league dweller for eternity.

This Monday match had a £5 entry fee which I lapped up; caused by the presence of the Sky cameras putting off potential supporters from attending, as is the sad reality throughout all 4 leagues. County were playing Brentford, whose fans were in great form, respectfully singing "There's only one Jimmy Sirrell" along with the Nottingham faithful.

To compliment the £5 ticket the £2 pie was a delicious and thoroughly desired chicken effort; warming me up as I took my place surrounded by many empty seats.

I didn't really recognise any of the County players except the 'keeper Russell Hoult. The former West Brom hero Hoult is one of those players with various legends about their private lives floating around to compliment any achievements made during their playing careers. A Baggies fan I know always brings out a detailed history of Russell Hoult sex stories when anyone asks, alongside his equally entertaining soliloquy 'The Troubled Life and Times of Lee Hughes' or even 'The Ginger Genius of Gary Megson.'

"Old Russ must be about 40 now," I muttered to the bloke next to me.

"Bet he's still a hit with the ladies though!" he replied.

Brentford went 1-0 up against the run of play, and half-time came with a short match began between County under 8s and Brentford under 8s. These kids were unbelievable. Crunching slide tackles, dropping of shoulders, step-overs. Honestly, if they weren't about 2 foot tall I would have put most of them in the County team.

During a dull second half I admired a hilariously awkward family outing unfolding in front of me. The dad, with a bushy moustache, kept making uncomfortable, borderline racist, jokes to which his son's girlfriend politely and nervously laughed to. He would also occasionally stand up and bellow abuse at the referee, usually calling him a word that rhymes with punt, shunt or Nicky Hunt.

County did eventually score through a dodgy penalty, leaving the customers moderately satisfied with their £5 tickets with the result being 1-1.

The fans were actually pretty loud, boisterous but also funny and acerbic towards their team. Songs such as "Two Pies on our shirt, 20 years of hurt never stopped us dreaming" warmed me to the tongue-in-cheek melancholy of the fans. This is all best summed up by the infamous 'wheelbarrow' song of "I had a wheelbarrow, the wheel fell off (and repeat)" bellowed out from the kop end. Rather than be an historic chant from the era of Jimmy Sirrell, the wheelbarrow song was born in Shrewsbury in 1990 when County were at their lowest ebb, the lyrics apparently summing up the mood of the time perfectly. Today, the wheel remains off the wheelbarrow for Notts County, but I hope they can fix it soon, it's what their history, their stadium, the remaining fans and the late great Jimmy Sirrell deserve.

NOTTS COUNTY 1 (Forrester pen 65)
BRENTFORD   1 (Poole 36)
Attendance 6,012

GAME 22
LUTON TOWN v Accrington Stanley
League Two
Saturday 18th October 2008, 3.00pm, Kenilworth Road, Luton

The time had come. I had been putting it off but as the 11th week of my quest delving into the football unknown began, I would now reluctantly enter much more familiar territory with Luton Town FC. Oh Luton. I can't say the word without an undercurrent of tragedy polluting my tone. Just three seasons ago they were in the Championship, looking a fairly decent outfit, nearly beating Liverpool in the FA Cup. Now they are destined for non-league football after the 30-point penalty given to them at the beginning of this season. Poor Luton. Poor lovely cuddly darling harmless beautiful sweet innocent Luton.

When I was about 12 I used to go to Kenilworth Road fairly regularly with my best friend at the time, Tony. Tony was a true geezer in the Del Boy/Kray twins mould even at that age. Now ten years on at 22 he predictably co-owns a second hand car business. We used to go to watch Luton with his dad Tony Snr in literally the best seats in the ground; the box right at the halfway line.

Walking from the station to the stadium with John and another friend, Dan, I realised I hadn't been to see Luton for about 7 years even though I kind-of consider them my 2nd team. And although I very seldom go to the town voted the official crappest in England (for what reason would I? The £12 all-you-can-drink nightclub is about it) I do live very near. In fact my road in Harpenden is actually called Luton Road. I won't tell you my house number. Knock on every door and you'll find me eventually. Come in! I'll make you a tea. Even provide a flapjack if I have any in.

The main reason I haven't been to see Luton is that it's a pretty unpleasant experience. The ground is situated in an extremely deprived part of the town, with disused sofas and various car-parts littering the streets. There is an uneasy coexistence in Luton between idiot meat-heads and Asian youths, which is not ideal with the football ground positioned right in the centre of the Asian community. I accidently witnessed horrible racial tension outside a pub in Luton on St George's day one year and it was a hugely uncomfortable experience.

Kenilworth Road itself is a horrible crumbling cess-pit bereft of the vintage charm of many other old league stadiums. Not counting the stand purely consisting of executive boxes the rest of the stadium offers limited visibility and no leg-room to compliment the rubbish that Luton spew on the pitch. The away stand can only be reached by squeezing down a single-file alleyway in between a row of terraced houses.

"£22.50??? To see *Luton?*" John angrily said to the ticket-office worker.

"Yes sir." The lady sighed back, as if this wasn't the first time she had heard this grumble.

John slammed his money on the desk.

"It's like giving to charity I suppose. They do need the money." I said, trying to make him feel better.

We took our £22.50 seats; wooden stumps with splinters poking out.

"Bargain," laughed Dan. Dan was at the match watching his cousin's best mate Harry Worley play at centre-back for Luton (how's that for a tenuous link?!). We sat with both of Worley's parents, who seemed both proud and nervous about their son playing.

"What's he like then Worley?" I asked Dan, out of his parents' ear-shot.

"Yeah he's a decent player. This is only his second game for Luton though so he's a bit nervous."

After 16 minutes Worley's feeble back-header fell straight to the feet of Accrington striker Paul Mullin who scored with an easy finish. Shit. This was embarrassing. I looked at John and we both nearly got the giggles.

"Awkward..." I whispered to him through gritted teeth, looking at the dismayed expression on Mr and Mrs Worley's faces.

Luton fans were doing their best to raise the atmosphere. The chant of "30 points, who gives a fuck, Luton Town are staying up!" was sang with enough spirit to make me almost believe it for a minute before coming to my senses. Another chant, "Oh Bedfordshire is wonderful! Oh Hertfordshire is full of shit!" sat much less favourably with me and my fellow Hertfordshire friends. Honestly, we'd only travelled 5 miles and now we were being told we were 'shit' because of our Hertfordshire roots.

"Sweet bloody Lord this is bad." John groaned as a defender managed to actually head the ball over the stadium. "Dagenham v Barnet now Luton v Accrington. Why am I only going to crap games with you?" He wasn't in the best of moods today.

Luton centre-back Ian Roper completely misplaced a pass and fell over whilst doing so. I hate to be rude, but Roper was pretty hopeless. He was fat. He had a fat belly and a fat arse.

"Jesus Christ! Roper is *crap!* He looks and plays like a bloody pub player. I'm better than him and I don't even get into the Harpenden Town C team," said John.

Luton actually managed to equalise before half-time, but 9 minutes into the second half Accrington deservedly went back in front after Roper got beaten for pace.

"You're shit Roper!"

"Go back to Walsall Roper you fat bastard!"

The fans were really turning on their own player. All of a sudden, amidst the abuse a frumpy frizzy-haired lady, sitting about 3 rows in front of us turned around.

"WILL YOU IDIOTS JUST SHUT THE HELL UP!!!"

The shaven-headed Luton fans were stunned into silence. The lady was cradling a young child in her arms whilst another played a Game Boy next to her. Something was weird about this though. She had taken the abuse about Roper quite personally, which the loutish fans quickly picked up on.

"Hold on! Why are you defending him luv? Are you Mrs Roper?"

The lady said nothing, and the group of men burst into uncontrollable laughter.

"She bloody well is! Mrs Roper! Fucking hell luv, get your husband on the Atkins diet will you?"

"Yeah you could do with that as well." They laughed and pointed at her.

It was cruel.

"Joke's on you you morons." Mrs Roper said, turning around defiantly. "You're the ones paying his wages."
The fans started cheering emphatically. Mrs Roper had balls, that's for sure. They began singing "There's only one Mrs Roper! One Mrs Roper!" and taking pictures of her. I didn't know whether to laugh or cry. Harry Worley's parents looked thoroughly grateful for Mrs. Roper, taking the attention away from their son's crucial mistake.
To sum the match up, Luton were awful and deserved to lose despite having some brilliant chances to equalise at the end. They simply weren't good enough and 30 points or no 30 points, relegation looks deserved.
We left pretty unsatisfied and saddened by witnessing the downfall of Luton with our very own eyes. It was sad, but if I had no pre-ordained geographical sentiment for Luton I am certain that I would loathe the club. What's not to hate?

- •• A horrible stadium in the hub of an intimidating and deprived area of the town officially voted worst in England (check)
- •• Awful seats/leg room/views ensuring an unsatisfying match-day experience (check)
- •• Horrendously overpriced tickets/food (check)
- •• Still many loutish, rude, Neanderthal supporters synonymous with the dark days of 1980s hooliganism (check)
- •• Throughout their history, various ridiculous mismanagement of the club including plastic pitches in the 1980s, a whole side of the stadium devoted to corporate boxes, and corruption running through the veins of the club culminating in a 30-point deduction and subsequent inevitable relegation and ruin (check)

But I can't hate Luton. And I can't hold any form of satisfaction at the demise of the club.
Luton, to me, is like an old friend who I do love, let also strongly dislike (everyone has one in their group of friends. If you don't – it's you). Yet despite my genuine dislike for them, I *have to* defend them, just because that's the way it is. I want to look after them and save them when things go wrong. The old friend is grimy, rough and anti-social, yet I love them because I have to. And seeing my friend's life collapse in front of my eyes is painful. The only way is down,

and although I want to help him, he is beyond help. There will be no redemption. R.I.P. Luton Town. For good and for bad, it's been emotional and I'll miss you.

LUTON TOWN **1** (Hall 34)
ACCRINGTON STANLEY **2** (Mullin 16, Gornell 54)
Attendance 5,492

GAME 23
NEWCASTLE UNITED v Manchester City
Premier League

Monday 20th October 2008, 8.00pm, St James' Park, Newcastle upon Tyne

My first significant milestone was in sight. At ¼ of the way through my journey I had seen a near riot at Stockport, a 9 goal thriller at Peterborough, unrivalled jubilation at Derby and dismay at Barnet, the exciting millionaires of Man City and devastating paupers of Luton. However, despite all this, the ¼ mark still meant I had ¾ to go to. Which is 69 more matches. And that's *loads*.

I woke up with a start at Annabel's house in Oxford on a frosty Monday morning. It was 8am and I was having a near-panic attack. I had been dreaming about the last day of the season, and my car breaking down on the way to Accrington Stanley, leaving me stuck on 91 for eternity.
"Annabel. Annabel." I shook her corpse-like body deep in slumber. "Annabel, what if it gets to the last day of the season and I haven't done it?! What then?"
"Phmmmmm," she helpfully replied.
"Exactly!! I need to start getting more in. God. Quick. What's going on tonight?"
I jumped over to her computer and checked the fixture list. Only one game on tonight, Newcastle were playing Man City. That must be sold out surely? Apparently not. I found out from the Newcastle website that you could buy tickets on the gate. Shall I do it? If I did go, then tonight's game neatly linked in with Hartlepool playing tomorrow, and perhaps even Chesterfield on the way home the next day.   Yes! This is exactly the reckless decision I should be making.
"Annabel," I gently said, rubbing her sleeping shoulders, "You know we were going to spend the day in Oxford and then go out for that meal tonight?"
"Hmmmph," she stirred, slightly waking.

"Well it turns out I have to leave right now to drive five hours away to the North-East to watch some football."

She definitely woke up at this bombshell.

An hour of reasoning and thinly-veiled promises of making amends later I was on the road up to Newcastle, five hours simply speeding by with Radio 3's Charles Mingus afternoon special.

I checked into my £15-per-night guest house which was much what you would expect for the price, but within a couple of metro stops from St James' Park. This was great! I entered the world of Geordie-life with a smile on my face at my rash decision to stand my girlfriend up and watch some football.

Unlike other big football cities such as Manchester and Liverpool, in Newcastle the ground is bang in the middle of the city centre. You almost feel that the rest of the city works around the stadium, given the level of importance the club holds with Geordies. Walking around Newcastle in the day the second thing that strikes you (after the bollock-freezing Easterly breeze) is the huge percentage of people; old, young, male and female, wearing Newcastle shirts.

I got to the stadium early but already there were thousands and thousands of fans soaking up the atmosphere. The metro station next to the ground has pictures of heroic former players, from Malcolm MacDonald to Les Ferdinand, decorating its walls, so as soon as you arrive you know you're in the football zone.

After a brief explore of the ground, including 'Shearer's bar' (where I had my first ever genuine Newcy Brown Ale) and the two-tiered massive club shop, I reached the ticket office and found a large steward approaching me.

"Alreet mate. You after a single ticket?"

"Yes." I replied meekly.

"That fella will sort you out," he said, pointing at a small, red-nosed, silver-haired man twiddling his thumbs.

"Hello." I said to the man.

"Alreetsonugottaneedforaticketlikecausigottaticketexecutivelikeho wayicannaeuse."

I nodded and said "Uhuh."

It turned out he was offering me and another man, a Scottish bloke called Alex, two spare platinum club tickets he was in possession of for a knock-down price! This drunkenly loveable but stern old Geordie seemed too good to be true. I apprehensively gave him my ticket money as he led me and Alex up some foreboding cold grey concrete back stairs to the platinum club area.

"Alreet lads. Meet me reet here in an hour under Pe'er Beardsley." He pointed directly above him to a signed picture of Peter Beardsley's Quasimodo face. He stumbled away leaving me with Alex in the platinum suite for a half hour. I smiled at him and he smiled back. I shrugged my shoulders and he nodded his head. This silent conversation had to end at some point.

"Pint?" I asked.

"Oh yes," he replied enthusiastically.

Ahhh. 'Pint'. The word to immediately remove any awkward silences between two males.

Alex and I chatted away over the afore-mentioned beverage for a while. He was actually a Rangers fan down in Newcastle on business, so we were two non-Newcastle fans cheering on Newcastle together.

"It's a funny old time for them I suppose isn't it," said Alex.

That was putting it mildly. Keegan had resigned in a passionate brain fart yet again, the Geordies had declared war on Mike Ashley and Dennis Wise's 'cockney mafia', and apparently the most sensible solution to steady the sinking Toon ship was to appoint Joe Kinnear as manager.

An interesting choice at the time. Even more interesting after he said 'shit' on Football Focus, causing the presenter Manish to splutter on his autocue like an embarrassed school teacher. Even *more* interesting after the infamous *Daily Mirror* interview in which he swore 52 times at journalists in 5 minutes, insulted pretty much everyone and projected himself as both tremendously insecure and under-qualified to cope with the pressures of the Premiership.

Without a win yet as 'interim' manager, Kinnear went all out to beat Man City and very nearly succeeded. My least favourite referee in the Premiership Rob Styles sent off Newcastle defender Habib Beye in the 12th minute and gave City a penalty, coolly slotted home by Mr £32million himself, Robinho.

I thought I had witnessed anger at other grounds before, but hell truly hath no fury like a Geordie scorned. There could not have been more disgust and anger directed at Styles if he had slept with each Geordie's wife, slapped their child and killed their favourite pet. He was public enemy number one two and three combined.

The boos and whistles were absolutely piercing for much of the first half, until Shola Ameobi, the human fork-lift-truck, bundled the ball in to equalise. The fans went wild for Ameobi.

"Howay Shola!"

"Think it went in off his arse! Hahaha! Canny!"

"Dinnae why Rooney's in the England squad ahead of him! Howay Shola!"

Half-time came and gave everyone a chance to cool down. In the booming atmosphere of St James's the noise levels were incredible. The equaliser had slightly eased the tension about Rob Styles though, and when Alan Shearer popped out to wave to the crowd and give away a charity bike at half-time there was far more warmth from the angry bunch of Geordies. The native wit wasn't quite at Scouse-level, but I did guiltily chortle when Shaun Wright-Phillips came to take a throw and a large topless man shouted at him "He's not even your real dad Shaun!"

Richard Dunne, who had a rotten match, scored an own goal to put Newcastle ahead, and Kinnear's gamble of playing 4-3-2 looked like it would pay off until the fantastic Stephen Ireland scored a last-gasp equaliser.

Geordies breathe football, love their club and probably do deserve to be in less of a mess than they are. But I also think that on some level they *quite enjoy* their consistent failure as it gives them something to moan about in the pub. At least they got a lot to moan about today I guess. Howay the Toon!

NEWCASTLE UNITED 2 (Ameobi 44, Dunne o.g. 63)
MANCHESTER CITY 2 (Robinho pen 14, Ireland 86)
Attendance 45,908

GAME 24
HARTLEPOOL UNITED v Huddersfield Town
League One
Tuesday 21st October 2008, 7.45pm, Victoria Stadium, Hartlepool

My feet were blistered and puffy. Right, that was it. I needed new shoes. Definitely. I had spent the day wandering around Newcastle, a city I had never been to before, and loving it. It was quite sunny at one point, and I managed to get into my best tourist mode; taking pictures of the Angel of the North (Gateshead flasher) and other landmarks around the city.

I was off to Hartlepool tonight, and I thought perhaps there would be fewer notable points of interest than in Newcastle. I was right. It was a very grey Tuesday evening and the people of Hartlepool just seemed to ooze melancholy pacing their way past the disused ports towards the Mecca Bingo.

I felt that an hour in Hartlepool had allowed me all I needed to see, so I made my way to the ground far too early. The 'unofficial' car park at the back of the Victoria Stadium was a bumpy muddy wasteland with huge clumps of metal jarring your tyres. There was an hour until kick-off. Balls. I wasn't feeling sociable so I sat in my car pretending not to be there while a group of kids were smashing bottles in the skate park a few metres away.

It was all very grim. My knackered old shoes were soaked by tripping into a sludgy puddle. There were no signs for the stands and the unfriendly stewards offered assistance very begrudgingly.

I came across the club shop, a fairly standard affair, but with a gleaming sign boldly proclaiming "The REAL Brian Honour book signing tonight". I didn't really know who Brian Honour was but I thought it must be an honour to meet the real him. And it's not often in life one truly receives a great honour like this.

I went up to the miserable bald man sitting by himself in the empty club shop.

"Brian Honour! It's...an honour." He didn't say anything so I just smiled. It was a *great* gag.

"You want a book signing?" he asked.

I looked on the shelves at the many many books in stock.

"How much are they?"

"£9.99."

I reluctantly decided not to buy his book. I had a copy of *Viz* in the car I hadn't even read yet. And although it was a *slight* honour to meet him, a man who probably once played for Hartlepool, I would save buying the book for a later date.

I found the ticket office and put on my trademark ridiculous accent to buy my ticket; an intriguing phenomenon which probably sounds a bit Welsh or Indian but is meant to be indistinguishable 'Northern' to fit in with Lancashire, Yorkshire, the Midlands, the North-East and everywhere in between. The bloke gave me my ticket;

"Thanks mate." I said in my special accent, the man giving me a rather queer look.

There was a bloke selling the unofficial £1 Hartlepool fanzine 'The Monkey Hanger' which I bought on the basis that it was cheaper than Brian Honour's biography. You can't escape the phrase 'Monkey Hanger' at Hartlepool. What used to be an offensive term has now been embraced by Hartlepool fans and taken as their own.

The phrase harks back to the 19th century when a French ship had been stranded on the Hartlepool coast. The legend goes that the only survivor was a monkey wearing a navy uniform, who the Hartlepool folk mistook for a Frenchman. They proceeded to hang the monkey after he was unable to answer their questions during the trials.

The fable of the monkey hanging stretches throughout the city with statues across Hartlepool. The Hartlepool Utd mascot is the tastefully named 'H'Angus' the monkey. H'Angus famously became the first democratically elected mayor of Hartlepool in 2002, and won a second term in 2005 on the manifesto promise of 'free bananas to school children'. Therefore Hartlepool, the town that hanged a monkey, now has a monkey as their mayor, which I suppose makes everything okay in the end. Let bygones be bygones hey?

Whilst most elements of the Victoria Stadium weren't exactly lovely, my mood improved vastly when the match actually started. Despite the seats having no backs to them the first 45 minutes absolutely zoomed by, and was possibly the best £10 I have ever spent. Huddersfield (playing in their gruesome gold away kit) went in 3-2 up after twists and turns throughout the half, some shocking defending and some incredible strikes.

The best of the 5 goals was a sublime volley scored by James Brown, the Hartlepool winger thoroughly deserving it after being brilliant during the half. Brown of course has his own moderate infamy from Hartlepool fan extraordinaire Jeff Stelling's frequent tributes to the winger on *Soccer Saturday;* singing his namesake's hit 'I Feel Good' whenever he scores.

My mood improved further with my half-time pie. The suffix of 'award-winning' was plastered in front of the steak pies, and they didn't disappoint, leaving me genuinely stuffed and satisfied. The second half was a tense affair but in the last ten minutes of the match Hartlepool scored an incredible three times, resulting in a 5-3 victory. The crucial goal, from former Huddersfield striker Kevin Kyle saw him celebrate wildly in front of the visiting fans as if to say "Yep, I was shit when I played for you, but look at me now!"

I was left breathless by this match. Even better than the 5-4 I saw at Peterborough. In fact, I was in such a good mood that as I sludged through the puddles back to my car, I managed to ignore the kids in the skatepark swearing at me, and nipped to the club shop to buy Brian Honour's biography, in great 'honour' of my experience with the monkey hangers themselves. Brilliant stuff!

HARTLEPOOL UNITED **5** (Kyle 26, 86, Brown 40, Porter pen 83, 89)
HUDDERSFIELD TOWN **3** (Dickinson 8, 44, Craney 38)
Attendance 3,771

GAME 25
CHESTERFIELD v Aldershot Town
League Two
Wednesday 22nd October 2008, 7.30pm, Saltergate, Chesterfield

Being a nostalgic rather than truly knowledgeable football fan I mainly associate Chesterfield F.C. with their heroic FA Cup run in 1997. This small 4th tier club from North Derbyshire nearly went all the way to Wembley, but were knocked out to Middlesbrough in the semi-finals after referee David Elleray failed to notice their shot that crossed the line when the scores were 3-3. It was great stuff nonetheless, with a youthful Kevin Davies being the talisman for the plucky side.

It has been 11 years since that 1997 semi-final against Ravanelli, Juninho and the rest, and in those 11 years Chesterfield have not really bothered my mind again. Driving down from the North-East I was glad I would get a chance to see what the club is actually like. Chesterfield are a club of a similar stature to Hartlepool who I saw the day before, but offer a far more instantly pleasant match-day experience. I parked up easily (with no rusty shards of metal in sight) and walked through Chesterfield, which seemed like an attractive little place from what I could tell, with the stadium placed nicely in the middle of town.

Built in 1871, Saltergate is one of the oldest football stadiums in England, and you can really tell. Positioned on top of an overgrown grassy mount, the stadium looks disjointed from the outside and even more slopey and uneven from the inside, which actually added to the charm of the place.

I had been a bit spoilt for goals and action in recent games, and this was no exception. Chesterfield coasted the match thanks to a brilliant display from their young winger Jamie Ward. The tiny Ward looks about 12, but his slight frame doesn't hinder him against your average 6ft2 League Two defender. His deserved hat-trick today rounded off a fantastic all-round performance that Aldershot just couldn't deal with.

I spent the match in and out of chat with a young guy there who was the spitting image of a chubby Frank Lampard in his early days at West Ham. As well as not acknowledging his girlfriend for 90 minutes plus stoppage time, he had the awkward intensity of Hannibal Lector.

"What's in your bag mate?" he asked me looking at my rucksack containing my North-East vital living equipment (spare pants, toothbrush, Brian Honour's biography etc).

"A BOMB?" he forcefully enquired, his head jolting forward at the word 'bomb'.

I awkwardly laughed this off, and Fat Frank looked pleased.

"Aldershot? AlderSHIT more like!" he said when Chesterfield went 2-0 up shortly before half-time.

"Yeah!" I said to this hilarious comment, because there was nothing else to say.

Counting out Fat Frank, the Chesterfield fans were a fairly normal bunch, a fair mixture of the cloth-cap wielding old gentlemen, the multi-tattooed alpha males and the speccy football nerds (myself). I did notice that there were barely any women there though; hard to explain, but I guess Chesterfield just have predominately male supporters. The crowd rowdiness and heckles were pretty tame.

"Lineo! Should have gone to Specsavers!" A man commented to enthusiastic laughter. Very gentle football banter that. It could have been written by a CBBC scriptwriter for a Blue Peter football piece. He said it twice more before the end of the match, the laughter slightly decreasing each time.

The Chesterfield full-back Jamie Lowry, who had had an impressive first half, was running after a ball going out for a throw when his momentum took him over the advertising boards right into the lap of a disabled supporter in a wheelchair.

"HAHAHAHAHA!" bellowed Fat Frank. "Did you see that?" he nudged me slightly too aggressively, "He fell right on the mongoloid!!! Classic!" This was a bit awkward now. He was making me uncomfortable enough to pull my own eyeballs out.

I popped in and out for my half-time pie, and found that there was something very odd about the terraces in the second half. The number of people there had definitely grown, there were literally hundreds more fans watching. They must have all somehow snuck in for free at half-time! It certainly made for a better atmosphere, particularly as Aldershot got a penalty in the first minute.

"Disaster. It's going to be just like Grimsby all over again isn't it?" Fat Frank said with all the tragic desperate sincerity of a man watching his next-of-kin die.

Fortunately for Frank's sanity Aldershot missed, and although they soon got one back Chesterfield, and Jamie Ward in particular, sprung into life to give the team a 5-1 win.

"Turned out alright in the end!" Fat Frank said to me with his devil eyes piercing into mine.

"Yeah it did." I replied honestly.

"We go here every week, do you?" he asked.

"Not every week, no." I replied, semi-honestly.

For the first time, his mute girlfriend suddenly sprung to life; "Well get more games in here before the new stadium is built. You won't get terraces like that in a couple of years when we're moved out of town." She said.

This was the brains of the outfit clearly. I was stunned. She was completely right, an old small club like Chesterfield belongs in an ancient terraced ground full of character like Saltergate. And when they move it'll be a carbon copy of all the other new grounds.

"You know what, I'll try." I said, completely honestly. I wanted to go again before it all gets destroyed. It made me quite sad to think about really.

Deep in contemplation I got in my car and began the long trek home after a quite brilliant 3 day, 18 goal, football trip, wondering where on earth my journey would take me next.

CHESTERFIELD   **5** (Lester 24, Ward 41, pen 53, 76, Niven 73)
ALDERSHOT TOWN **1** (Hudson 50)
Attendance 3,079

GAME 26
TOTTENHAM HOTSPUR v Bolton Wanderers
Premier League
Sunday 26th October 2008, 3.00pm, White Hart Lane, Tottenham, North London

Using all of my scrounging abilities I managed to get hold of a Tottenham v Bolton ticket a few days before the game, unaware that the match would be of far greater significance than I initially expected. The amazing breaking news the night before the match was that Juande Ramos had been sacked as Spurs manager and replaced immediately by Harry Redknapp. Didn't see that coming! It had all happened so quickly.

Tottenham's start to the 2008/2009 season was the worst by any Spurs team for 80 years; winning 0 drawing 2 and losing 6 of the first 8 games, the team were deservedly languishing at the bottom of the table.

The newspapers and football websites have been full of Tottenham jokes (What do Spurs have in common with a toothpick? They both have two points) with the BBC online football coverage even having its own separate Tottenham joke section in 'quotes of the week'. Humiliating times to be a Spurs fan, but brilliant for the rest of us.

Liverpool aside, Tottenham Hotspur irritate me more than any other team in the 92. I'm sorry Spurs fans, I'm just being honest. It's the fault of my many Tottenham-supporting friends really. A good handful of my mates are Spurs fans, and without fail start every season with the words 'this will be our year'. Duffy, (who came to Chester with me,) is a Spurs fan who last season argued with complete sincerity that Spurs's back four was superior to Man United's Premiership/Champions League winning defence. And that Juande Ramos is one of the top three managers in the world.

My dear best friend Robbie, although lovely in his own special way, is the most obnoxious Spurs fan I have ever met. If you get him drunk enough he will stand on a pub table, spilling numerous pints in the process, and shout "YID ARMY! YID ARMY!" at anyone who walks past. Actually I think he does that sober sometimes as well.

I don't necessarily *hate* Spurs fans, I just find their false optimism/skewed view of their own brilliance intolerable.

I had intended to go to the match with Robbie, who unfortunately couldn't come back down south from working on his punk music dissertation at Leeds uni, so I instead went down with two of my more pleasant and introverted Spurs-supporting friends, Sammy and Rhys.

Sammy and Rhys are brothers and season ticket holders, although by their own admission are 'rich Harpenden boys sitting with the quiet fans'.

"You'll win today definitely." I said bluntly. "If ever Spurs are going to break this horrible run it'll be against Bolton."

"I dunno. I'd take a draw," said Rhys.

"We just need to avoid defeat, not get humiliated and then we can build from that!" Sammy continued, "It's been pathetic this season. Every single player is underperforming."

"Anyone in particular?" I enquired.

"Jermaine bloody Jenas." Sammy replied without hesitation. "They are all overrated though, especially the new players. What we need is some stability in the team. Every season we sell half the squad and replace them, and hopefully Redknapp can change that."

I laughed. "Wheeler-dealer 'arry though? Surely not!"

What I had realised is that failure brought out the best in Spurs fans. No cries of 'this will be our season' had been heard recently, and Sammy and Rhys were graciously pessimistic and, even better, *realistic* about what a struggle of a season Spurs had in store.

Making my way into the Lane I noticed a real sense of nerves yet excitement from the fans. No one was sure where Harry would be today, but right on cue he came out and waved at the crowd before taking his place on the Tottenham bench. I find it incredible that the formalities behind such a transfer can happen so quickly. Just 15 hours ago Redknapp was still Portsmouth manager, preparing for their game against Fulham, and now he was here in the dugout at a new club, apparently having actually picked the team today.

There was an incredible vibe around the Lane, and as the game kicked off the fans were already letting Harry know they approved of him, and interestingly being loud and clear about who they wanted him to sign by singing frequent 'Jermain Defoe, he's a Yiddo' chants.

Another Spurs chant, predictably rude, inaccurate and derogatory about the legend that is Sol Campbell would not have sat as well with Harry. It was only a couple of weeks ago that Campbell got such homophobic abuse from Spurs fans at Portsmouth that Redknapp slammed the Tottenham support in the media. Interesting how it can all change in such a short space of time isn't it?

I think this was my 6th or 7th time at White Hart Lane, but I have never heard the stadium make as much noise as when Pavlyuchenko nodded in a David Bentley cross in the 17th minute. You could see what it meant to the fans, who had their first glimmer of hope in about half a year that things might be on the up again. It was a decent match, with Tottenham 'keeper Gomes in fantastically erratic form, flapping at crosses and presenting Bolton with numerous chances that a better team would have scored. Gavin McCann saw red for two bookings in the second half and from then on Tottenham had the long-overdue win fairly secure, with Darren Bent notching the second from the penalty spot.

Whilst Spurs fans were buzzing, all was not well in the away end, with 'Megson out' chants ringing towards the end of the match. Looking at what instant impact Redknapp had on the Spurs players it shows the kind of effect a new manager can have on a team's confidence.

On the way home we got chatting to an extremely drunk man with a tattoo on the top of his bald head. He saw Rhys's Tottenham shirt and asked the score.

"2-0 win! Great start for Harry Redknapp." Rhys said, with slight apprehension.

"Redknapp ..." the man said cross-eyed, dramatically pausing to finish his profound statement. "should be *ashamed* of himself! He has no loyalty. None whatsoever. No sir.

I'm a great judge of character. Never trust him..." he said with a knowing wink before falling into a chair behind him.

Well, regardless of the topic of loyalty, he certainly had a good start as manager. There was cautious optimism from the crowd too, perhaps this would be the turning point for the unrealistic expectations of Spurs fans?

At this moment, I got a phone call and squeezed my hand into my pocket to answer it. It was Robbie.

"Yessss mate! Yiddddos! This is it T, it'll be our season now! Harry will take us up the league! Top half! Maybe get into Europe! We'll win a cup!"

Honestly, one victory. It's all it takes.

TOTTENHAM HOTSPUR 2 (Pavlyuchenko 17, Bent pen 76)
BOLTON WANDERERS 0
Attendance 35,507

GAME 27
IPSWICH TOWN v Charlton Athletic
The Championship
Tuesday 28th October 2008, 7.45pm, Portman Road, Ipswich

Now I'm no weatherman, but I know for sure that on 28th October you should not find yourself driving up the traffic-jammed A12 in a panic that Ipswich v Charlton might be called off due to snow. Snow in October?!

The radio was tantalisingly torturing me by saying Northampton v Colchester had been postponed and more were likely to follow. Balls! I had been driving for a silly amount of time to potentially arrive at Portman Road and find the game has been postponed. What would I do when I got there? Drive around the stadium aimlessly? That was a bloody stupid idea; Ipswich is the *last* place where I would want the police to think I am kerb-crawling.

Fortunately the game went ahead as planned. Despite the ice-cold conditions, it was a decent match between two teams who are struggling in ex-Premier League purgatory; the Championship.

So many clubs have struggled after relegation from the Premiership. As well as today's teams the likes of Coventry, Southampton, Crystal Palace and Norwich have proved that it is hugely difficult to form a new promotion-threatening squad after relegation.

Recent seasons have been so disappointing for Ipswich it's easy to forget that a mere seven years ago the Tractor Boys were three points away from qualifying for the Champions League. The team played quite well today, but were lacking any killer instinct up-front. With the greatest respect to Jon Stead (apologies in advance Jon...) he is *not* a goalscorer. In fact he's not a striker. In fact, he's probably not a footballer. In fact, he's absolutely crap. His body language on the field was awful, he looked disinterested, he couldn't pass, or shoot, or do anything. You get my drift. With Stead partly to blame, Ipswich should have scored a bucket load but only managed the one, a floating free kick from Owen Garvan.

I was sat behind the goal, and a few feet away from Ipswich 'keeper Richard Wright. When I did a week of work experience at Sky Sports News last summer I spent one entire day editing a piece about Wright moving back to Ipswich from West Ham. This involved the riveting activity of sifting through hours of footage of Wright in training, trying to find a suitable 4 second shot of him looking busy. There's a limit to how much looking at Richard Wright a man can take, so I tried to avoid looking at him today.

With my face engulfed in my scarf I felt like a grumpy snowman. My breath seemed to be freezing in the air as I exhaled. "Oh look," I thought, "Jon Stead is being substituted. Does he deserve me to pull my icicle fingers out of my jacket pockets for applause? No, he most definitely does not." I warmed myself with a Chicken Balti Shire special (quickly becoming my pie of choice) and trip to the toilet in which I was surprised to find Chlamydia awareness posters up. Those Ipswich youths may be promiscuous, but at least they are aware of the consequences. It sure beats the lapdancing club posters in the Southend toilets anyway.

The match turned with Counago's penalty miss when Ipswich were 1-0 up, which allowed Charlton to inevitably get back in the game.[1] Charlton fans were singing 'We only want one shot!' which merited a round of applause from the home support. And about a minute later they scored with their first shot of the match. 'We only need one shot!' the Charlton fans sang, which this time did most definitely not gain a round of applause from the home support.

My old mate Richard Wright did not take kindly to conceding this goal. He furiously picked up the ball and booted it in the crowd behind his goal where I was sitting. The ball smacked a lady in the face, which probably merited an apology from Raging Richard. Have some manners Richard! Some people spend a whole afternoon looking at footage of you doing absolutely nothing. The least you can do is behave like some kind of role model!

With full-time approaching, two fans behind me were going into pretty detailed tactical analysis.

---

[1] For all you stat-fans out there this was my 7th penalty I had seen in the last 7 games. I was becoming a penalty-magnet!

"If Volz could overlap his winger then it would draw the defender out, allowing Walters to dictate the game more."
"Lisbie's natural habit to progress from the flanks wide means we are essentially playing 4-5-1, but without the central midfielders to sufficiently benefit Stead's layoffs with his back to goal."
It was impressive stuff, although this was counteracted by the kid in front of me who spent most of the match staring at the Charlton fans performing the 'wanker' sign.
Far from being tractor boys, Ipswich are a smart club with an impressive, well designed stadium for any division and a good breed of supporter. I just hope they don't stagnate in Championship purgatory for ever and ever and ever.

IPSWICH TOWN   **1** (Garvan 37)
CHARLTON ATHLETIC   **1** (Bailey 82)
Attendance 20,352

GAME 28
BIRMINGHAM CITY v Coventry City
The Championship
Monday 3rd November 2008, 7.45pm, St. Andrews, Birmingham

The worst song before a match I have encountered so far is 'Blue da ba dee da ba di', the 1999 hit from Europop stalwarts Eifel 65, which raped my ears at St Andrews. Birmingham play in blue. I get it. It was quickly followed by *Mr Blue Sky* by ELO. Come on folks. At least play *Blue Monday* by New Order.

Yep, it was time for a trip to the second city for some football treats. Looking at Birmingham's position in the Championship table would suggest that all was well at St Andrews, with the team riding high in 2nd automatic position, well placed to mount another successful promotion challenge. However, from actually going to see Birmingham play I got a completely different vibe. The endless negatively from my Birmingham supporting friend Amy summed up the general mood; "It's a lost cause! We're worse than useless," she often says in her slightly posh Birmingham accent (plummie Brummie I like to call it) even when the team seem to be doing quite well.

The first and most glaring problem is, surprisingly, with the team. On paper Birmingham's starting 11 is full of Premier League standard talent, but they just don't click. It was a fascinating match against Coventry watching players such as Larsson, Jerome and McFadden massively underperform. Birmingham would have been spanked today if it wasn't for Lee Carsley playing his heart out in the middle. The players were poor; McFadden in particular was awful. He's a player who I've always admired but showed such an incredible lack of effort, and no glimpses of the talent that made him Scotland's key player. It didn't help Birmingham's cause that the back 4 was as shaky as Michael J. Fox's toothbrush as well (is that too un-PC? I think I've gone too far...). Only Nicky Hunt, the on-loan Bolton right-back who I maintain is the worst player in the Premier League, reached an acceptable level of performance. In fact the one time bean-pole Nicky did manage to get forward, he delivered a Cafu-esque burst from the back and a cross that Beckham would have been proud of. He's certainly never done that in his eight bloody seasons at Bolton.

All was not well. There had recently been a press statement from McLeish urging more supporters to attend Birmingham matches, with attendances dropping to an average of almost 10,000 less than the previous season. The £15 adult tickets would be reduced to £10 for Saturday's match against Charlton, which really is quite extraordinary when you consider that Luton Town adult tickets are set at over £20, similar to many other League Two clubs.

The fans that *were* there literally spent the full 90 minutes moaning about their team. They absolutely loved moaning! They've inspired me to moan about them right now! Moan moan moan. I think moaning suits the Birmingham accent as well. It seemed a lot of the fans vented their anger towards the porn baron owners. I've always been suspicious of David Gold and his wispy beard, neatly cultivated from selling dildos. Ditto his two sidekicks David Sullivan and Karren Brady, both quite frighteningly formidable presences in the board room.

I went to get the obligatory pie, of which I had been informed by Amy were always undercooked, and in the bar area found a big crowd gathering around two people fighting! Both shaven headed and laden with gold (more scummie Brummie than plummie Brummie) and wearing blue Birmingham shirts, one floored the other with a punch, and then began booting him in the stomach when he was grounded.

This literally beggared belief!!! What on *earth*? What made it even more farcical was that the three or four stewards around were just watching with curiosity rather than intervening at all. Finally the police arrived and sorted it out, but I was stunned. With your team playing as terribly as that the last thing you need is the fans to start decking each other.

The second half was an improvement in terms of effort from Birmingham, but they just couldn't make the pressure count and find a goal. The highlight of the half was when Carsley, the only Birmingham player to emerge with any credit, went up for a header and accidently floored his lumbering team-mate Cameron Jerome with an elbow.

"Cheers Lee!" a Blues fan shouted, "can you get McFadden next?" Coventry's goal came from ex-Birmingham favourite Clinton Morrison, who got a fantastic reception at the beginning of the match, only to commit the rather rude act of scoring and then celebrating. He was massively booed after scoring, but shrugged his shoulders and came out a winner overall.

Situations change for football clubs, and maybe the mood around St Andrews will improve sometime soon. Tonight though, the main thing I found about Birmingham is that whilst everything should be okay, it isn't, and the crowd just loved to moan about it. Whether a plummie Brummie or scummie Brummie, what is universal amongst Birmingham fans is that they are all, most certainly, glummie Brummies.

BIRMINGHAM CITY 0
COVENTRY CITY   **1** (Morrison 53)
Attendance 17,215

GAME 29
WALSALL v Luton Town
Johnstone's Paint Trophy Southern Section, Semi-Final
Tuesday 4th November 2008, 7.45pm, Bescot Stadium, Walsall

The history books will show Tuesday 4th November 2008 to be a momentous date. The day a black man and a white man did battle for the people they represent, the fate of the nation depending on the outcome and the consequences affecting the foundations of contemporary society as we know it.

Barack Obama vs. John McCain? Oh no.

Across the Atlantic Ocean in a battle arena known as 'Walsall', there was a more crucial, titanic encounter happening.

Michael Ricketts vs. Ian Roper.

Well, probably not. Nobody would remember the evening where these two overweight titans of the lower-league English game locked horns for the most coveted of prizes; the Southern final of the Johnstone's Paint Trophy. But I would remember, on a rather depressing night sitting by myself watching Walsall v Luton.

You would be hard pressed to find an uglier stadium that the Bescot (or 'Bank's Stadium' as the sponsors would have it called). An uninspiring grey slab plonked in a big car park, enticing you in with its promise of inevitably mediocre football. It looks more like a warehouse than a football ground, and is just as disappointing on the inside, with pillars restricting the view of every other seat. It was built in 1990, meaning that it is probably technically a 'new' stadium, but without any of 21st Century benefits such as 'good design' or 'decent facilities'.

You can't escape these bloody sponsors either. As well as the stadium carrying the name of its sponsor, each of the 4 stands are named after various other money-pimps. How about sitting in the 'Floors 2 Go Stand'? Or soak in the famous atmosphere of the 'West Bromwich Building Society Stand'? How about you away fans, have the evening of your life in the 'Homeserve Stand'? But for the best

Walsall experience, why not sing along with the die-hards in the legendary 'Txt 64446 Health Stand'? Oh God it was soulless.

Walsall FC was one big daytime television advert screaming for more money from somewhere. Anywhere. In fact the club are currently in plans to put a massive illuminated advertising board on the back of the Homeserve Stand, visible from both sides of the M6, which would be the largest sign by any European motorway. Dream the dream Walsall FC, you could be the club with the *largest illuminated advertising sign in Europe!!!* Forget those stupid clubs who dream of winning titles and major silverware, you've hit the nail on the head with your dreams of reaching advertising greatness.

Walsall FC didn't impress me, neither the club nor the team. The game itself was awful, but what it lacked in anything closely resembling quality, it made up for in crunching tackles; the Walsall left-back in particular snarling at his prey after scything them down. The ref was letting everything go; even when there was a scuffle on the pitch he just stood back and let them sort it out themselves like the handbag-wielding men they are.

Michael Ricketts stood there like a useless lump of dough as Ian Roper majestically rose above him to head the ball clear.

"Michael, Michael!" bellowed Walsall manager Jimmy Mullen.

"Michael. TRY HARDER!" he said with a longing desperation, as if he has said it 100 times before.

Now I have a bit of a vendetta against Michael Ricketts. He is actually a naturally talented footballer, with an eye for goal who could have made a decent career for himself if he wasn't too lazy, both on the pitch with the effort in his performances, and off the pitch with his constant battles with his flabby gut. He scored 15 goals between August and February in Bolton's first season back in the Premiership, including a winner at Old Trafford, and deservedly won that sole England cap. And then he got too big for his boots (quite literally), fell out with Big Sam and claimed he was worth over £10 million. And now he is getting outplayed by Ian Roper in the Johnstone's Paint Trophy.

Roper was in his element tonight. He played for Walsall for a whopping 13 years before joining Luton last summer. I couldn't believe this judging by his performance I saw for Luton against

Accrington last month, but he's a Saddler's legend! He even got granted a testimonial! A testimonial...of which you can buy the DVD! The Walsall website still basks in the glory of the Roper years;

Saddlers' supporters can relive the highlights of Ian Roper's Testimonial Year with our brand new DVD! This DVD is a must-have for any Ian Roper fan.

Fan-bloody-tastic! A must for any Ian Roper fan! I'm an Ian Roper fan! (Well I'm certainly a fan of his ballsy wife I had the encounter with at Luton). I immediately put in the order for my Ian Roper DVD, a bargain at only £12.99. I would have to order some more as presents for all the other Ian Roper fans I am friends with.

 Half-time came and I went to a depressing 'social club' style indoor bar area monitored by the two most unnecessary doormen in the history of unnecessary doormen. It was dimly lit with circular tables, two small bars, a stage and lighting equipment. What events worthy of a stage and lighting ever go on in this asylum of misery? People were huddling up together to keep warm in their hats and scarves, and volunteers were giving out coffee and tea. It was like a refugee shelter. If tea and coffee cost £1.50 each at a refugee shelter and there was a shit football match going on in the background.

The second half livened up a bit, due to the incredible sight of man in a skinny purple inflatable monster suit who occasionally went jogging around the pitch, much to the enjoyment of myself and the rest of the tortured Walsall crowd.

By the Walsall bench there was a huge bucket full of energy drinks for the players. A member of the crowd asked the Walsall dugout if he could have one, half-jokingly.

"£1 mate. Cheaper than the shops!" The Walsall staff member said, in all seriousness. Honestly, it's all about the money with this club. Things weren't going so well for my old friend Roper around this point. He was down with a face injury. He was bleeding! Oh Ian. His face was a bloody mess.

"Never mind Ropes, you never were very pretty were you?" A Walsall fan said in a droll Brummie accent while Roper was receiving treatment at the side. Ropes looked up, and gave a sly laugh to his beloved former-faithful, blood dripping from his crooked nose. His old fans gave him a storming standing ovation as he was forced into being subbed. What a hero. I wonder if his wife was here to see his wonderful reception? There's no one for her to shout at today, that's for sure.

It was nearly bonfire night, and fireworks began to explode over the ground as the game reached its end. The fireworks began on the pitch as well, as Luton grabbed a winner in the 90th minute. Which was about what Walsall deserved. A club with many advertising opportunities, but little character, especially now Lord Roper has departed. I don't think I'll be back soon.

WALSALL   **0**
LUTON TOWN   **1** (Jarvis 90)
Attendance 1,844

GAME 30
LEEDS UNITED v Northampton Town
FA Cup First Round

Friday 7th November 2008, 7.45pm, Elland Road, Leeds

Leeds United are a unique club. While Millwall claim that 'no one likes us, we don't care', it is Leeds that generate more venomous hatred from opposing fans than all the other clubs put together. 'We all hate Leeds scum! We all hate Leeds scum!' is a chant almost ubiquitous throughout English football. From Huddersfield to Yeovil, from Man United to Hartlepool. No region of the country is exempt from being Leeds haters, but I have always struggled to understand *why* this is.

I was driving myself and John up to Leeds and he was getting restless, showing his nipples to passing cars on the M1 to see their reaction. "It's amazing! Some laugh at you, some look disgusted! The split is almost exactly 50/50!"

"What does that say about the great British public?"

"That half like nipples and half don't I guess."

I was looking forward to our trip to Leeds. Both my brothers Ali and Greg were there for the weekend as well as my old mates Robbie and Liam and their uni crowds. It would be a testing weekend of Yorkshire football and casual binge drinking.

"Why do you think it is that everyone hates Leeds scum?" I asked John, primarily to distract him from his nipple-flashing.

John looked at me pensively. He had gone to university in Leeds so was better placed to comment on the intricate character of Leeds fans than me.

"I think they're just kind of scummy aren't they? Like the dirge of Leeds. Scummy folk. Big old shitty Leeds scum." John's a Man United fan incidentally.

I wasn't really in the place to comment but I felt extremely sorry for Leeds fans about their plight. When I was first getting into football Leeds were considered one of the league's real big guns. From winning the title in 1992 through the days of Tony Yeboah's thunderbolts to the 2001 Champions League semi-final defeat against Valencia, Leeds were a force to be reckoned with.

The incredible decline started at the turn of the century when Peter Ridsdale lost his mind, spent £7million on Seth Johnson and about the same amount on tropical fish. He left the club in crippling debts, resulting in two relegations, a 15-point deduction and an all-round spectacular collapse.

"Don't you feel a *bit* sorry for Leeds fans? From Champions League semi-finals to mid-table League One in 6 years? Please don't show your nipple to that group of threatening looking youths." I pleaded to John as we arrived in Leeds.

"Not really. Could be worse. Think of Luton."

We pulled up at Robbie's house opposite the gigantic mosque in the Hyde Park region.

"Eyyyy lads!" he warmly greeted us standing at his door, his cheeky grin and bright ginger hair not having changed one bit since we last saw him. Shortly after we arrived my brothers, Liam and some assorted mates arrived, and a few drinks later a group of 9 of us jumped in a couple of taxis for Elland Road.

The first thing you notice about the stadium is how huge it is, particularly compared to other League One grounds. Situated in a quite poor part of Leeds, the vibe around Elland Road is not immediately friendly, with a larger than usual police presence.

Despite Leeds's reputation for providing a fairly menacing match-day on par with the likes of Millwall, Cardiff and West Ham, none of the group were bothered by it all, even the two girls with us seemed unfazed by the potentially intimidating Elland Road. We grabbed our tickets and headed through the turnstiles.

"Wahey! I knew I'd manage it!" said Greg, smiling from ear to ear. He unzipped his coat pocket to reveal 4 cans of Stella.

"How did you know they wouldn't search you?" asked Ali.

"Honest face." Greg said pointing at his blemish-free, butter-wouldn't-melt gob.

The little scamp! 5 minutes around John and Robbie and he's acting like them. Honestly. Poor influences. My disapproval didn't stop me from nabbing a tin from him though.

From the inside, Elland Road has a definite shabby 'shit chic' feel to it. There is no leg room, basic facilities and the ground has the old earthiness of Goodison Park or Loftus Road but with less charm. The crowd seemed tiny in such a big stadium, but most of the fans were squeezed in the Don Revie stand behind the goal, where we all remained stood for the entire 90 minutes. The Leeds fans were in great voice for the match despite a large amount of people choosing to watch the Friday night FA Cup game on Setanta Sports. "If you're watching on Setanta you're a c**t!" chorused the Leeds fans, apparently loud enough for it to be picked up live on Setanta. The match kicked off, and Northampton scored a shock opener, but ruined their good start by stupidly going down to ten men in the 29th minute after Giles Coke's two quick yellow cards, allowing Leeds to get back in the game and score a penalty before half-time.

This gee'd up the Leeds fans, with deafening chants ringing from the terraces, ranging from the funny to the rude, the intelligent to the highly offensive. The funny anti-Chelsea chants made us all laugh at Liam (a Chelsea fan) but these soon turned into pretty disgraceful anti-United chants about 1958 Munich and the runway, which we all declined to join in with. Not endearing behaviour from the scummy Leeds fans there.

Half-time had come, Greg's illegal tinnies had been consumed so it was off to the bar. The bar area was absolutely rammed, we were packed like Yorkshire cattle in what felt like a working men's club from the 1970s. It smelt strongly of farts, and the lager tasted a bit like farts too.

"Mate, are you German?" a rat-boy Leeds fan asked Liam in the bar.

"No. I'm from Kimpton." Liam replied timidly.

"Why are you wearing a German jacket?" he said, pointing at Liam's khaki jacket with German flags on the sleeves.

Liam just looked at the ratty Leeds fan with contempt.

"Don't worry mate," the fan shouted to his friend at the other side of the bar, "he's not German, he's just wearing a German jacket."

I was holding John's beer. Where was he? He returned grinning.

"Where have you been?"

"I went for a crap. Grim. Don't go to the toilets at Elland Road though unless you have to, that's my advice," John announced to the group, the girls looking at him with mild disgust.

Back out for the second half, the crowd noise was relentless. "You shit bastard!" was the insult of choice to the Northampton goalkeeper upon taking his goal kicks, a subtle and select alternative to "You fat bastard" or "You're shit aaaaah". Points to Leeds for originality.

It was a slow but tense second half, Leeds pressing Northampton but mainly resorting to long-shots, spurning chances that Tony Yeboah would surely have buried back in the day.

The pressure had obviously got to the Leeds fans because all around us there was a large group of lads smoking weed right next to us. The cheek was amazing! Far more bold than Greg smuggling in the tinnies. In the 29 games prior I hadn't seen a single fan even have a sneaky fag in the ground, and here I was at Leeds witnessing *several* pot-smoking supporters getting away with it. I suppose if any fans need it to cope with their team's misfortunes then it's apt that it's Leeds.

The match finished 1-1, leaving the few (and silent) Northampton fans happy.

"Off for some drinks then to the house party in Headingley then boys?!" John said, tiny-eyed. He and Robbie had got 'chatting' to the lads sitting next to us during the match and were feeling all the happier for it.

"Billy Bremner! Ginger legend!" Robbie said, hugging the statue of Bremner outside Elland Road.

It was a terrific, and fairly unique, experience watching Leeds United. It's a great old club; the crowd were so loud and passionate, but also, well, (how can I put this kindly).... a bit scummy. NOW I understand.

LEEDS UNITED **1** (Robinson pen 37)
NORTHAMPTON TOWN **1** (McGleish 9)
Attendance 9,531

GAME 31
HUDDERSFIELD TOWN v Port Vale
FA Cup First Round
Saturday 8th November 2008, 3pm, Galpharm Stadium, Huddersfield

I woke up spooning a snoring Robbie, dribble dripping from his mouth to my hand. With a start I jumped up and shuddered, brushing myself down thoroughly. Ugh. Where was I? Leeds. That was it. I felt rough.

In a zombie state with a pounding head I climbed down the stairs, hands feeling the walls to make sure I didn't fall down. I focused my eyes on the various bodies conked out on the living room floor surrounded by beer cans; Ali, Greg, John, Liam. All dead to the world. The one upside of sharing a bed with Robbie is that I didn't have to sleep on the living room floor I suppose.

Shit, what was the time? I looked at my watch. 1.30pm. No!!! Huddersfield! Quick!!

I got a prang of *deja vu* of the morning after my birthday going to Leyton Orient a mere 7 weeks ago. I turned on the living room light and pleaded with the corpses.

"Lads! Huddersfield v Port Vale! Come on...you said you would come!"

Liam stirred. "Sounds shit," he grunted, and turned his head away from me, beginning to snore again.

"Ali, Greg, my dear loyal brothers! Come on! Please! I need someone to make sure I don't conk out at the wheel."

They both told me where to go. Not very brotherly. I ran back upstairs.

"Robbie, come on mate! Huddersfield Town eh? You know you want to!"

He didn't want to and didn't enjoy being woken up. I was becoming increasingly unpopular amongst my closest friends and family.

Right, last try... I stood over a sleeping John and shook him viciously. "JOHN! No one else will, but you're bloody well coming to Huddersfield! I know you may feel crap, but I feel as rough as you do, and it's *your* fault I decided to go to every ground in the country, so it's *your* responsibility to escort me to Huddersfield and make sure I don't die on the way. Or I will actually disown you as a friend." I manhandled John into my car and we began the short but stomach-churning journey from Leeds to Huddersfield.

"Why am I here? Bet Huddersfield is a shit-hole," John groaned, looking like a tramp and unwelcomely sparking up a fag in my car. He definitely didn't have the energy for nipple-flashing today.

John's mood not improving, we parked up and realised we had no money for the machine. A couple of friendly looking blokes came up to us.

"Alright there lads?" one said in a thick Yorkshire accent. Pure Huddersfield this fella.

"Well, we haven't got any money for the machine! A bit annoying really." I said.

The older of the two nodded to the sky and reached into his pockets. "Here you are mate, on me," he said, handing us the £2 needed. What a hero! I offered to pay him back later after the match but he wasn't having any of it, saying it was only a couple of quid and wishing us well for the match.

"Legends!" I said to John.

"I know! Dispels the myth about stingy Yorkshiremen doesn't it!"

We wandered towards the stadium and it boldly came into view. It was magnificent, almost Reebok-ish but a bit weirder. The official Huddersfield Town website has a marvellous section describing their odd ground. And I quote;

"From almost any angle of approach, the first glimpses are of weirdly white, skeletal arches looming above the rooftops of Huddersfield's weathered sandstone terraces or between its gasometers and chimneys. Do these incongruous white structures form part of a bridge, or perhaps a fairground ride?"

Wonderful! And there's more;

"The stadium cuts right into its surrounds. The familiar soft colours of a West Yorkshire townscape are now but faded pastels next to the shiny, hard, metallic, almost clinical blues, yellows, reds and greys of the stands. If skies are grey the details seem cold and mechanical.

Under the sun, they shine like American motorhomes. Clearly, this is like no other stadium you have ever seen before."

The website was spot on about the Galpharm Stadium. Huddersfield is an honest, quite old-fashioned Yorkshire working town, and the ground, certainly resembling an Alton Towers ride in parts, looks almost futuristically out of place. Looking from the stadium outwards you get incredibly contrasting views too, of either an ugly boggy industrial part of the town or vast extended countryside.

The team were under recent new management but looked good in the opening stages of this FA Cup tie, playing lovely fluid one-touch football, and coming back from going 1-0 down to tearing Port Vale apart.

"You know what?!" John said to me as the sun beamed down, it becoming an increasingly lovely fresh autumn afternoon. "THIS is what a hangover Saturday should be about. Getting out of the house, watching some footy, refreshing your mind and cleansing your soul."

"Exactly mate!" I smiled at John, "It's days like this I thank you for opening my eyes to how I should spend my year."

"You still won't manage to do it though."

"J, if I managed to get up today after last night's debauchery to watch Huddersfield Town, I can manage anything the rest of the season has to throw at me."

John looked worried. I couldn't wait for him to lose the bet and admit Sam Allardyce is a misunderstood tactical genius. He was going to pay.

Huddersfield went all guns blazing in the second half, and quickly went 3-1 up with a Robbie Williams goal that certainly entertained me; it was an angel of a strike.

Huddersfield were absolutely coasting, and should have gone 4, 5 or even 6 up with a succession of missed opportunities.

This was all very good, but as the sun was setting over the fabulously peculiar Galpharm Stadium something amazing happened from the previously-rubbish Port Vale FC. 3-1 down with 11 minutes to go, being outplayed in every area of the field, they produced the most incredible comeback.

First David Howland scored a Cantona-esque chip from outside the box, then five minutes from the end against all the odds Louis Dodds scored a scorching thunderbolt equaliser from outside the area. Even more incredibly, Port Vale missed an open goal with the score at 3-3 in the 90th minute. AND THEN, 4 minutes into injury time Marc Richards scored a free kick.

Port Vale won!

I couldn't believe it. Honestly, it was mind-blowing. Port Vale fans were understandably going wild. I've barely ever seen a celebration like it. As neutrals, surrounded by distraught Huddersfield fans, John and I sat wide-mouthed. An old man sitting next to us was furious. "I've been watching this lot since 1968 and nothing changes," he said to us, "I knew we hadn't sewn it up even when it was 3-1." I guess that such a collapse was not a one-off for Huddersfield. Come to think of it, I saw them surrender a 3-2 lead at Hartlepool and end up losing 5-3. Wow. 15 goals in two Huddersfield matches! I should see them every week!

A couple of visibly shocked Huddersfield players came over to clap the bewildered supporters. A huge row of fans were lining the advertising boards as the players approached.

"You useless pathetic bottling twats!!!"

"How could you let that go? Against Port fucking Vale?! You should be ashamed!"

The insults ranged from the personal to the general, the fair to the unfair, the articulate to the, predictable.

"Nobhead!"

John and I were still in shock as we drove back to Leeds. The best thing about it is that the tickets were only £6! Without question the best £6 I have ever spent, even better than the super special mixed kebab I had had the previous night.

We arrived back at Robbie's just before 6pm, to find Ali, Greg, Liam and Robbie all slumped on the sofa watching Jeff Stelling reflect on the day's events. They all looked mildly pissed off they hadn't come. "You hear the score?" John smugly enquired. They didn't answer.

I was happy.

If in doubt kids, go to the weird and wonderful Galpharm Stadium to see Huddersfield Town and their chaotic defence on a sunny Saturday afternoon.   The best hangover cure I can possibly recommend.

HUDDERSFIELD TOWN   **3** (Collins 41, Craney 51, Williams 65)
PORT VALE   **4** (Dodds 27, 85, Howland 79, Richards 90)
Attendance 6,942

GAME 32
COVENTRY CITY v Plymouth Argyle
The Championship
Saturday 15th November 2008, 3.00pm, Ricoh Arena, Coventry

"Park in Tesco!"

"I can't park in Tesco there's match-day restrictions!"

"Park in Tesco anyway!"

"There's bloody match-day res.."

"JUST PARK IN TESCO!"

I parked in Tesco and looked at the big sign saying 'Match-Day Restrictions'. Coventry City's rather ugly and poorly named big new stadium the Ricoh Arena was in sight over a hill in the rain sodden stadium complex. I already resented it.

The sign read something like:

No parking on match-days. Unless proof of purchase over £25 from one of the retail outlets. Put receipt in car window. Fine of £1000000.[1]

"Right. I've got an idea," said Annabel, fed up with my constant circling of the Tesco car park. She got out of the car and went into one of the clothes shops while I waited outside. What on earth was she doing? She came out 3 minutes later with 3 colourful tops.

"There. Put the receipt in the window and let's watch the football." Whilst I'm good at anything football related, Annabel's a bloody genius at shopping.

So Coventry City...Coventry City. What inspiring words can I say about Coventry City? Well they used to be in the Premiership. But not anymore. They used to have Steve Ogrizovic in goal! But not anymore. There was a rumour that circulated in 2003 that Ogrizovic was kidnapped in Kazakhstan but this turned out to be untrue. They used to have a lovely old stadium called Highfield Road. But not anymore. I went there and saw Bolton draw 2-2 when I was a nipper.

---

[1] That was the gist of the sign anyway. Perhaps not word-for-word accurate.

I'm struggling really. I have previously referred to the Championship as being quite a depressing league with loads of fallen Premier League regulars now in mid-lower table 2nd tier purgatory, and I think Coventry are the finest example of a team suffering from this.

I had dragged an unenthusiastic Annabel along on this rainy Saturday, but the blow was softened by a heroic steward at the gate.

"Excuse me mate, which way's the ticket office?" I asked the beefy shaven-headed steward.

He looked around suspiciously.

"Wait there a minute," he muttered before walking off.

Annabel and I shrugged at each other and waited for about 3 or 4 minutes before he came back holding two tickets.

"Here you go," he said handing them over. "This bloke I know is giving them out for free."

Wow! What a bonus! I was delighted! A bruising old duffer with a heart of gold. "Thanks a million mate." I said.

"It's alright. If you see me inside buy me a coffee. Milk two sugars," he said stone-faced. I couldn't detect whether he was joking or if this was an intricate part of the deal.

It was a wonderful stroke of luck anyway, and made the whole Coventry experience a hell of a lot more bearable.

It was clear from the outset that the match wasn't going to be any good. Annabel and I were more entertained by the kid sitting next to us with her own Coventry City pullbag full of various weird and wonderful merchandise. At one point she got a piece of A4 paper out of the bag and wrote 'Come on Sky Blue City' in biro.

After a half of absolutely nothing to note except the eerily quiet atmosphere it was pie time. The pies would make me feel better surely. The stall was called 'Nice as Pie!' which wasn't a particular fathomable pun.

"One steak and kidney pie please!" I jovially asked, handing over 3 pound coins.

"Sorry, we don't accept cash." The blank-faced female assistant replied, her mouth slightly open exposing a tongue ring which looked a bit pus-filled.

"You don't accept cash?"

"No. Only card." She said pointing at a huge sign, 'We only accept card'. Maybe I should have noticed this. Why on *earth* was this the rule? What idiot decided this? It was even more annoying because I didn't have a card on me.

"ANNABEL! ANNABEL!" I shouted outside the queue. "Can I borrow your card to buy my pie?!"

I wasn't her favourite person today.

Out of the corner of my eye I saw that legend of a steward standing at the top of one of the entrances to the arena. He made eye-contact with me.

"And one coffee."

I received my card-paid goodies and walked up to our shaven-headed friend.

"Here you are mate, milk two sugars, just how you like it!" I said with a wink. Perhaps a bit of an ill-advised wink. I don't think he knew who I was; a weird stranger who knows 'just how he likes' his coffee, but he gladly accepted it with a smile on his big face. That's karma for you right there.

I had my sub-standard pie and visited the surprisingly rank toilets, designed so you have to brush the back of at least one pissing man when walking out. There are many disadvantages of new stadiums, but you would think an improvement on the toilets would be an obvious plus point. Not here.

"Those toilets were horrible." Annabel said as we met up again.

"Oh really, mine too."

"They didn't have any mirrors! Were there mirrors in yours?" she asked.

"Yes, there was a queue of Coventry City metrosexuals preening their hair." I replied, getting a playful punch in the ribs.

Something about Coventry just depressed me. 18,000 isn't exactly a *bad* attendance for the Championship but in the grand Ricoh arena it looked empty and the fans struggled to generate any form of atmosphere. I suppose the match may have contributed to this. It was AWFUL. An uninspiring shocker. There were sighs coming from Annabel's direction every couple of minutes.

"No complaining. Free tickets remember!" I reminded her.

It was awful though. A bloody horrible goalless encounter. We left 3 minutes from the end to miss the traffic and as we were walking down the stairs we heard a muted cheer from what sounded like the Plymouth end.

"Bollocks. We've missed a goal haven't we?"

87 minutes of absolutely nothing and then a missed goal. Never leave early folks.

It was yet another 0-1 home defeat in the Midlands I had witnessed; I was beginning to think that the scoreline of 0-1 was representative of the region as a whole. I didn't hate Coventry, they aren't a very dislikeable club, but equally there is very little to get excited about a team that seem to have frustratingly accepted Championship mediocrity.

COVENTRY CITY   0
PLYMOUTH ARGYLE 1 (Noone 87)
Attendance 18,528

GAME 33
LINCOLN CITY v Kettering Town
FA Cup First Round Replay
Tuesday 18th November 2008, 7.45pm, Sincil Bank Stadium, Lincoln

Sometimes travelling to certain parts of England can be a bit of a chore, and certain places are perhaps best left undiscovered (naming no names Luton). Visiting Lincoln on the other hand was a joy; a city I had never been to, and was chuffed that the team remained in the Football League.

I remember when planning 92 Pies thinking it rotten luck that I would miss out on the quaint cathedral cities of Oxford, Cambridge and York, whose clubs are all playing non-league football nowadays. Fortunately Lincoln came to my aid, and I spent the pre-football part of my Tuesday soaking in all the charm Lincoln had to hit me. The Steep Hill area, with the ghostly grounds of the castle and cathedral bewitched me in an early-evening wintery way; it created quite a magical image of Lincoln.

The football ground on the other hand.....

Well, it's not *that* bad. Walking down the vast hill to the bottom of Lincoln you reach Sincil Bank Stadium, lying on the bank of the canal and integrated almost invisibly into rows and rows of small terraced houses. There are two big modern sloping stands coexisting with the charming 'Poacher's Corner', a miniscule stand in one corner of the stadium which can seat about 100 people. It was a bit of a mishmash but I liked it.

At the gorgeous top of the hill earlier in the day I had decided to treat myself to a very special pie, from the 'Browns Pie Shop and Restaurant' next to the Cathedral. This was posh. £7.95 a pie! I was starving, it would be worth it. I glanced at the menu.

'Game bird pie with orange madeira and thyme'.

'Lamb redcurrant and rosemary pie'.

Exotic! I wanted something they probably wouldn't have at the football ground, so went with the 'Local braised rabbit pie with onion and elderflower'. I don't think *Pukka* do a variety of that. Maybe they should though, because this braised bunny was bloody delicious.

Back down the hill though I was freezing my balls off at Sincil Bank and eyeing up the food stall. I started questioning my own non-codified pie constitution. Surely that glorious rabbit pie a couple of hours ago counted as my Lincoln City pie?! It was in the city of Lincoln after all wasn't it? I decided that it counted and took my place amongst the brave folk braving the cold for the FA Cup replay fixture versus non-league Kettering Town.

With 'Nellie the Elephant' inexplicably playing on the PA, the compère was doing his best to raise the damp pre-match atmosphere by greeting each stand.

"Let's have a big cheer from our visiting friends from Kettering!!!" he kindly requested.

"WANKER! WANKER! WANKER! WANKER!" the Kettering fans replied.

The poor bloke was consoled by the mascot, Poacher the imp (modelled on the legendary 'imp' figure that is synonymous with Lincoln cathedral and the city in general) and moved on swiftly.

There was a bit of tension in the air actually because last week Lincoln's not-very-shy manager Peter Jackson (who caused amusement for me and my pals at Chester City) claimed in the post-match press conference that when the teams met last week a Kettering fan was making monkey noises at his black players and at assistant manager Iffy Onuora. Kettering's chairman Imraan Ladak strongly denied this allegation, and blamed Jackson for inciting the home fans.

I don't know if it Jackson was right to be upset or if he was overreacting (which I *can* imagine him doing), but it all led to a very frosty atmosphere between the two sets of supporters.

"Racists! Racists! Racists!" the Lincoln fans shouted at the Kettering fans, an odd step in the right direction if the term 'racist' is now an insult on the football terraces!

Jackson himself wasn't shying away from the occasion, and looked like the pinnacle of modern fashion in a grey trouser complimented by a black jacket and bright orange tie. I could also see my old mate Super Frank Sinclair sitting next to Jackson. Maybe I would go say hello! Update him on the book! He would *definitely* remember me from Chester.

I postponed my Sinclair-stalking as the game kicked off and I concentrated on a first half that was pretty poor. The samba-style drums were banging away from some committed Lincoln fans but the game wasn't rocking like the drums were. The standard between the League Two and Conference sides was similar, the biggest difference that Kettering were prone to a few more amateurish lapses in concentration.

The goalless first half was approaching the end, and a very old man came up to me selling the 50/50 golden gamble tickets. He had the word 'Cyril' written on his cloth cap in glitter pen, which for some reason tickled my funny-bones and made me snort with laughter to myself.

"One ticket please Cyril." I said, handing him my pound.

"How do you know my name?" he asked with complete sincerity.

"It's written on your hat in glitter pen." I replied.

Cyril took off his hat and looked at it. "So it is!" he grinned before walking off bellowing "50/50 jackpot! Last chance! Roll up! Golden gamble!"

Lenell John-Lewis, who had been strong in every department (boom boom), scored for Lincoln as the second half began, but the Imps were living dangerously. Kettering had already hit the post twice in the second half before they deservedly equalised with 20 minutes to go.

The game was bubbling up nicely but I couldn't enjoy the match. There was a niggling voice in my head that had been going away at me.

"Not having a pie Tom?" "Pie from a posh pie shop Tom?""Gotta be a pie at the football stadium surely Tom!" "Doesn't count Tom!" "ONLY 91 PIES TOM!!"

Bollocks. I walked up to the food stall and looked at the menu. I wasn't even hungry. Wow! They did Lincolnshire sausages! That's brilliant! Lincolnshire are my favourite sausage (apart from perhaps Cumberland). I didn't even want a bloody pie, I wanted a sausage.

"What pies have you got?" I begrudgingly asked the lady.

"Meat and potato and chicken and mushroom is all we've got left." She replied.

"No 'Local braised rabbit' or 'Game bird with orange madeira?'" I asked hopefully.

She didn't respond so I just ordered the meat pie and went back to my seat slightly pissed off at myself for adhering to my own rules so bloody strictly.

I felt sick whilst eating my sub-rabbit-standard pie. Extra time and penalties loomed, but in the final minute of injury time the magic of the FA Cup struck (on a very small scale) and non-league Kettering scored a scrappy winner, sending out the relative giants of Lincoln City in the process.

I left Lincoln feeling a lot of love for the city, a casual indifference for the football team and a strange kind of 'embarrassing uncle' love for Peter Jackson. I had certainly eaten far too much pie though, I felt impishly sick.

LINCOLN CITY　　**1** (John-Lewis 54)
KETTERING TOWN　**2** (Westcarr 68, Christie 90)
Attendance 3,953

GAME 34
GRIMSBY TOWN v Bournemouth
League Two
Friday 21st November 2008, 7.45pm, Blundell Park, Cleethorpes

It was time for another adventure. I was anticipating a big pile up of awkward fixtures at the end of the season if I didn't start pulling my finger out a bit. So I planned another 5 matches in 5 days, venturing forth to Grimsby, Middlesbrough, Sunderland, Barnsley and Doncaster.

These five Northern towns do not scream 'glamour' to most people, but I was willing to enter these strange regions with an open mind and embrace whatever hit me, starting with visiting the fishiest club in the UK, Grimsby.

I had a feeling Grimsby might be a bit, well, 'grim'. I did a bit of research (*Wikipedia*) and found that three of the 'notable residents' of Grimsby were listed as Roy Chubby Brown, Jeffery Archer and Ian Huntley. That probably wouldn't be *everyone's* ideal dinner party line-up. I found out however that Grimsby Town FC is not based in Grimsby at all, but is based in Cleethorpes, a delightful(ish) seaside resort just outside Grimsby.[1] I'm not sure mid-November is an especially bustling time for Cleethorpes tourism, especially considering that on this particular Friday there was a sleet storm for the majority of the day.

Unsurprisingly I easily found a cheap guesthouse and checked in, asking the nice landlady directions to Blundell Park.

"Can't miss it love, carry on straight over the roundabout and it's on your right. Shame you didn't tell me this on the phone, I could have gotten you a free ticket! We have links with the club, the young trialists and new youth team players get put up here."

"Oh wow. Never mind! Thanks a lot anyway." I said, hiding my irritation.

---

[1] Leading to the popular whim that 'Grimsby are the only club in England who play away every week.'

I wrapped up very warm to brave the snow and trudged over to Blundell Park, an ugly grey block next to a McDonalds surrounded by mass terraced houses and an equally large amount of fish and chip shops.

Grimsby Town, officially nicknamed the Mariners and unofficially named the fishy people, are a club rooted in fish. The town of Grimsby was founded by a Danish fisherman called 'Grim'. The area around the stadium smells incredibly fishy. There were queues coming out of every one of the multiple fish and chips shops, and the McDonalds next to the ground was next to empty (and the few people inside would probably be ordering the fillet o'fish sandwich). It quickly became apparent to me that Grimsby fans are an unusual bunch; the weird and wonderful inhabitants of Cleethorpes were out in force. My favourite were a group of 4 men a few rows in front of me who were *all* bearded, with one in particular having a chest-length beard. He must have been a fisherman dressed like that; wearing an old green anorak and muddy wellies!

Bournemouth took the lead early on, but Grimsby equalised through a Jamie Clarke thunderbolt. My fishy friends were delighted, and started doing 'Cotton-Eye-Joe' style barn dancing with each other.

"Bloody Hell! When did we last score a goal that good Bill?!"

"1934!"

There was a Sky Sports reporter behind us doing a live link after the equaliser, to which all 4 men bellowed 'show us your cock!' repeatedly, causing an unintended smirk from the reporter, and big laughter from the surrounding fans.

Grimsby went one better and got another goal, their second in 3 minutes, on the stroke of half-time. A spiky-haired young lad sitting in front of me went to get his parents two cups of tea just before half-time, and came back having missed two Grimsby goals. Poor kid had all the surrounding fans pointing and laughing at him.

I was hoping that there would be a special fish pie to devour at half-time but alas I was not to be rewarded. Same old steak and kidney it is then. I found myself standing behind the hairy men in the queue, and thought I would start some small talk.

"Yeah lovely old place this!" the 2nd hairiest said to me looking at the crumbling yellow turnstiles and smiling.

"We're meant to be moving stadium to Grimsby town in a couple of years, but to be honest I don't really want to leave. This place suits us."

After about 4 minutes of chat I couldn't wait any longer. I needed confirmation that they were fishermen.
"Oh no! We're all in advertising," he said to me completely straight-faced. The men walked off with their beers nodding goodbye.
With my brain befuddled by that bombshell the second half began with great action, including comical defending by both sides, which probably explains why this was a match between the 90th and 91st placed teams out of the 92 (with only Luton below. Poor Luton).
Grimsby went 3-1 up, but had their first home win since March cruelly snatched away from them as 10-man Bournemouth scored through Darren 'retirement dodger' Anderton and Lee Bradbury to bring them level, and break 4,000 fishy hearts.
You could sense that the term 'long suffering' was invented for Grimsby fans (well...along with Luton fans of course. Poor Luton) and if any team were going to throw away a 3-1 lead against a 10-man Bournemouth side it was going to be Grimsby. It had been 14 home games without a win, and yet again the fans would go home to their fish suppers empty handed.

It was a bloody freezing evening at Blundell Park. It was snowing, and the wind coming from the North Sea was bitter enough to make my 5 woolly layers ineffective. Even the ref at one point took out a long handkerchief and blew his red nose. Despite this however, I absolutely loved watching Grimsby; with their obsession with fish, the positive and laid-back attitude of the crowd and the chants ("We only sing when we're fishing" being my favourite). The best thing of all however was looking up from the match action and seeing the lights of a ferry cruising past the stadium from the sea behind the ground. It was a fantastic contrast of images, and reminded me (slightly) of seeing the Thames from Craven Cottage.

It was the fans that set Grimsby apart though, the endless positivity from a group of supporters who have experienced such crap times recently. I hope they get to sing when they're actually *winning* as well as when they're fishing some time soon.

GRIMSBY TOWN   **3** (Clarke 42, Bennett 44, Atkinson 61)
BOURNEMOUTH   **3** (Bradbury 6, 89, Anderton 79)
Attendance 4,353

GAME 35
MIDDLESBROUGH v Bolton Wanderers
Premier League
Saturday 22nd November 2008, 3.00pm, Riverside Stadium, Middlesbrough

Where am I? I don't recognise this flowery wallpaper. Or the dark green carpet; the kind that wouldn't show up a blood stain. Ah! The guesthouse in Cleethorpes. Grey old ghost-town Cleethorpes.
I looked out of my bedroom window, anticipating a sunny walk on the beach before heading up to Middlesbrough.
It was snowing. Fairly heavily.
This wasn't in the script! What about the ice-cream vans, sandcastles and sun-drenched promenades?
I popped to the bathroom, but was met in the corridor by a man whose slickly gelled black quiff suggested he simply *must* have been an Elvis Presley impersonator.
He was completely naked.
This was a disturbing and quite inexplicable moment in my life, so I ran back into my room, grabbed my stuff together and immediately left for Middlesbrough, quite excited about heading back up to the North East after such a fun visit last time (and equally excited about getting as far away from the naked Elvis impersonator as possible).
Middlesbrough hasn't got the best of reputations, and driving in I didn't fail to notice the old steelworks and neglected machinery sites littering the outskirts. Going further into the city centre I reached the Riverside Stadium and immediately wondered how on earth Steve Gibson sells this club to the international superstars who arrive here. The ground looks alright, but the area surrounding is hardly exotic. Far from being scenic the riverside itself was a sludgy hell-flow, probably carrying its fair share of corpses (both human and animal). The ground is built on a former petro-chemical storage facility, which might be what attracted Juninho, Ravanelli et al.
It was a fresh afternoon, the snow had stopped and the sun was threatening to pop out so I took a wander around the stadium. The executive car park was absolutely rammed with Ferraris,

Lamborghinis and other various super cars. I wondered if any of them belonged to David Wheater.

I wandered to the exquisite gates at the front of the ground, a lovely touch in that they were the gates from the old stadium Ayresome Park, relocated to the Riverside. As I was admiring them, I was astonished to see the chairman Steve Gibson speed-walking through them! Steve Gibson! The richest man in Middlesbrough, the man widely regarded as the best football chairman in the UK. Even better, he was wearing *red leather* shoes! Dapper *and* charming. I ran over to speak to him!

"Steve!" I said warmly. Shit, perhaps this was over-familiar. He was an authority figure after all.

"Mr Gibson," I corrected myself.

"Hello," he said smiling, but continuing to walk.

What would I say?

"You're doing a great job sir." *Sir?* Suck up. "What do you think about today?"

"2-0 win I think!" He optimistically replied, reaching the executive door for the stadium.

"One last thing!!! Could I have a picture with you please?" I asked hopefully.

"Of course." Steve replied. I stuck the camera out arm length and gave my best cheesy grin for a picture of me and the 644th richest person in the UK.

Which (I kid you not) was the precise moment my camera decided to run out of battery, the lens retreating into itself and wilting like a limp cock. Steve Gibson and I were standing like fools, staring at an outstretched dead camera.

"Sorry," Steve said, patting me on the shoulder and trotting into the executive area in his amazing red shoes. Damn it! The camera doesn't bloody conk out for external shots of Grimsby's arse-ugly stadium does it?! Only when I meet a Premier League chairman!

Pleased I met my first ever owner of a club (Abramovich was next on my hit list) I went through the turnstiles, only for my ridiculously large bag to get stuck. There was a week's worth of stuff in my bag, too big apparently for the Boro turnstiles. I was stuck for what seemed like an age, trying to shimmy my way through unsuccessfully. Two humiliating instances in the space of a few minutes. Thanks Middlesbrough.

I took my seat in what I found was a rather bland inside to the stadium; just as ordinary as most modern grounds. Boro were playing an out-of-form Bolton side, and the atmosphere inside the Riverside was muted, especially as Bolton went 2-0 up in the first 10 minutes.

I felt like crying! 2-0 after 10 minutes! Ginger Mourinho waving his magic wand again! Boro fans were more politely unhappy rather than 'hell-hath-no-furious', but were undoubtedly all pissed off at Gareth Southgate's team.

It must be incredibly frustrating being a Boro fan watching the underperforming superstars week-in week-out. Today in the chilly Middlesbrough climate against Bolton Afonso Alves was the biggest culprit; a £12million striker that looks like a Conference player.

Sometimes the aura and atmosphere of a crowd can dictate the way their team play, and the low-energy, low-enthusiasm crowd today couldn't enthuse the low-effort players. At half-time, getting my pie, there was nothing in the way of banter in the food-queue, just the world-weary sighing faces of supporters losing 2-0 at home to Bolton.

Despite there being no efforts by the crowd to gee their team forward, Boro scored through a scruffy Pogatetz goal, and all of a sudden the noise was deafening from the home support.

"CUMMON BORO! CUMMON BORO!"

The Fratellis 'Chelsea Dagger' theme blazed out and the crowd went wild, jumping around and celebrating, singing the 'na na na na na' chorus. They were people absolutely transformed by a goal! Supporters were cheering ferociously for their team to get another. There was suddenly a terrific atmosphere about the place that the Riverside was holding in brilliantly.

Then Bolton scored through Elmander 1 minute later and everything from the home end went silent again.

I looked over with envy at the Bolton fans (fantastically loud and energetic all match incidentally) taking the piss out of the Boro fans by singing their own Fratellis celebration song back at them.

The match ended a deserved 3-1 defeat for Middlesbrough, and their fickle fans.

Almost everything about Middlesbrough underwhelmed me. I would like Southgate to make it as a manager but I fear he won't. You can tell he's a decent bloke, but I will never forgive him for those Pizza Hut adverts he made mocking his penalty miss. It wasn't (and still isn't) a laughing matter Gareth. My 10-year-old cousin Rory recently said, whilst we were watching Boro lose on Match of the Day, "I always thought Southgate was really cool." Poor deluded lad. Southgate is not cool. Boro aren't cool. Naked Elvis impersonators aren't cool. Gibson's red shoes on the other hand..... *they're* cool.

MIDDLESBROUGH   **1** (Pogatetz 77)
BOLTON WANDERERS 3 (Davies 8, Taylor 10, Elmander 78)
Attendance 24,487

GAME 36
SUNDERLAND v West Ham United
Premier League
Sunday 23ʳᵈ November 2008, 4.00pm, Stadium of Light, Sunderland

The snow had settled and Durham looked absolutely stunning. It was one of those winter mornings where the sun beams down to create a beautiful fresh day. With Middlesbrough on Saturday and Sunderland on Sunday I thought Durham would be a pleasant alternative to stay for a couple of nights, especially as my friend Lizzie is still at uni there. Not that Middlesbrough and Sunderland aren't delightful. Their charms are just a bit more of an acquired taste.

The cathedral and castle looked incredible sun and snow-kissed, but my afternoon of soaking in the glory of Durham had to come to an abrupt halt, because 12 miles up the road a football match was about to take place. And that's the reason I was here.

"It had better be worth it..." I said to Lizzie as I left for Sunderland.

"Are they good teams?" football-novice Lizzie asked inquisitively.

"Yeah they are fairly," I replied, "it'll be a good one, I've got a feeling!"

For good measure I put on my Sunderland shirt before heading off to the Stadium of Light. What's that? Why do I have a Sunderland shirt? Well at last year's Glastonbury Festival I was a tad squiffy and passed a second hand clothes stall which was selling a Sunderland shirt for £2. £2!!!

"It'll come in use at some point!" I slurred to my pals Collo and Paul in the mud-drenched field, both clearly jealous that they didn't have a football kit to buy.

And a mere 17 months later here I was, getting my £2 worth of use out of my Sunderland kit! Except that it was freezing and I was wearing 4 layers on top of it. Still, it's the *principle* isn't it?

If the £2 shirt was a bargain, then the £17 Premier League football ticket was (in context) a bargain also. Bearing in mind I paid £1 more for the League Two match at Grimsby a couple of days ago I was extremely happy with my cheapo Sunderland ticket.

The Stadium of Light is a magnificent stadium in many ways. It looks monstrously large from the outside; a brilliant piece of architecture. With the 'into the light' gate and the various odd statues, the Stadium of Light manages to feel historical despite being a new ground. This continues inside, with the different bars being named after various Sunderland legends, such as 'Monty's magic diner' after Mackem goalkeeping legend Jimmy Montgomery, and 'Ian Porterfield's golden goal bar!' after, erm, Ian Porterfield.

The stadium wasn't full, but I was still fairly awe-struck by it as I took my seat. I sat watching the hugely wealthy players warm up, and I noticed how many of both the Sunderland and West Ham players are the Premier League 'undesirable' types[1]. Lee Bowyer, Craig Bellamy, El-Hadji Diouf, Lucas Neill, Djibril Cisse, Carlton Cole, Anton Ferdinand. I wouldn't lend my car/girlfriend to any of them.

The ground was sparkling as the sun was setting, and a ghostly chill had entered the immense arena. There was an eerie majesty to the Stadium of Light. The fierce and spooky music of 'Dance of the Knights' from Prokofiev's Romeo and Juliet (OK, the *Apprentice* theme tune as I actually know it) built up the importance of the occasion as the players came out. The music promised great things. But great things were not delivered.

For this was a steaming turd of a match, an example of two Premier League teams playing without confidence, desperate not to concede and neglecting any attacking finesse for the quest of a clean sheet. It was a match not worthy of the great stadium, and the atmosphere remained flat throughout.

Behrami took the lead for West Ham in the 20th minute with a scuffed shot, but from then on almost nothing happened, (except for Behrami again missing an open goal in the second half).

Sunderland's tactics under Roy Keane looked incredibly limited and the players were poor, especially the red-mohawked Cisse (or as he is officially known Lord Djibril Cisse of the Manor of Frodsham). Andy

---

[1] Wankers.

Reid, still carrying the weight from last Christmas, Easter and Thanksgiving combined, was the worst culprit; his final ball being anything but Premiership class.

The Sunderland fans were about as miserable as the Boro fans the previous day, but there was definitely more noise generated around the Stadium of Light. The fans weren't really chanting or singing many songs, but rather they gave a constant running commentary to each other about the match.

The fans were certainly passionate though, that's for sure. I opened my coat briefly to reveal my (still muddy from Glastonbury 07) Sunderland shirt. I felt quite proud! For about a minute. It was bloody freezing!

Sunderland lost 1-0, and the Mackem jeers were absolutely piercing for referee Mike Dean, who despite being absolutely slaughtered did quite a good job in my humble opinion. The fans used him as the excuse for a poor defeat though. In fact it was the most noise I've heard to protest against a referee since, well, Newcastle.

However magnificent the Stadium of Light is, getting away from it is HARD. I was in a solid stream of traffic for bloody hours.

"Could be ages until I'm back Lizzie," I said, illegally phone-driving.

"Okay, fabbo, wizard, I'm in the Durham castle bar, see you later," posh Liz replied.

Sitting in the traffic, longing for that drink in the castle bar, my mind wandered to the fact that I had now been to 10 matches without seeing a home win! My away-win count was becoming statistically incredible. I was an unlucky mascot, clubs should dread me coming! Another interesting stat is that this match was West Ham's first win since against Fulham 2 months ago, a match I was at. So in the last two months, where I have attended 24 games, poor West Ham didn't win. Maybe I was their *lucky* mascot? Maybe I just needed to stop over-analysing things and get a life.

SUNDERLAND   **0**
WEST HAM UNITED **1** (Behrami 20)
Attendance 35,222

GAME 37
BARNSLEY v Burnley
The Championship
Monday 24th November 2008, 7.45pm, Oakwell, Barnsley

I left the North East thoroughly satisfied with my weekend spent alongside depressed Middlesbrough and Sunderland fans. As I headed down the A1 towards Yorkshire I wondered whether the depression would continue onward to Barnsley and Doncaster? Barnsley is pure Yorkshire. It oozes Yorkshire out of its pores. I don't think anything could have possibly made it any more Yorkshire. Maybe Michael Parkinson? Cloth caps? Whippets? Kes? Brass bands? Dickie Bird?

Alas none of these popped up, but you can feel the early 20th century history of Yorkshire Barnsley driving through; it is an old mining and glassmaking industrial town, and the cobbled roads and high chimneys were prominent driving towards Oakwell.

I parked up with plenty of time to spare, and sat in my car until the last possible minute to escape the rain. It was pummelling down. The old ground was much bigger than I thought it would be, with lots of improvement work having gone on in the 1990s. 10 minutes 'til kick-off I braved the thundering sky and entered the ground, alongside some Yorkshiremen grumbling about the weather, and indeed sporting the odd cloth cap for good measure.

A recent unwelcome incident was affecting the atmosphere at Oakwell. Iain Hume, the Barnsley striker, had been seriously ill in hospital for the past two weeks; suffering a fractured skull and internal bleeding after getting elbowed in the head by Sheffield United defender Chris Morgan. Oakwell frequently erupted into a 'For Iain Hume stand up!" chant, and there were signs scattered through the crowd saying 'Get well soon Iain' and similar messages. There was massive controversy over the incident, with particular criticism being reserved for Morgan; a player born in Barnsley and who made over 200 appearances for his home town club before moving to Sheffield. "If you hate Chris Morgan clap your hands," chorused his former-supporters.

Barnsley were still basking in the glory of last season's FA Cup run in which they beat both Liverpool and Chelsea, but they were struggling in the league this season, and had recently looked like a team on the down. Burnley however most certainly *are* a team on the up, having also incredibly just beaten Chelsea, this time in the Carling Cup[1], and were also doing pretty well in the league.

In an accent so thick it can't be stirred, the Barnsley fans were cheering on their team in the pissing rain, and the first half was one-way traffic; Barnsley scoring and dominating until half-time. A series of poor decisions by the referee led to him being fiercely booed, jeered, and abused off at half-time by both sets of fans. The 'respect campaign' that the FA have been banging on about is clearly not working (although in this case the ref *was* complete shite and deserved everything he got).

I was sopping wet. My seat in Oakwell was one of the few not covered, and my waterproof coat, it turned out, was not acting like it was particularly waterproof.

"Ey look at those shoes son!" a big-nosed man said, nodding at my pathetic holey footwear.

"Yeah they're not great," I replied, fearing pneumonia.

"Look at these," the man said, pulling up his trousers to reveal solid man-boots, "that's a proper shoe!"

"I'll bear that in mind thanks."

Shoe-miliated and feeling wet, a good old reliable *Pukka* pie warmed me up, but I needn't had worried because the second half was positively *scorching!* Barnsley came out all guns blazing and scored twice in the first 6 minutes. The atmosphere had risen, with a fair amount of good-natured yet meaningful abuse between the Barnsley and Burnley fans, only uniting for the predictable 'We all hate Leeds scum' chant. A fair few Burnley fans were chucked out by some heavy-handed policemen, but the atmosphere never really got truly tense, (unless you were the referee I would assume).

---

[1] Meaning that at the time Barnsley and Burnley were 2 of the last 3 teams to beat Chelsea domestically!

Barnsley were coasting towards victory; Jamal Campbell-Ryce and former Real Madrid midfielder (honestly!) Diego Leon running the game in the middle of the park. With 20 minutes to go however, Burnley suddenly sparked into life, and began playing with all the fluidity that saw them beat Chelsea, scoring twice in 4 minutes and producing an incredibly tense finale. Burnley really should have equalised on numerous occasions, missing some stone-cold sitters, but Barnsley held on and won by a just-about deserved 3-2 margin. As I sprinted back to my car, my shoes now resembling small foot-spas, I thought that Barnsley v Burnley certainly had all the passion I would have hoped from a Yorkshire/Lancashire derby. More satisfyingly for me my home-team hoodoo had been lifted with the first home victory I had seen in 11 games! Huzzah! Now on for Doncaster to maul Forest tomorrow night! As long as it stops bloody raining, that's all I ask for.

BARNSLEY 3 (Macken 18, Whaley 48, Leon 51)
BURNLEY 2 (Paterson 69, 73)
Attendance 10,678

GAME 38
DONCASTER ROVERS v Nottingham Forest
The Championship
Tuesday 25th November 2008, 7.45pm, Keepmoat Stadium, Doncaster

Visiting Doncaster Rovers' remarkably bowl-shaped new ground I learnt a valuable life lesson. Always carry some cash on you when you go to the football.

I had arrived at a car park, handed them my last £5 and reached the Keepmoat Stadium's ticket office only to find that they didn't accept cards. This was annoying. I ran back to my car and zoomed off to find a cash point with 25 minutes until kick-off and counting.

Zooming around this newly built area of Doncaster my eyes were peeled but there were no ATMs anywhere! What was I going to do; beg for money at the side of the Keepmoat? Even McDonalds didn't do cashback. They *did* do an apple pie for 99p however, which I managed to pay for with the last of my coppers.

It was only 10 minutes until kick-off and I needed some dosh, otherwise I had just travelled many miles to the town of Doncaster just to see its McDonalds. Which is a thought that made me borderline suicidal.

Fortunately I found a shitty pub a few miles from the stadium and managed to park on double-yellow lines, run in and find a cash point! Yes!!! Maybe I could stay for a quick pint and get to know the locals? 7.40pm. 5 minutes 'til kick-off. Perhaps not.

Driving back to the stadium I reached the car park, and the same attendant I had paid £5 a mere half hour ago, a long haired man who looked like an American deep-south country singer.

"£5 please mate."

"Hey, yeah I just had to go and get some money." I said.

"You left the car park though," he said cruelly, holding out his hand for a £5.

"But I was just in here a minute ago. I gave you my last fiver! I've still got the ticket!" I showed him.

"But you left."

"But..."

"But it's £5 or you're not coming in."

I looked at him with a furious stare, cursing venereal disease upon him and his family. He looked in my car.

"Have a McDonalds did you?" he asked sarcastically, noticing the paper bag. "What did you have?"

"Apple pie." I said through my gritted teeth, handing him his cursed money.

He looked at me with distain. "Apple pie? What did you get that for? Get a Chicken Supreme if you go to McDonalds. Or at *least* a Big Tasty. Damn fine burger that."

I escaped an in-depth conversation with my new nemesis about the merits of the McDonalds pound-saver menu and ran to the stadium. I hoped I wouldn't miss any goals.

Of course little was I to know (although I probably could have guessed) the match between 23rd and 24th in the Championship would finish goalless. It was a really poor game between two promoted teams too frightened to try and go for a win.

The main problem with the match was that neither team had a single player who looked like they could score. And goals tend to win football matches.

Doncaster fluffed a chance. South-Yorkshire drawls were swearing around me.

"If we had Kevin Phillips we'd be in the play-offs this season. He'd have 40 goals for us by now," exaggerated the fat fan next to me, but you saw his point.

As far as new stadiums go, the Keepmoat is fairly bog-standard. Situated next to an almost (but not quite) picturesque lake, the bowl-shaped ground isn't very tall, grand or particularly attractive. The floodlights were quite interesting however; large blocks hanging over the pitch at an angle which seemed to defy gravity.

Half-time featured some dancing girls with bare midriffs foolishly braving the below-freezing temperatures. Soft Southern wally like me, I was wearing 5 woolly layers and still shivering my balls off. 'You're not famous anymore!!' sang the Donnie fans to Forest. That was slightly amusing, but about as lively as the crowd got.

The game was petering out to the goalless finish it was written in the stars that it would be. Doncaster 'keeper Neil Sullivan at the ripe old age of 38 was keeping the crowd amused with some good interaction.

The final whistle was greeted with a sigh of relief, but despite the unsatisfying match I appreciated the scale to which Doncaster Rovers FC has changed over the years. It was exceedingly bold for a small club like Doncaster to get involved with a new stadium like the Keepmoat. Only 10 years ago they were non-league having finished bottom of Division 3 with a -83 goal difference. Fans carried a coffin through Doncaster town centre to symbolise the death of the club. I wish I got the chance to visit Donnie's old stomping ground, the fabulously derelict Belle Vue. The history of Belle Vue is littered with various hilarious disaster stories, the finest being the former chairman Ken Richardson being convicted of arson after attempting to burn down the ground in 1995.

The 15,000 all-seater Keepmoat is very pleasant, organised and efficient, I guess everything their old ground or their old team wasn't.

A duller Doncaster Rovers for the 21st Century perhaps. I had power-walked back to my stupid unofficial £5 x 2 car park. My long-haired archenemy was standing there a smile on his face.

"Good match then? What was the score? Worth the money?"

I said nothing to him and drove off, narrowly avoiding running over his foot after a last-ditch change of heart not to try and hit him. I looked on the floor and saw my apple pie wrapper, and made a decision that a Big Tasty McDonalds might cheer me up. A 'damn fine burger' apparently.

DONCASTER ROVERS   0
NOTTINGHAM FOREST   0
Attendance 12,612

MILLWALL v Aldershot Town
FA Cup Second Round
Saturday 29th November 2008, 3pm, The New Den, Bermondsey, South-East London

Hmm...
I wasn't particularly looking forward to this one.
MILLWALL.
The word doesn't connote sunshine and fairy wings and football fans holding hands in blissful harmony.
In fact if you ask almost anyone in the country what they associate Millwall with you would probably get a flurry of images of rioting fans in the street, pitch invasions, chairs being ripped up, meat-heads throwing bricks through pub windows and the like.
Of course Millwall fans have cleaned their act up in recent years. They had to. Former chairman Theo Dragon Paphitis introduced a scheme in which fans had to carry a membership card to watch a home match, with all their details on the Millwall computer system. The most severe incident of recent years was the battle with Birmingham fans outside the New Den in 2002, probably the worst example of English football hooliganism so far this century. But surely incidents like that are isolated enough for me not to fear my trip to the Isle of Dogs?

It was an FA Cup weekend, and Millwall had been drawn against Aldershot Town, the first *ever* meeting between the two clubs. Given this fact, the Aldershot fans were more than up for the occasion as you would expect. Millwall away in the cup? A bit of a tasty draw... As I arrived at London Bridge station the police presence was absolutely huge. On the train the Millwall fans were separated from the lively Aldershot elite by a row of policemen between carriages. On reaching Bermondsey station the police wouldn't let us off, for fear of a fight escalating with the Aldershot fans a few carriages down. A group of only about 40 of us were held back for 10 minutes by the police. I looked around, there were a couple of families, women, children, an old couple, and generally pleasant looking people.

"Bit much isn't it?" I said to the bloke next to me.

"Yeah just a bit. Always the way though isn't it, too much Bill around. Not needed," he replied. I had noticed on the short train ride that all the Millwall fans only refer to the police as 'Bill'. Not even 'Old Bill', just 'Bill'.

"Come on Bill! Let us get to the ground! This ain't exactly the firm is it?" my new friend said to the police, gesturing at the women and children and causing a ripple of laughter from the group.

"It's only Aldershot! You'd think they were bloody West Ham or something!"

Finally the police let us go, "Follow us," ordered the unyielding senior officer.

"Jesus! It's Captain Mainwaring! Come on everyone! Left, right, left, right, left, right!" the cheeky bloke shouted to the group, again getting a big laugh, but a stern look from Mainwaring.

It turned out that a couple of the guys in our small group were in fact Aldershot fans, but the police didn't believe them so wouldn't let them go! The whole debacle made me think that perhaps sometimes such a large police presence causes more problems that the fans themselves.

It was a very grey afternoon, some games across the country had been called off due to fog, and this part of South-East London had a smoggy, Victorian, 'Jack the Ripper' feel about it. The New Den is placed bang in the middle between the dense dark metallic greyness of the train line and an old industrial power station incinerator site. It is an intimidating large ugly stadium but I can bet it's nothing like as terrifying as Millwall's former ground the Old Den was.

From reading about the Old Den it seemed that the crowd were fearsome, but often in quite a productive way; intimidating the opposition team to actually make them play worse through shit-your-pants terror. I would have loved to have gone to the Old Den and sampled the blazing inferno of the passionate fiery old dockers that were the typical Millwall fans.

I know it was just an FA Cup 2nd Round tie against the minnows of Aldershot, but the atmosphere in the New Den was completely flat.

For all the hype and pre-conceived reputation of Millwall fans, they were actually very quiet and static, despite playing like a winning side throughout the match. There were no songs really except for the occasional 'No one likes us we don't care,' and their long note of 'Miiiiiiiiiiiii'; a strange phenomenon at Millwall matches that is usually rather tuneful.

The game itself was a bit of a dud, Millwall never looked like getting out of second gear, and Aldershot looked overawed by the occasion. The fan sitting in front of me didn't give me the greatest of images of Millwall supporters. He was watching the game with his mate and his bonny baby, a tiny little thing that must have been less than a year old. He spent half the match bouncing the baby on his lap and kissing him, and half the match shouting threats at the Aldershot fans and calling the referee a c**t.

The baby was wrapped up in a blue Millwall scarf, his destiny pre-ordained before he knows what a football is.

There was a light moment at half-time with a bunch of kids doing a relay race around the side of the pitch; one of the racers was a very portly ginger boy, running at tortoise pace and losing against a much smaller girl. The poor boy's boobies were wobbling, and he was on the receiving end of lots of laughing from the Millwall contingent. That'll scar him for life.

Millwall won 3-0, a scoreline which flattered the quality of the match, but represented their dominance and shows why they are doing so well in League One this year.

As for a day out however I wouldn't particularly recommend Millwall and the New Den. I remained tense for the majority of the match, I couldn't help it. At least I didn't get cordoned in by the police on the way back. And there were no riots between the Millwall and Aldershot fans. Shame really, I was secretly quite excited about seeing a few chairs thrown at some policemen. Or Bill. Maybe some time later on in the season huh?

MILLWALL   **3** (Alexander 30, 77, Grimes 88)
ALDERSHOT TOWN   **0**
Attendance 6,159

GAME 40
MORECAMBE v Cheltenham Town
FA Cup Second Round

Tuesday 2nd December 2008, 7.45pm, Christie Park, Morecambe

With a spring in my step, I happily bounced my way to Christie Park to watch Morecambe FC! What a treat! 92 Pies was making sense to me, I had woken up this morning thinking I would not be able to get a game in today, only to find out that the FA Cup rescheduled dates meant I could fit in going to Morecambe tonight and Carlisle United tomorrow night!

I knew nothing about Morecambe that doesn't involve tragic cockle-pickers or Eric Morecambe, yet 4 ½ pain-free hours driving later I was here! I strutted towards the football stadium excited about some lower-league gold. Until...

Swoooooooooooooooooooooooooooooooooooooooooooooooooooooo ooooooooooooooooosh!

  Arse

    Over

      Tit

I extravagantly slipped over a few feet outside the stadium. Damn that spring in my step! I slipped over to produce a comic pratfall Eric and Ernie would have been proud of; landing on my tail bone, hearing a crushing, agonising crunch before everything went black.....
I should begin this chapter a couple of hours earlier really.

I am in a small guesthouse, overlooking the bay, watching the local news station and praying for the pitch inspection to produce a positive result. November had turned into December, and winter had truly arrived. There was snow in the air and a blanket of frost on the fields, the gritters were out in force and Morecambe bay was frozen over.

Please Mr Weatherman, give me some good news. Please tell me that the FA Cup second-round match between Morecambe and Cheltenham Town is not postponed. An impromptu 220-mile trip to Morecambe isn't *quite* worth it if there's no game to be watched, however picturesque the frozen seagulls lying dead on the bay are. The owner of the guest house, a friendly small chap called Neil, was adamant the match would be postponed.

"Definitely. I was going to go tonight but I've told the wife I'll have a look at the bills with her. That's how certain I am it'll be called off."

That wasn't very helpful. I had a feeling the staff at Morecambe will have busted their collective nuts to keep this match on; especially as this FA Cup tie had already been postponed once, a week earlier, due to fog. After a tense hour of local news, I was overjoyed at the announcement that the match would go ahead, and saved a thought for Neil sorting out his bills.

Which was about the point where I left you; momentarily passed out on the icy pavement outside the 88th largest ground in the Football League. I came to, and saw about 6 or 7 Morecambe fans looking over me.

"You alright mate?" I vaguely heard a North-Lancashire accent say, my vision re-emerging.

"Yeah, I think so," I mumbled as a couple of the fans helped me to my feet. I felt pretty woozy and my back had definitely clicked out of place

With my dignity scraped across the floor with the gritty ice, I stumbled my way into the ground behind one of my helpers who said "I'm keeping this one just in case," about his ticket stub, anticipating another abandonment.

Christie Park is located in a nice residential part of Morecambe which adds to the community feel of the club. The ground itself looks non-league, with creaky old terraces and, in the case of the East Stand, a flat slab of concrete for people to stand on. The pitch was obviously very hard and bobbly in the frost, leading to an unsurprisingly scrappy match.

There was an interesting mix on the PA before the game began, starting with the town's favourite son singing 'Bring Me Sunshine'. You really couldn't escape Eric in this town. Eric actually links my home town Harpenden with Morecambe, as he lived in Harpenden for most of his life, only a few miles away from his beloved Luton Town.

The game started well with Morecambe scoring a great looping header to the muted cheers of the crowd who braved the freeze, and the goals kept flowing in the first half, with three more (including two penalties) before half-time. The atmosphere was quiet but comforting, and I do enjoy being in a stadium small enough so that you can personally here the players call each other twats. Also, brilliantly, I heard one Morecambe player call the veteran Cheltenham striker Barry Hayles 'a fat prick'.

I had enjoyed the first half at 2-2, but half-time couldn't come quickly enough for me, because it was pie time. And what certainly *isn't* non-league about Morecambe is their pies. The massive meaty pie (courtesy of local manufacturers 'Potts Pies') came on a full plate with gravy, and was simply the best I have had.

It was delicious.

Thick chunks of meat, delicious crispy pastry, and everything complimenting each other perfectly on a freezing cold night.

If this wasn't enough, Morecambe also, spectacularly, did hotpot! Again, a full plate of the finest stewy goodness Lancashire had to offer. All served by extremely friendly ladies in their own little booth. If you're going to eat food at a football club, make it Morecambe.

The second half dragged a bit as the temperature dropped further. Cheltenham had gone ahead and didn't look like conceding another goal.

An old gent standing next to me got out his hipflask and put some whisky in his Bovril. Bovril-whisky! Tremendous. That'll warm you up. The fans stuck it out until the end, with the game finishing 2-3, but the Morecambe players were enthusiastically clapped off by the fans who should feel proud at braving the cold to watch their team. Ice dripping down from my nose and my back in aching agony, I made it back to the guesthouse and went straight towards the raging fire in the living room. Neil was sitting there with his specs on, looking over some paperwork.

"How was it?" he asked, "better than doing the bills or not?"

"Yeah marginally," I said, shivering "five goals, a couple of penalties, pretty good game if a tiny bit nippy."

"They're a decent club, Morecambe. I'm more of a rugby man traditionally, but since I moved here we've had lots of football fans in and they've always been lovely folk. My eyes have been opened!" A good assessment from a rugby man I think. If the appeal of tiny Morecambe FC can convert the doubters and the egg-chasers then that says something about our beautiful game. Plus I bet they never serve pies that bloody good at the rugby.

MORECAMBE   **2** (McStay 5, Howe pen 27)
CHELTENHAM TOWN   **3** (Vincent 23, 54, Finnigan pen 36)
Attendance 1,758

GAME 41
CARLISLE UNITED v Crewe Alexandra
FA Cup Second Round
Wednesday 3rd December 2008, 7.45pm, Brunton Park, Carlisle

Breakfast ended at 8.30am, so I stumbled down to the dining room at 8.28 looking far from a million dollars with my crooked back and bagged eyes. Neil had rustled up a full-English of epic proportions, despite the fact that I was probably the only person staying in the guesthouse. The dining room had been decorated in red ribbons and red flowers.

"It looks nice in here; very festive." I said to Neil.

"Oh yes. We're hosting a conference here this afternoon for the local Tory councillors you see. I thought decorating the room in red might wind them up a bit."

I saw from his expression that he wasn't joking.

"Well good luck with that!" I said, taking a bite of my sausage.

"So where are you off to today?" Neil asked.

"Carlisle. Got a cup match against Crewe."

"It'll be called off. Definitely. I wouldn't bother heading up there if I were you," he helpfully advised.

I said farewell and headed to my car, completely frozen over. No de-icer, no scraper. Shit! I took off my sock and began scraping the ice off my windscreen with that, only to remember I had forgotten to bring any spare socks. This wasn't a great start to the day. Maybe Neil was right, the game would be called off, I *shouldn't* head up to Carlisle.

But I did head up. And I went via the Lake District, spending the day driving through the beautiful sun-kissed but freshly icy National Park. Wearing only one sock. I felt wonderful during the day, wandering lonely as a cloud through what must be the most gorgeous region of England, albeit a region with very few sock-shops.

I was still a bit paranoid about the match though. I phoned up Collo.

"Alreet la!"

"Collo, what are you up to today?"

"*Football Manager*, I'm breaking through with trying to get Notts County to the Premiership. Just signed Barry Hayles on a free transfer, I've got a good feeling about this year."

"Right OK, could you keep the Carlisle Utd website up, checking news on the pitch inspections for the Crewe match please?"

"Sure thing mate. Why do you want to know though?"

"I'm going to Carlisle."

"Oh."

Many hours later there was still no word from Collo about a postponement, so I nipped on up from Keswick to Carlisle, fingers firmly crossed that my brilliant day in the Lakes would be rounded off with some more low-quality FA Cup football.

Against all the odds, I breathed a huge sigh of relief at about 6.30pm. Collo let me know that the match was definitely on whilst I was walking through Carlisle town centre, past a bar called *'Party Party! – It Does Exactly What it Says on the Sign!'* with one fat man drinking a pint by himself in the window. It made me proud to be English.

I was fairly excited about watching Carlisle United, a club I will always associate with their miraculous escape from Football League relegation in 1999. Needing a win against Plymouth, the match was 1-1 going into injury time, when on-loan goalkeeper Jimmy Glass came up for a corner and scored the goal that saved Carlisle from non-league football. Fairytale stuff.

Brunton Park is situated just outside the centre of Carlisle, in a nice leafy residential area. It's an interestingly designed ground from the inside; the different stands ranging in shapes and sizes, with the terrace and seating areas seamlessly and oddly merging together. My favourite thing by far about Brunton Park was the fact that (wait for this...it's good...) *the club shop has its own cat!*

The folk at the turnstiles didn't like my big bag. "I didn't know we did overnight camping here son!" one steward laughed while the other one looked at me with great suspicion. I made it in though and took my place alongside the Carlisle elite, looking around to see if I recognised any of them from when I accidently sat with them in Rochdale. I didn't. I watched the officials warm-up and tried to predict which one out of the three is the ref. You can always tell!

They possess an odd authority over their meagre linesmen colleagues.

The players were coming out to, quite tremendously, a re-worked version of 'One Step Beyond' by Madness. "Hey you! Don't watch that! Watch this! Carlisle United! One Step Beyond!"
The match never quite lived up to this great pre-match song however. Crewe had reappointed Super Dario Gradi again, and the team came out all guns blazing, going two goals up in the first 12 minutes against a hapless Carlisle side. Carlisle were uninspiring; their silver fox Graham Kavanagh had a nightmare in centre midfield, looking twice his 35 years.

'Can the driver of the Crewe Alexandra team coach please return to his coach,' the PA announced. At which point, 10 minutes from the end of a match stagnating at 0-2, I thought it was about time the driver of a green Peugeot 206 (me) returned to his car.

I was bollock-freezing, I had witnessed some very low-quality football, but this spontaneous trip up to the very North-West had made me feel brilliant about myself. What an adventure! Now for the massive massive drive back to Harpenden. *TomTom* said the estimated time of arrival 3:23am. Time for the emergency Red Bull in my boot to come out!

CARLISLE UNITED   0
CREWE ALEXANDRA 2 (Miller 3, 12)
Attendance 2,755

GAME 42
CHELTENHAM TOWN v Crewe Alexandra
League One
Saturday 6th December 2008, 3pm, Whaddon Road, Cheltenham

I realised I was being a bit of a lousy boyfriend at the moment, so thought I would treat Annabel to Cheltenham Town vs. Crewe Alexandra. Surely the tension of the League One relegation six-pointer is the stuff every girl's dreams are made of?

Brushing up on my Cheltenham knowledge I realised there is more to the town than steeple chasing. The club are in a fair amount of trouble, rooted to the bottom of League One and fighting off the threat of administration.

The sun was beaming into the car and it was a very pleasant drive from Oxford to Gloucestershire. After being told it was impossible to park anywhere near the stadium and the park-and-ride was necessary (and subsequently ignoring said advice and parking in a street 3 minutes from the ground) we arrived at Whaddon Road.

As if to emphasise my pre-conceptions of Cheltenham Town the ground was what I would patronisingly refer to as being 'cute'. It popped up amidst the houses, dwarfed by the green trees surrounding it.

"WHY HELLO YOU!!!!" said an old man in a pineapple bikini fat suit, jumping out at me and Annabel. His face was caked in make-up, and if the pineapple bikini wasn't enough he was wearing a sombrero and a multi-coloured cape. Is this normal behaviour in Cheltenham?

"I'm scared Tom..." Annabel muttered.

"Me too," I whispered back, as the lipstick-smeared man stared at us like a mass-murderer.

"ARE YOU EXCITED ABOUT THE MATCH?!" he shouted, the terrifying smile not flinching.

"Sure..." I said, retreating backwards slowly, my hand in a vice-like grip with Annabel's.

"AND ARE YOU EXCITED ABOUT THE PANTOMIME SOON TO OPEN IN THE CHELTENHAM EVERYMAN THEATRE STARRING ME?!"

It was slowly making sense why this man was wearing a fat suit and had pineapple boobs.

"Thrilled," I smiled, taking his flyer politely.

It was an icy but beautiful afternoon, especially with the view of the Cotsworld Hills from inside the stadium. In fact I would be as bold as to state Whaddon Road offers the most pleasing internal view in the Football League I had seen so far.

We saw some bloke apparently plays the next door neighbour in the Royle Family queuing up for a cup of tea.

"Why have you gone red?!" I asked Annabel.

"I don't know, it just happens when I see someone famous! I'm easily starstruck."

I looked at her with one eyebrow raised.

"I know, I know, but it always happens. Like that time I saw Darren Day in Tesco."

"I've heard the Darren Day story already."

I looked at the Cheltenham players warming up.

"What about Barry Hayles! Do you not get star-struck with him?"

Annabel had curiously never heard of the spritely Barry Hayles; Cheltenham's most exciting talent on show.

With the man from the Royle Family out of sight the pre-match entertainment came from our old pineapple-titted friend wandering the pitch waving to the crowd. This time he/she was accompanied by a man in a red disco-suit on stilts, juggling.

"What the fucking hell is that?" the fans sang at the panto dame, in a rather humiliating ritual, with the man on stilts only receiving a "There's only one Peter Crouch!" chant.

Pantomime characters cleared from the pitch, the match began with Crewe having two players stretchered off in the first 7 minutes. Crewe, after losing two key men so early, looked a shadow of the team I saw beat Carlisle 3 days ago. In fact Cheltenham also looked a shadow of a team I saw beat Morecambe 4 days ago. Oh God. I had seen both these incredibly un-glamorous teams twice in the space of half a week. Unintentional lower-League-One stalking. I had reached a zenith of sadness. I doubt how many bloody Cheltenham or Crewe fans had been to 2 of their teams games in half a week, let alone *me*.

This relegation battle was predictably a dull and cagey scrap, won by Cheltenham through a scuffed effort from Drissa Diallo.

"Not great is it?" I sheepishly said to an unimpressed Annabel. Oh God. Coventry v Plymouth now this, she wasn't picking the good ones. We were more interested in looking at a nearby steward.

"That steward really reminds me of someone..." said Annabel. I thought for a minute...

"Harry Redknapp!"

"That's it! Looks *exactly* like him!"

She really did look *exactly* like Harry Redknapp the poor woman.

After being initially surprised with League One's quality, I had now seen the darker, more dismal side of the league with the performances of the three C's of Crewe, Carlisle and Cheltenham; the gulf in class between these and the likes of Leicester and Leeds astronomical.

The lack of quality on the pitch didn't really matter though. Cheltenham Town FC is a delightful little club with a family friendly atmosphere who seem to be punching above their weight. I hope the football Gods are kind and they sort their finances out sometime soon. In the meantime at least they've got pineapple-breasted dames to cheer up the place.

CHELTENHAM TOWN **1** (Diallo 48)
CREWE ALEXANDRA **0**
Attendance 4,052

GAME 43
CRYSTAL PALACE v Southampton
The Championship

Monday 8th December 2008, 8pm, Selhurst Park, Croydon, South London

Spontaneity once again smacked me in the face, this time at approximately 3.45pm on a gloomy Monday whilst watching Countdown.

In the dictionary corner alongside lovely Suzie (the thinking man's crumpet) was Jo Brand, who was telling a story about her love for Crystal Palace FC, and how she attends home matches with bags of shopping from the Sainsbury's superstore on the corner of the ground. Linking in the 'big shop' with some mediocre Championship football! That's time-saving. I began farting around on the internet about various Crystal Palace titbits, and found out that they were playing *tonight!* A mere 4 hours from now! How on earth did that manage to escape my schedule?

Train route sorted, I downed my tea just after the conundrum (F O A M I C I N G) and made my way to see South London's finest. Selhurst Park is a stadium which is often derided as one of the blander and more depressing in the country; an opinion often backed up by the fact the ground is in the Borough of Croydon, arguably one of the more soul-zapping parts of London.

On reaching Palace though I was pleasantly surprised by the ground. Selhurst Park comes into sight amidst the houses with the huge impressive curved roof of the Holmesdale Stand; a great-looking structure fit for a 21st Century stadium.

There was a really friendly atmosphere outside the ground, and for the first time this season I felt rather Christmassy. Palace had a huge tree outside decorated in red and blue, and a Salvation Army band playing some Christmas classics on their horns. It was all rather heart-warming.

My mood was soured upon reaching the ticket office though. Balls. I didn't have any cash again. Did I not learn anything from Doncaster? Surely a club of Palace's size would take card?

"Sorry sir, we don't take card," the blank-faced man said.

"Damn. Do you know if there's a cash machine anywhere near?"

"Erm.. no not that I know of. I'm new here..."

This was very unhelpful.

"Hold on...I know of a cash machine nearby!!! Jo Brand said there's a Sainsbury's on one corner of the ground! Must be a cash point there!" I said to the ticket man, probably bemused at why Jo Brand and I were in discussion about Sainsbury's. Either that or he had no idea who Jo Brand was.

I wandered off and found Sainsbury's on the opposite side of the ground. Result. Lovely delicious cash point.

Money kerfuffle over I entered Selhurst and the match kicked off in brilliant style for Palace, going 2-0 up in the first 15 minutes. The first goal was a delightful Shefki Kuqi lob, and was followed by Kuqi's trademark celebration of diving chest-first onto the floor. I tried that once after scoring a goal when I was a kid but winded myself and had to get substituted. "There's only one Shefki Kuqi! One Shefki Kuqi! He used to be shite, but now he's alright, walking in a Kuqi wonderland!" sang the Palace fans. Does a player enjoy hearing a chant like that or not?

The crowd banter was slightly limited but sets of fans were at their funniest when clocking the television pundits working in the Sky booth just between the Holmesdale Stand and the away section. Dougie Freedman was representing Palace, and (naturally) Matt Le Tissier for Southampton. Le Tiss looked dejected watching the game after going 2-0 down so early, and the "You fat bastard" directed at him from the Palace fans probably didn't help improve his mood.

"Dougie, what's the score? Dougie, Dougie, what's the score?" the Palace fans sang incessantly at Freedman until he put two fingers up on one hand and a clenched fist on the other, to a huge ripple of laughter from the home crowd.

Half-time was spent queuing for a pie that turned out to be a bit crap. I tried striking up conversation with a few Palace supporters but they weren't really having it, which was a bit disappointing. Where have the friendly Palace fans gone?

The second half meandered, Palace were comfortable and the only animated man in the stadium was Neil Warnock, who was ranting and raving and bouncing so much I thought his head might explode. At least he couldn't blame the officials about anything tonight as Palace went 3-0 up to secure their victory.

Despite the fact that the atmosphere was a bit dead I think that Selhurst Park gets a bit of harsh press. It's not exactly *lovely*, but it's not all that bad either. AND like Jo Brand said, you can link it in with getting a Sainsbury's shop in, stock up on some pastries to munch so you don't have to queue for 20 minutes for a lukewarm pie like I did.

F O A M I C I N G was 'Magnifico' by the way. I didn't get it.

CRYSTAL PALACE   3 (Kuqi 9, Beattie 15, Ifill 75)
SOUTHAMPTON   0
Attendance 13,799

GAME 44
NOTTINGHAM FOREST v Sheffield United
The Championship

Tuesday 9th December 2008, 7.45pm, City Ground, Nottingham

Nottingham Forest are a fantastic club, with a rich history and loyal fan base. Which makes it all the more unfortunate that I *hated* going to watch them. For the first time, my journey was feeling like a real chore.

It was bollock-freezing, and Forest yet again proved that their brand of relegation-battling Championship football is marginally worse than watching paint dry; providing me with my previous worst match against Doncaster, and now my new worst match against Sheffield United.

The fans deserve better than this. Back in the mid-90s when I had just 'chosen' Bolton as my team my brother Ali chose Forest because he liked the name. The family actually went to the City Ground to see Forest play Newcastle, with their new signing Alan Shearer up front. The game was goalless (naturally), but certain Forest players were genuine cult heroes; the likes of Brian Roy, Alfie Inge Haaland, Ian Woan, Steve Stone, Mark Crossley. Tremendous! Oh and how could I forget the temperamental genius of Pierre Van Hooijdonk?

I had made my way up the traffic-clogged M1 towards Nottingham and parked nearby the bustling riverside stadiums.

"How much is the cheapest adult ticket?" I asked the lady in the ticket office.

"£25."

"£25?! How about student discount?"

"£11.50."

"So less than half price?"

"Yes."

"One student ticket then please," I asked, without the lady even asking to see my non-existent student card. Financial confusion all round at the City Ground.

I made my way in, and *Mull of Kintyre* was playing on the sound system as the teams lined up. *Mull of Kintyre?* That's a bloody terrible choice. It made my bad mood even *worse*. Jesus I was cold. I swear there was smog looming over the Trent like an unwanted predator.

20 minutes had gone, without a single incident to note. Nothing. I looked around. Every single other fan looked miserable too. There were a handful of Chinese lads sitting a few rows in front of me, who were by far the most excited members of the crowd; taking pictures, clapping enthusiastically. If only they knew how glorious it can all be. They need to experience a bit of Huddersfield v Port Vale or something similar to really get their blood pumping.

The fans in general weren't digging the game and I didn't blame them. The most lively they got was when title-winning boxer Carl Froch, Nottingham born-and-bred, was presented to the crowd before the match. He got a much bigger ovation than the players. The mood dropped further when Brian Howard scored a scuffed scissor kick for Sheffield United after some inept Forest defending. I was so thankful for the half-time whistle. I could warm myself with a pie, however sick I was of them, and pretend to wait for a friend outside the warmth of the toilets. Heavenly.

Robbie called me at half-time, pissed.

"How's the match?"he shouted, clearly at a crowded bar.

"A piece of absolute steaming dog shit."

"Oh right! Mate... Gary Megson has won manager of the month!"

"Wow!" I replied. "That's either made my day or ruined my day!"

"One for the gingers! Wow! Look at O'Hara's goal from midweek, Yid Army!"

"Are you watching Sky Sports News in a pub Rob?"

"Yeah I finished my dissertation today."

"So you're celebrating by watching Sky Sports News at a pub?"

"Sure am mate. Shit! De La Red is out for the season!"

Robbie, (who's surname is Redway, which compliments his striking red hair) recently took on having people refer to him as 'De La Red' as his "MC name" after the Real Madrid midfielder.

"Is that so?"

"Heartbreaker. Oh Look. Wolves 'keeper Carl Ikeme has signed a new contract to keep him at the club until 2012."

"Are you just going to narrate Sky Sports News to me?"

"Yep. Until Adam gets back from the toilet. Yids playing Man Utd tomorrow, we're not going to bed until then. All day bender!"

"Congratulations Robbie."

"Cheers mate. Ads is back. 'Til next week."

"Laters"

"Oh and by the way, Ross McCormick is out of Cardiff's trip to Burnley with a hamstring injury."

"I know. I saw that already on Georgie Thompson's teatime bulletin." Oh Georgie. What a lady. We both paused in silent contemplation for a few seconds.

"See ya later T."

"Bye."

The tannoy announced that Derby were losing to Wolves, which was greeted with another storming cheer. Well, I suppose with nothing to cheer about your own team it's only fair to gain a little bit of pleasure from the suffering of your biggest rivals.

The second half was just as bad, albeit with a couple of missed sitters to liven it up a tiny bit, the biggest culprit being Rob Earnshaw. Oh Rob, what happened to you? One of my favourite bits of football trivia is that Earnshaw is the only man to score a hat-trick in all 4 domestic leagues, the FA Cup, the League Cup and at international level. Some feat, especially considering he did it all in 5 years. He sure as heck-fire didn't look like scoring a hat-trick tonight though. The problem with the Forest team was that they were crap at all the absolute basics you learn when you're 10 years old. Needless offsides, foul throws, taking free-kicks with moving balls, teammates going up together for the same header. Simple stuff that Calderwood's team just couldn't manage.

The full-time whistle was music to my ears sweeter than any symphony Mozart could have even dreamt of. Awful, awful awful match. Yet ANOTHER 1-0 home defeat I had witnessed in the Midlands. This was getting weird. I couldn't wait to get home. Walking back to my car a few Nottingham rat-boys came up to me.

"Oi moite can I borrow 20p?"

"No."

"How about 50p?"

"No."

"How about your phone."

"No."

I managed to shake them off, like a pack of manky eager stray dogs. Their accent was horrible. It was the worst of the worst. My mate Paul always said Nottingham chavs had the filthiest accent in the U.K. but I didn't believe him until now.

Getting back to my car made me so happy. It was over! No more Notts Forest for Tom, potentially *ever* again. I wished the club well, just not with me in presence when the team is as shoddy as this. Brian Clough will be spinning (and no doubt cursing) in his grave.

NOTTINGHAM FOREST 0
SHEFFIELD UNITED   1 (Howard 31)
Attendance 19,541

BRIGHTON AND HOVE ALBION v Milton Keynes Dons
League One

Friday 12th December 2008, 7.45pm, Withdean Stadium, Brighton

Going to see Brighton play is, for lack of a better word, *different*. This became apparent as soon as I arrived at the Withdean Stadium; the atmosphere was less 'football' and more 'PTA-organised school sports day'.

The leafy middle-class suburb just outside Brighton was the backdrop, with jolly fans trying to control their children from running around everywhere screaming and honking their honkers.

The stewards looked like volunteer parents rather than the typical shaven headed hard-arse or disinterested student. They rubbed their gloves together, nuzzled into their scarves and raised eyebrows at each other in a 'gosh isn't it cold!' gesture.

The Brighton Withdean Athletics Stadium is of course not intended for football, but has been accommodated by the only club in England eligible for charity at a homeless shelter, Brighton and Hove Albion. After two seasons playing at 'home' 70 miles away in Gillingham, Brighton moved to the athletics stadium where they have remained for 9 years.

Straight away the Withdean doesn't feel right. The running track surrounding the pitch removes any threat of an atmosphere, the pitch itself is actually the wrong size, and the horrible unsheltered temporary-scaffolding seating shakes violently whenever someone stands up. The East stand in particular is a monstrosity, the most breathtakingly bollocks stand I have seen; two crumbling, ugly, awkwardly different sized misshaped prisms plonked next to each other.

There is no alcohol served, no parking anywhere within 100 miles of the stadium (slight exaggeration allowed), no noise upon leaving the ground as to not disturb the neighbours, and no music allowed from the PA. The burger vans forming a circle in the club car park and temporary toilets screamed out 'village firework evening' rather than 'professional football match'.

To get to my seat I had to climb a hill, battling wayward tree branches and rouge woodland creatures. I reached the top of the grassy knoll and noticed the massive bouncy castle-style inflatable football game next to the pitch! This was getting too much for me.

When they weren't smacking footballs at the bouncy castle the sugar-rushed kids were trying to pull down the shorts of the seagull mascot and kick him in his bird-balls. The poor mascot was surrounded by endless chubby Brighton-and-Hove devil children, thick snot smeared from their nostrils across their cheeks, pupils dilated from too much candy floss.

I was pondering over how to help the giant seagull when a man in a cloth cap approached me, fat and bearded. He looked at his ticket. "R42?" he growled, pointing at my seat. I looked around. It was 40 minutes until kick-off and there was no one sat in 25 seats to the left or right of me, or in 3 rows either in front or behind me.

"Yes," I replied. He gestured towards his precious seat with a grunt and a point. And I got up and moved a few seats down, watching him eat his egg and beef burger from R42, a crap seat far back and near the corner flag.

I got chatting to two more accommodating Brighton fans who were making me laugh, being derogatory about the opponents MK Dons. "Who give a shit about MK Dons anyway? What's the point of Milton Keynes? They don't even have an accent." I laughed into my pie and nearly choked. It summed up Milton Keynes so perfectly that a town is so uncharismatic that they don't even have an accent.

Watching Brighton was a multi-cultural experience. Sitting around me there were Japanese, Austrians, and I met *two different* groups of Norwegians. I had no explanation for this, but a Mecca-style pilgrimage to watch MK Dons' Norwegian sub Tore Andre Flo seemed excessive. Although they did pipe up when Flo came on in the second half....

The match was really good. There were 6 goals and decent passing football (predominately from MK Dons rather than Brighton), and there was much enjoyment from a full-on 22 man handbag fight. Despite punches being thrown by players from both teams, the ref thought booking 4 players was more suitable than producing a red card.

Nothing felt right about the Withdean. It felt like fairly useless aliens had landed with the intention of forming a football club but getting all the basics (food, toilets, seats, and shape of the stadium) wrong. The fans were so placid and well behaved in their odd open stadium, although it didn't help that the team played uselessly after going ahead in the 2nd minute. I doubt Mickey Adams can have possibly thought defending a lead for 88 minutes would work.

The odd thing about the evening was that I came out having really *enjoyed* it. This might be my only ever trip to the Withdean, and for a one-off experience the ramshackle, weird and often inappropriate running of Brighton from an athletics stadium is a more fulfilling experience somehow than going to a cloned football-by-numbers ground. And although it was unusual and not ideal, it felt like these PTA-type people rallied round Brighton during their money problems and made it actually possible to host a high standard of football in a makeshift ground, which deserves huge commendation.

So whereas I like going to the Withdean as a one-off, I feel hugely sorry for the poor Brighton fans who go every week; being deprived of any form of an atmosphere, out in the open and so far from the pitch. They have been playing there for 9 years, which is far too long, and I hope the new stadium does get built soon. Even just to allow the fans a bloody drink in the ground to help them get through it all!

BRIGHTON & HOVE ALBION 2 (Johnson 3, Fleetwood 88)
MILTON KEYNES DONS   **4** (Llera 26, Johnson 46, Leven 69, Puncheon 90)
Attendance 5,691

GAME 46
PORTSMOUTH v Newcastle United
Premier League
Sunday 14ᵗʰ December 2008, 1.30pm, Fratton Park, Portsmouth

"Play up Pompey! Pompey play up!"

I had been looking forward to this one. There was something about Portsmouth that represented a bygone age of when the big clubs were as shabby as the smaller clubs.

What a different half a year makes in football. A mere 6 months ago there were crowds singing 'Arry Redknapp's name on the streets of Portsmouth as he brought the FA Cup back to the town. Those days seem a lifetime away from Tony Adams's shoddy team that would meet fellow strugglers Newcastle on this bright winter Sunday afternoon.

'Fratton Park' is 'Krap – Nott'arf' backwards, and whilst it indeed is rather crap, it is also oddly enchanting. Entering the wonderful mock Tudor entrance you get hit with the quite unique stadium. On one side of the ground you reach the turnstiles by passing through an extremely narrow alleyway. With graffiti sprawling over all over the walls of the stadium, and sharp menacing barbed wire over the alleyway, it resembles a disused prison rather than an UEFA-Cup standard stadium. AC Milan played here a couple of weeks ago, yet it looks in worse nick than most of the League One grounds.

You go through turnstiles that are electric (Portsmouth's solitary entrance into the 21ˢᵗ century) and realise the ground is even shabbier on the inside. The back area is all outside, with rogue ladders, pipe drips, potholes and rats carrying the Black Death (I might have made the last one up).

I was sitting behind the goal quite near the front, gladly not any further forward as the front row at Fratton Park has the fans below-pitch level; their heads bobbing up from the trenches to watch the action. Pre-match joy came from an elderly couple coming on the pitch to celebrate their 50th wedding anniversary by having their picture taken with Herman Hreidarsson. Congratulations Henry and June! The penalty area was amazingly slanted, with the goal net actually sloping down-hill. I was shocked to see this in the Premier League, but also oddly warmed by it.

The players came out and the famous Pompey Chimes song was being bellowed throughout the ground with a distinct ringing sound in the background. Where was that coming from? And then it dawned on me... that twat with the bell (not my nickname for him incidentally), the bloke with the big hat and blue wig and million Pompey tattoos. Nobby Portsmouth! Him! That guy! You know! The man *officially known on his birth certificate* as John Portsmouth Football Club Westwood. I glanced briefly to my left and saw him and his posse behind the corner flag in their own little booth, a mere few feet away from me.

JPFCW is an intriguing character; a man with over 60 Portsmouth tattoos, PFC engraved in his teeth, and who hasn't missed a game, home or away, in over 24 years, yet is a supposedly gentle fellow who runs an antique book shop.

"Stand up! If you hate the scum stand up! If you hate the scum!" JPFCW was roaring huskily by himself. His mates around him followed, banging their drums and blowing their bugles in the process.

"Fucking scummers!"

No love lost between Southampton and Portsmouth. Skates v scummers. A relatively new rivalry in English football, but certainly one of the most vicious. One that can turn a peaceful antique book dealer into hate-filled tattooed blue sea-monster.

The first half was a goalless affair, but one of the most exciting goalless halves of football I think I've seen. Portsmouth were playing very well but Crouch and Defoe were guilty of missing a truckload of chances. Newcastle looked dangerous on the counter attack, with Obafemi Martins hitting the post. All performed to a rapturous crowd and the soundtrack of a never-ending bell.

At half-time I had the unpleasant experience of getting some food and going to the toilet. The tiny bogs were from the third world. There was a thick layer of piss on the floor streaming towards a gutter; it was a bit like that foot-pool you have to go through before going swimming. Oh, and I was wearing my holey shoes again. Grim. There's also the issue of the food kiosk which is literally that, a tiny kiosk, ensuring a preposterously large queue going up the stairs into the stands and beyond.

I was wandering back to my seat when I noticed a huge queue of Chinese people lining up to get their picture taken with JPFCW. This is a man who is a local celebrity because he supports a football team and dresses funny. He'll be on Big Brother next year probably.

The second half began and we saw a bit of long-overdue Michael Owen magic to put Newcastle ahead, scoring with a deft chip over David James. Portsmouth kept probing Newcastle; Crouch and Defoe missing even more chances, before Martins got the Geordie's second goal. James was at fault for the goal, diving too early, and booted the ball out of the ground in frustration. To confound his misery he got booked for his troubles.

Newcastle had sewn up the game and the home crowd had gone a bit quiet, all except the crew behind the corner flag. I had another look. The Chinese followers had gone. The game had died, I thought to myself there was nothing to lose. Go and speak to him Tom! I apprehensively approached the booth, blagged past the steward, went up to Nobby Portsmouth and told him what I was doing.

"92 grounds," he muttered, smelling ever-so slightly of stale beer, his tattoos and blue hair gleaming in the afternoon sun, "well you're at the best one now mate." He smiled a warm smile, not significantly toothy enough for me to see his Portsmouth enamel engraving.

"I'm John," he said putting out his hand, "crap game to come to though, we've been bloody awful." He turned around and started ringing his bell again. The drummer and the bugle player, both looking a bit drunk, kindly nodded at me and carried on playing their instruments. With little in the way of instruments I just clapped along enthusiastically, until John gave me a massive Portsmouth toy lion to wave around.

Newcastle scored their third in the final minute to which John uttered a single expletive and began ringing his bell again. It was another David James error that let Guthrie's shot through his hands.

"He's been a liability today," said John. I think he's a liability most of the time personally, but I decided not to say this in front of his own fans.

Full-time went and John patted me on the back as I gave him his lion back.

"Harry's a disgrace for going, an absolute disgrace. He could have built something brilliant after the cup win. But with Adams the team don't look happy[1]. Diarra will probably go in the transfer window[2] and we'll end up fighting a relegation battle all season[3] and go broke at the end of it.[4]"

John looked mournful as he took off his huge checked hat. "Well…" he said with a dramatic pause, one of a man of infinite knowledge and experience after not missing a game for 26 years, "that's football isn't it." And shook my hand as he wandered off.

Despite the shaky times for Pompey my trip to the south coast had been one of my favourites so far. The stadium was crap; it had a sloped pitch, uncomfy cramped seats, the worst facilities in the Premiership, graffiti and barbed wire surrounding it, BUT with more old-fashioned charm, personality and essential character than any other top-flight ground.

Fratton Park has contradicting pleasures, but what's for sure though is that the Premier League would certainly be a lot blander without Portsmouth FC and Fratton Park. And John Portsmouth Football Club Westwood and his bell of course.

PORTSMOUTH   0
NEWCASTLE UNITED   3 (Owen 52, Martins 77, Guthrie 89)
Attendance 19,416

---

[1] They weren't.

[2] He did. As did Defoe.

[3] They did.

[4] Big time.

GAME 47
SHREWSBURY TOWN v Wycombe Wanderers
League Two
Saturday 20th December 2008, 3.00pm, New Meadow, Shrewsbury

I woke up to the all-too-familiar sound of Collo snoring on the couch opposite mine. Where *were* we? Wallpaper doesn't look familiar. Collo is covered in icing sugar. Why for the love of God is Collo covered in icing sugar?

My friend Jack, a quite unique character who is a tall, thin, mysterious, handsome, quiet, and very odd trainee pilot/ice cream man walked in and drew the curtains.

"Morning!" he said in his Mr Bean-like drone. Oh yes, we were at Jack's house in Wales! We went out for his birthday last night.

"Jack, why is Collo covered in icing sugar?"

"Me and you decided to cover him in icing sugar when he fell asleep."

"I see."

I checked my phone.

"Jack, why do I have a picture of me and Lembit Opik as my screensaver?"

"We were with Lembit Opik last night, remember? He was asking us for drinks and chatting to those sixth form girls."

"Oh yes, it's coming back to me."

Jack lives in Newtown, where it is not uncommon for his MP to be out on the lash by himself, hanging out with whoever will have him. I remembered something quite shocking that Lembit told me last night, that I am scared to put in print for fear of libel. But it involved the word 'pussy'. My head was predictably pounding and I feared that a trip to Shrewsbury Town's spanking new stadium would not solve my problem.

I begrudgingly drove back to England with Collo and Jack in tow, a momentous occasion which was Jack's first ever football match.

"Excited Jack?"

"Not really," was the frank response.

As if the monster of a hangover wasn't enough, the journey wasn't exactly a fun one. The powers that be in Shrewsbury Town deserve a big slap concerning match-day parking. They built this new stadium out of town on a large site with nothing nearby, yet they provide zero parking spaces for fans without a special permit.

The car park at the ground holds nearly 1000 cars, was less than half full, but no cars were allowed in it. Where is the logic? After a painfully lengthy search for the 'park-and-ride' coach car park we finally reached the stadium.

What we did notice from our aimless driving around was that Shrewsbury is a lovely medieval market town, full of attractive listed buildings and a distinctive personality.

It's a shame absolutely none of this is reflected in the new football ground.

Opened in 2007, the New Meadow is a less-gay version of the Gay Meadow, with gay in this case meaning historical, interesting and charismatic. I never went to Gay Meadow but it was apparently a joyous away day for fans of the wonderfully ramshackle lower-league grounds; something that this new stadium does not even come close to achieving.

It ticks all the dull boxes of being clean, safe, shiny and comfortable, but is this really what you want from a day out at the football? I'd rather have a leaky pipe dripping on my head and mice nibbling at my toes at a half-interesting ground than sit in a stadium with the personality of a cardboard box for 90 minutes.

Shrewsbury fans, to be fair to them, were in good spirit before kick-off. The mascot was giving out honkers, and Jack thought it would be funny to honk his in mine and Collo's face for the majority of the match. It wasn't. Shrewsbury, lying in the play-off places were up against unbeaten runaway leaders Wycombe.

The game was alright but pretty forgettable; Shrewsbury's delivery was good but they looked absent up front, even the league's top scorer Grant Holt.

"Enjoying this Jack?" Collo asked at half-time, Jack's face pie-deep in meat and potato.

"Not really. Why are the fans so mean to each other?"

The atmosphere had not been particularly hostile, but I suppose from Jack's perspective there were lots of 'wanker' signs and indeed 'wanker' chants being directed between supporters. I guess I'm completely sanitised to it all now. I could make out 'You're Welsh and you know you are' from the Wycombe end too, that might have been upsetting Jack.

"The pie's good though," he said, mouth full of meat, and/or potato. "My compliments to the chef."

5 minutes later Jack (who eats at least 5 takeaways a week yet is still stick-thin) went back for his second pie. Unbelievable.

Wycombe scored quite early in the second half which turned out to be the winner, meaning yet another 1-0 home defeat in the (sort-of) Midlands. I was racking them up!

The New Meadow is a ground I simply can't and won't say anything nice about. It is an identikit monstrosity of mediocrity. The 4 individual stands all look the same, and are far apart enough to make it nigh-on impossible for any atmosphere to be held in the ground. There is nothing nearby; no pubs, restaurants, statues, museums, flying trapeze circuses or *anything* to stimulate the mind; just a big grey unused car park. I understand that Shrewsbury haven't got the finances to make it their new ground spectacular or wonderful, but could they not make it a) a tiny bit unique, b) a tiny bit attractive, or c) a tiny bit convenient to travel to/from.

My experience of Shrewsbury Town FC wasn't horrible. It was fine. It was OK. Like ready salted crisps or a successful dentist check-up, it was *fine*. In the Football League fine isn't good enough, you need something special about your club, ground and team, which I found nothing of at Shrewsbury. Sorry.

SHREWSBURY TOWN   0
WYCOMBE WANDERERS 1 (Harrold 55)
Attendance 6,160

TOP And so the adventure begins - game 1 at The Valley, Charlton Athletic
LEFT Super Frank Sinclair at Chester City
BOTTOM LEFT Digger the Dog at Dagenham & Redbridge
BOTTOM RIGHT Message to the FA from the Luton Town fans

Galpharm Stadium, Huddersfie

NEWCASTLE UNITE

St James Park - home of Ne
United

Me and John
Portsmouth Football
Club Westwood

LEFT Arsenal's Emirates Stadium

ABOVE Outside Old Trafford, Manchester United
BELOW Clarence the Dragon looks out over Sixfields, home of Northampton Town

Sunset at the Recreation Ground, Aldershot Town

TOP LEFT A pie and a pint at Moor, Burnley
BOTTOM LEFT A Premier Lea ground? Blackpool's Bloomf

Braving the elements at the Britannia Ground, home of Stoke City

Accrington Stanley. Who are they?

hite elephant
e Northern
ington Arena

Deepdale, the home of Preston North End

You'll never walk alone - the famous Kop at Anfield, home of Liverpool

Sunderland fans making a point away at West Brom

Pitch invasion at Brentford's Griffin Park on the day they won League Two

Me and John at Brentford

Friends and family join me for the final game - Bolton
Wanderers v Hull City

The 92nd Pie!

GAME 48
ARSENAL v Liverpool
Premier League
Sunday 21st December 2008, 4.00pm, Emirates Stadium, North London

It had taken 48 matches but I was finally going to get my first delicious taste of 'Big Four' action. This was a goodie. Arsenal v Liverpool. If I hadn't just eaten some Shreddies I would be literally foaming at the mouth.

The thought of going to see Arsenal excited me, despite it being an occasion I am rather familiar with. I went to every Bolton game at Highbury since we returned to the Premiership in 2001, and it was a ground that I absolutely adored. It was so seamlessly immersed into a row of terraced houses that you could walk past one of Europe's most famous stadiums without even realising it was there if not for the floodlights; something I found magical.

The atmosphere, whilst sometimes not very loud (hence the nickname 'Highbury the Library') was usually still special in some way; the giant clock looming over the crumbly old ground. I never saw Bolton win at Highbury but I always came out happy. Watching Henry, Bergkamp, Pires and the rest in action was a joy. Indeed, the 'Invincibles' season of 2003/2004 barely seems to get mentioned very much nowadays. Perhaps that team (and Wenger of course) don't get enough credit for what they achieved that season.

But Highbury is gone. One of England's most charismatic old grounds has been replaced by a giant 60,000 seater bowl-shaped arena named after an Asian airline. Surely the Emirates Stadium is a soulless, atmosphere-free, overlarge hub representing all that's wrong with the personality-bereft corporate 21st Century money-making Premier League?!

No.

I loved Highbury. It was the best. But the Emirates runs it close, albeit in a very different way.

Firstly, and most obviously, the Emirates Stadium is magnificent. There's no other word for it. The design is continental, a huge bowl in the centre of an arena super-zone. The whole Emirates area is absolutely massive; you can get lost just walking around the stadium. The two-tiered club shop is suitably spectacular, selling every item in the Argos catalogue, but with the Arsenal crest on it. The packed shop has 11 lines for the tills numbered from 1-11 with each line 'named after' a suitable gunner legend (1 Seaman, 2 Dixon, 3 Winterburn etc).

I texted my brother Greg to tell him that, thinking it might amuse him. Greg went out with Lee Dixon's daughter for about 3 years, so always enjoys a bit of Lee banter. In fact the only other time I have been to the Emirates, I was in the Bolton end whilst Greg was in Matt (he of Little Britain fame) Lucas's box with Lee. Lucky bastard. *AND* he met Thierry Henry![1] I wish *my* girlfriend's dad was a former England and Arsenal footballer rather than a carpet-shop owner.

I met my cousin Markie a good couple of hours before kick-off to soak in the atmosphere. Markie is 12, good at every sport imaginable, and has an immense mop of curly ginger hair. And he supports Liverpool.

"Alright cuz! I said, giving his ginger scalp a rub like a patronising older cousin, "you excited about the game? Scared that we're in the Arsenal end?"

"Yeah a bit. I don't know what my reaction's going to be when Liverpool score," he said confidently.

Walking around the Emirates I think it still feels historic despite being only a couple of years old. It is crucial that the new ground is still in the area, with the old Highbury site just around the corner. The big block 'Arsenal' sign and the huge cannons at the front of the stadium are a nice touch, helping to maintain the personality of Arsenal Football Club.

With the afternoon winter sun beginning to set the bright red ground looked fantastic, all four tiers of the ground beginning to slowly fill up, the curvy top of the stadium just above the chronological drawings of every major trophy the club have one, with room left for future victories. The facilities are as lush as you would expect; the absolute crème-de-la-crème being the cushioned seats.

---

[1] Greg told me that he smelt beautiful. Va va voom!

"This is the life hey!" I said, cracking my knuckles and stretching, thinking of Shrewsbury Town yesterday and being very glad I wasn't there now.

The pre-match music was scene-settingly perfect, a bit of *Move On Up* by Curtis Mayfield followed by Elvis's *Wonder of You* as the 22 international superstars came out to thunderous applause from both sets of fans. The Emirates crowd were in tremendous voice as the match began, but Liverpool started the brighter; Gerrard missing a couple of good chances early on.

"He's not looking lethal your 'super Stevie'... "I teased my 12-year-old cousin. A mere few seconds later Robin Van Persie scored an absolute belter with his right foot, flying past Reina and sending the crowd wild, except for Markie who sat on his hands biting his tongue whilst everyone around us was cheering.

The link up play between Fabregas, Van Persie and Adebayor was looking sharp, and Arsenal were the better team until Robbie Keane scored a goal equally as fantastic as Van Persie's; a route-one volley struck with absolute venom. Markie just poked me in my sides and grinned from ear to ear.

The goal was a bit controversial in that Keane should perhaps have not been on the pitch at all following a cynical foul earlier on in the match. Keane had been enduring a hostile reception from the crowd due to his Spurs connections but had shown his composure by scoring the first crucial goal of his, as yet, short Liverpool career.

Arsene trudged off at half-time looking fairly annoyed at letting the lead slip, but the match had been a cracker. Half-time entertainment came in the form of some 'Citreon dancing robots' which defied any kind of conventional advertising techniques. I had a £4 pie that, whilst not even nearly worth £4, was actually rather good.

"How's your 'hotdog and chips'?" I sarcastically asked my young cousin, nicking some of his chips in the process.

"What's wrong with that?!" laughed Markie, "I just didn't get a pie because I don't want to be like you."

The second half didn't live up to the quality of the first, which can mainly be attributed to the half-time injury of the inspirational Cesc Fabregas. To make it worse, Adebayor was sent off after an hour for a stupid second yellow card, meaning there was a distinct lack of quality on show. Arsenal's three-man central midfield of Diaby, Denilson and Song is OK, but lacking title-challenging inspiration, or indeed experience. Are any of these players world class? They were all better than Lucas for Liverpool though that's for sure.

"For fuck's sake Lucas," said Markie, using words that I *certainly* didn't use when I was 12, "I could do a better job than him."

The match finished at 1-1, a fair result for these two equally matched Premier League big guns. The match left me doubting Arsenal's title credentials, their squad isn't quite there yet to compete with United and Chelsea.

The Emirates Stadium is in a different world from any other of the previous 47 grounds I'd been to this season, and is £430million well spent. It is a superb ground fit for a superb team, something Arsenal still have some way towards becoming.

Despite this though, I maintain you should always trust Arsene Wenger. He knows what he is doing. The empty spaces on the curved Emirates trophy haul will not remain empty for much longer with the sulky French professor in charge, I am certain of that.

I said a farewell to Markie (he met his dad, don't worry, I didn't just leave him in North London surrounded by Arsenal fans) and headed home. Walking back to Arsenal tube station I felt a nudge in my arm. "Do you miss it mate?" a stranger said, nodding at a row of houses. I was struck by the realisation that it was Highbury. Or at least the remnants of Highbury. I hadn't even noticed. Only the front mural still existed, but was covered with scaffolding. It was like looking at a dead body.

"Yeah I do actually," I said honestly, Arsenal fan or not. "But I think the Emirates will do Arsenal proud over the years."

The stranger nodded, smiled and walked off, catching up with his mates and singing a Gooner song.

ARSENAL   **1** (Van Persie 24)
LIVERPOOL **1** (Keane 42)
Attendance 60,094

GAME 49
READING v Cardiff City
The Championship

Friday 26th December 2008, 3pm, Madejski Stadium, Reading

British institution #138 – sarcastically applauding a dropped plate.

British institution #139 – morris dancing

British institution #140 – apologising when someone bumps *in to you*

British institution #141 – Sir David Attenborough

British institution #142 – going to the football on Boxing Day.

That's right folks; Boxing Day football is a bloody British institution. So by that logic I am a crappy football fan, having *never* been to a football match on Boxing Day. In my defence we always spend Christmas with my cousins in Surrey, which is quite far from Bolton, but still that's no excuse. Aldershot's just around the corner!

So I woke up with my mouth tasting of sherry and sprouts (form an orderly queue ladies), the temples in my head pounding and my paper cracker-hat drooping over my eyes. I slept in my paper cracker hat. Oh dear.

Yet despite these familiar Boxing Day emotions I had a different buzzy feeling; for I was off to the Madejski Stadium with the family for a post-Christmas slice of merry Championship joy.

I rounded up the troops; both brothers, 3 cousins (including Markie for his 2nd game in a row) and a very hungover Uncle Rupert. Mum and my Auntie Steph were making turkey sandwiches for our journey. Ugh! No more turkey.

Reading looked like being one of three standout teams in the Championship this season, along with the runaway leaders Wolves and the constantly flattering-to-deceive Birmingham. The team had retained many of the stars from their two fantastic seasons in the Premiership; the likes of Harper, Doyle and the feisty Hunt brothers, and looked good bet for a swift return to the top flight.

A hungover car ride later we arrived in the town dreams are made of; Reading. When the Madejski Stadium (named after the surprisingly difficult to spell Reading chairman John Madejski) came into view I was left a bit underwhelmed. For some reason I had it in my mind that the Madejski is a Reebok/Galpharm like example of impressive, almost futuristic new football stadiums. I was a bit disappointed to see how ordinary it looked. Maybe with the Emirates, New Wembley and other newer, spankier grounds popping up the Madejski looks less special than it did 10 years ago.

The ground is plunked off the M4, with absolutely nothing nearby except a few car parks and a wind turbine. The fans were walking in orderly single file up the hill towards the stadium, some wearing London Irish Rugby Union shirts (who share the ground), passing the Waitrose and John Lewis advertising signs. Call me a football snob but it was all so middle-class and bland and beige and safe.

And there was the *membership card* scheme that I had to spend the best part of a day organising. Membership card? At Reading? It's not exactly bloody Millwall is it?! I had to buy 7 cards before being able to order tickets. Why? Search me.

We entered via our membership cards and went straight to the bar. The headaches were kicking in but Rupert had a cure for this.

"Five pints of Guinness please," he ordered. 12-year-old Markie and 10-year-old Rory looked at their father with pleading eyes.

"Not for a couple of years lads," he said responsibly.

The man at the counter gave Rupert his change and looked at Rory. "Here mate, I've got a joke for you," he said, "What does an ugly baby look like? Why don't you ask your mother!"

Little Rory paused looking unamused.

"Only joking lad! Give me five!" he jested, putting up his hand for Rory to high-five, only to pull away and leave Rory hanging when he reluctantly obliged to humour the buffoon.

"Errr..right. Thanks," said Rupert taking the beers looking unimpressed with the borderline bullying of his 10-year-old son.

"See ya later granddad!!!" the nobhead said, waving us off.

The Guinnesses (or Guinni? Is that the correct plural?) were going down a bit questionably. I was sweating out a turkey/Guinness hybrid of smell. We took our seats, high up and next to the Cardiff fans which I was pleased about, it's always good to be near the away fans for some good quality baiting.

So we had all (the under 12s excluded) downed a Guinness for Christmassy charm, taken our seats and eagerly anticipated a Boxing Day treat!

89 minutes (plus 15 minutes for half-time) later...

We were all (the under 12s excluded) feeling groggy from the Guinness. The match was very poor and the fans were sedated. Nothing really had happened. It all felt rather limp, especially for a big Boxing Day fixture. It had been a testy game, the Cardiff fans being quite lively with their abuse directed at Michael Duberry, getting called a grass[1] all game.

The Reading fans were beginning to scatter out as the 4th official held up the board for injury time, when suddenly Michael Chopra, nipped in from nowhere (with a hint of offside) to score what would surely be the winner for Cardiff. The celebrations were beyond wild, they were going absolutely crazy with fiery Welsh passion. They were taunting us theatrically. I would have felt bad if I was actually a Reading supporter.

All hope was lost, Cardiff had claimed a last minute scalp. Surely?

Although a minute later Reading won a corner. The 4th minute of injury time. Desperation. Reading goalkeeper Adam Federici went up for the corner.

The ball came in, scrambled around for a bit and eventually reached the right boot of Federici.

Who stabbed the ball home.

The goalkeeper.

Scored.

Cue a thoroughly un-gracious return of taunting celebrations back to the Cardiff pack of wolves. The Reading fans, previously almost mute for 94 minutes, had gone as wild as the Cardiff fans had a mere minute earlier. The *goalkeeper* had scored! Un-bloody-believable.

---

[1] Relating back to the notorious Lee Bowyer/Jonathan Woodgate affray trial of 2001 where Duberry testified against his teammates.

The game kicked off again and the final whistle went almost straight away. The Reading players sprinted back to the hero Federici, who was in the goal right in front of the Cardiff fans. Stephen Hunt and Michael Dubbery hugged Federici and clenched their fists towards the furious Cardiff supporters.

They were winding them up big time, right in front of their faces. The fans were getting seriously angry as Duberry, abused for the whole match, was cheering in their faces and patting the top of his arse at them.

The Cardiff fans began throwing coins and bottles at the Reading players as they began to leave the field. The police and the stewards tried to restrain the Welsh but that just incited them further. The scenes that followed were pretty shocking, as the Cardiff fans started storming the pitch.

About 100 or so were on the pitch behind the goal, the police were receiving some punches and scuffles were breaking out. We, (we being the Reading fans) were the tier above watching with amazement; partly excited, partly amused, partly nervous. It really was quite exhilarating to watch, particularly when the police horses came onto the pitch to calm it all down.

We managed to escape eventually and headed back to the car park. Two coaches of Cardiff fans drove past us; swearing, pointing threatening gestures, and trying to get off the coaches when stationary in traffic for more fighting. It wasn't nice to see when you are less detached from it, particularly when young Rory got a bit scared, and understandably so. Normally in an incident like this you would say it is isolated and only a handful of idiots, but the sheer amount of Cardiff fans behaving like morons does make you question it.

My opinion of Reading is secondary compared to the exhilarating scenes from the 89th minute onwards. The fans weren't great, the ground was pretty classy but ultimately lacking character, there was little to love, but who cares? We saw the goalkeeper score and a near-riot take place! What could possibly be more entertaining than that?

"How was the game boys? We saw it was 0-0 with a few minutes to go..." Mum said as we came back.

"Haha. Well it got a bit more interesting..."laughed Ali.
"Good tell us about it over dinner, we've made a turkey curry."

READING   **1** (Federici 90)
CARDIFF CITY **1** (Chopra 89)
Attendance 22,770

GAME 50
ALDERSHOT TOWN v Dagenham & Redbridge
League Two

Sunday 28th December 2008, 3pm, Recreation Ground, Aldershot

Santa Claus had come to town and buggered off back to the North Pole again, and the post-Christmas bloated lethargy was starting to die down. We had spent the last couple of days practising furiously for our 'homecoming' Christmas gig with our shoddy yet oddly popular band 'Black Sheep'. In the midst of all the practising I forgot I had a football game to go to. Which one was it?

Oh yes, today was Aldershot Town v Dagenham and Redbridge. Not a lot of people would believe this is a League football match where Oxford v Cambridge or Torquay v York isn't. On paper it doesn't ooze glamour. After a morning desperately trying to remember songs I had to escape the band session, and managed to convince our bassist Liam to make the short trip with me around the M25 to the Recreation Ground.

"Are they better than I might expect then?" Liam, a Chelsea fan, said.

"Well it depends on how low your expectations are mate." I replied. "I've seen them a couple of times away already this season actually."

"Oh right, how'd they do?"

"Erm... lost 3-0 at Millwall and lost 5-1 at Chesterfield."

Aldershot Town are actually a very new football club. The original Aldershot, a Football League stalwart, went bust in 1992 but Aldershot Town rose from the ashes like a Hampshire Phoenix and this season is their first back in the Football League. Their rise through the lower divisions is a fairytale story, albeit a fairytale that probably has a slightly less catchy narrative hook than Cinderella or Snow White.

The Recreation Ground is a tiny ground full of character; the stand we were in behind the goal holds in the atmosphere perfectly, with a fairly low curved roof and enclosed side allowing the chants to echo in the air brilliantly.

The tiny cramped terraces, with tetanus-inducing rusty old poles supporting the roof, were packed full of Aldershot fans in fine voice. However difficult it is to incorporate the word 'Aldershot' into a football song, they managed with aplomb, encouraging their team to take the lead after 16 minutes.

"Hello! Hello! We are the Aldershot boys." Far too many syllables. Dagenham and Redbridge equalised with a brilliant free-kick, leading to a surreal silence through the ground. I think there were only about 12 Dagenham fans in.

After buying our much-desired pies we walked back in to the terraces, squeezing through the masses and found a different spot to stand in.

"What is the terrace etiquette?" asked Liam, "Will someone accuse me of 'stealing their zone of concrete?'"

Half-time was a pretty entertaining affair. The dreadful, half-arsed mascot (what was he, a bird?) was lobbing sweets at the kids in the crowd so hard I thought he might knock them out. Then the Aldershot PA announcer had the bored sarcastic demeanour of Jack Dee, and made for a funny half-time. He hosted the 'crossbar challenge', with two youngish lads taking part, one from Aldershot, one from Dagenham.

Firstly the Aldershot lad missed his 3 attempts wildly. The next attemptee stood up.

"Alright son, what's your name?" he asked the Dagenham lad of about 15.

"Sam."

"Tell us an interesting fact about Dagenham and Redbridge Sam."

"They're quality," he replied, consonant free, in an East London drawl.

"'They're quality'. Glad to see this country's education system is still doing well. Go on give it a go Sam."

Sam missed by miles, and got roundly heckled by the Aldershot fans despite being a kid.

"Well lads, what can I say? You've let yourselves down, you've let your families down and worst of all you've let your clubs down. You're a disgrace. Get off the pitch." The announcer said, causing a ripple of laughter.

The best thing about the second half was the interaction between Dagenham 'keeper Tony Roberts and the crowd. Roberts, a former Welsh international pushing 40, faced the fans behind the goal and pulled a ridiculous gurning Benny Hill-style facial expression every time he had a goal kick.

"You fat bastard! You fat bastard!" Liam and I were joining in with the crowd, directed at Roberts. With the play up at the other end, Roberts turned round and lifted up his shirt, revealing a tight stomach which he was obviously holding in. He then produced a kind of 'strongman' pose, showing off his muscles. Whilst he was doing all this Aldershot began to attack, so he quickly turned around and sprung back into his goalkeeper mode.

About ten minutes from the end there was an announcement on the PA that was probably the funniest thing I've heard at a football match.

"This is a message for Dagenham and Redbridge supporters. Can all Dagenham supporters travelling on the official club coach please be aware.... the coach has broken down."

The Aldershot cheers were phenomenal! I just loved the way it was worded, especially 'be aware'. It actually gee'd up the Aldershot crowd so that the last 10 minutes had the best atmosphere of the entire game.

Aldershot, unbeaten at home for 11 months, had dominated the match but Dagenham scored what turned out to be the winner with a couple of minutes to go. Tony Roberts, the 'keeper without the belly, celebrated wildly in front of the furious Aldershot fans, doing a forward roll and an attempted cartwheel. At least the stranded away fans would (eventually) go home happy.

As the match finished to a chorus of boos the sun was setting spectacularly; producing a beautiful orange glow, the skeletal tree branches showing up into a moody silhouette. It was just great. A perfect winter sunset, surrounded by a couple thousand angry people from Aldershot. I was at my most content.

Aldershot appealed to me. Any League club with houses on one side of the pitch instead of terracing, a train line on the other (which received *many* balls on it today) and huge trees with sprawling branches hanging over the pitch gets a thumbs up in my eyes.

"Oooh. Pretty angry aren't they?" whispered Liam as the Aldershot fans began their collective swearing at Roberts, Dagenham, the ref, their own team and whoever else was to blame for them losing at home for the first time since January.

"Yeah. We'd better shoot off." I said, realising that everyone was piling out and we couldn't really afford to get stuck in traffic. "What time's the soundcheck?"

"They want us at the pub for 6pm!" laughed Liam.

"Hahaha! In their dreams!"

Maybe *that's* why we never made it as a band... Come on though! Who in their right mind would turn down Aldershot Town?

ALDERSHOT TOWN **1** (Hudson 16)
DAGENHAM & REDBRIDGE **2** (Taiwo 27, Nurse 87)
Attendance 3,697

GAME 51
WATFORD v Scunthorpe United
FA Cup Third Round

Saturday 3rd January 2009, 3.00pm, Vicarage Road, Watford

2009 was here, we were three whole days in and I had not yet been to a football game *this entire year!* This was not acceptable. Yet I was lying in bed with tonsils the size of Russell Hoult's gonads. I'm aware this isn't a nice image, but that's just exactly how I felt. Tonsillitis just *had* to arrive during the FA Cup third-round didn't it, selfish germs.

FA Cup third-round day is probably my favourite of the entire football calendar. Apart from maybe the *draw* for the FA Cup third-round. You desperately want Chasetown to get Man United away, or various other ties to throw up magnificent David v Goliath shocks. I had planned to attend the most juicy of the third-round ties, but after being struck down with illness I begrudgingly stuck to the match that involved the least travel; Watford v Scunthorpe. A tie that was probably the 32nd most exciting of the 32 going on this weekend.

I got out of bed, climbed over snot-tissue-mountain and put on about 20 layers of clothes, still shaking as I did so. Annabel had agreed to come with me, being the impeccably patient human being she is.

"Thanks so much for this," I said as we got in Annabel's bright yellow Fiat Punto, the exact car that gets mocked in *The Inbetweeners.* The car has no speedometer, the passenger window doesn't go down, fifth gear doesn't work and the clutch has been replaced three times. So I don't know why I was surprised when it didn't start a mere hour before kick-off.

"Aaaargh! How annoying," said Annabel. "I guess you'll have to drive!"

Now I was in no fit state to drive at all, but I had already abandoned one Watford effort this season, and another one might drive me to suicide.

John and I had been out in Oxford for a Halloween party back on, erm, Halloween. We got very very drunk dressed as Mario and Luigi, John had passed out in a room with 5 strangers who drew all over his body in marker-pen, and I lost my spanner and spent an hour drunkenly searching for it.

We woke up feeling like our heads had been raped by the four horsemen of the apocalypse, yet I managed to drive us to Vicarage Road to watch Watford v Blackpool. Yet despite getting there with an impressive 10 minutes to spare, we couldn't find *anywhere* to park. ANYWHERE whatsoever! So we went home a bit depressed. Especially when we found out the game was a 4-3 cracker.

With the pain of that Halloween still in mind I took behind the wheel and made it to Watford! Sure I drove abysmally, nearly crashed twice, killing myself and my girlfriend, but I still made it. Two unsuccessful trips to Watford would have been very damaging for my soul.

I've been to Vicarage Road several times before, and the matches there have been absolutely rubbish every single time. My Dad is technically a Watford fan, and used to go with my Grandpa during the days of Elton John and Turnip Taylor. Back then the club were the most exciting thing Hertfordshire had to offer outside Hemel Hempstead, but now endure a painfully mediocre existence in the lower end of the Championship. Being a Hertfordshire lad I should probably feel some sort of fondness towards the only team from my county in the 92, but I don't. In fact, if anything, I prefer Luton.

Vicarage Road is currently undergoing building work on their crumbling East Stand, and with cranes everywhere it looks even uglier than usual. The building work was sufficiently vast for the sign for the ticket office to be replaced by one written *in pencil*. If only I had brought a rubber with me.

The first half was a blur of nothingness for me. I confess I spent most of this match blowing my nose and grumbling to Annabel, but I'm pretty sure there wasn't a shot. I wished I was in bed. There was a group of drunk blokes dressed as nuns near us having a jolly old time! They were quite entertaining I suppose.

"Break him down!" said Annabel, getting in the spirit when no one else around us was.

"Break him down? He's not a car!" I sarcastically commented, my illness probably not making me any more charming or witty.

"You know what I mean! What do I mean?"

"Close him down?"

"That's it. Oh yeah, break him down sounds a bit violent doesn't it." The highlight of our Vicarage Road day out was predictably at half-time, with an absolutely epic band coming on; probably about 50 or 60 people performing brass marching music. I loved it! It almost made me forgive the football (and the pretty mediocre pie that I was in too much pain to swallow).

Second half did produce a goal through Watford's Gregor Rasiak, but the match didn't improve. Certain Watford players just looked completely disinterested in this low-key FA Cup tie; with McAnuff and Priskin particularly un-arsed. It was pathetic. The Watford fans (despite being quiet and few in numbers) deserve to get *some* effort for their money.

The match had finished 1-0, propelling Watford into the 4th Round of the Cup where they would probably lose away at Coventry or something. This game, I can safely predict, won't have a lasting effect on the world, except for the fact that it perhaps made me infect some men dressed as nuns with my tonsillitis.

"How are you feeling?" Annabel kindly enquired, rubbing my back.

"Like I want to never go to a football match again." I moaned as we reached the car for the unwelcome, but thankfully very short drive home.

I learnt very little today, except that Watford games are indeed always dull, the stadium is looking worse by the year, and attending low quality football when you feel horrible isn't much fun. Whilst not being quite as skanky as their fierce rivals Luton, Watford are more *average*, which is probably actually a worse crime for a football club. But in the end...they're both a bit crap really.

Crap enough to make me support *Bolton* as an alternative for goodness sake.

WATFORD   **1** (Rasiak 67)
SCUNTHORPE UNITED   **0**
Attendance 8,690

GAME 52
NORTHAMPTON TOWN v Huddersfield Town
League One
Saturday 11th January 2009, 3.00pm, Sixfields Stadium, Northampton

The heating in my house was broken. I was sleeping wearing a thick fleece and tracksuit bottoms. It was the big freeze 2009, and I was both big and freezing.

Before my tonsillitis I had a week of new-year football planned, but in the midst of the snowiest winter England has officially ever had, icy pitches and subsequent cancellations were happening every day. Fortunately instead of sitting around eagerly praying for the pitches to hold out, I was actually doing the complete opposite. The thought of going to lower-league football in the cold whilst ill wasn't exactly appealing.

But living just a few stops south of Northampton on the M1, and with Northampton v Huddersfield surviving the ice, I had a rush of blood to the head and drove to Sixfields against my better judgement. The amount of effort my weakened body had to pull together to scrape all the ice off my car window should have pre-warned me that it wouldn't be a particularly cosy day out.

Listening to the radio on the way up I heard that out of the 22 games scheduled for either League One or League Two today, only 6 were going ahead. Whilst going to see Northampton v Huddersfield was a bit of a chore I was looking forward to seeing my old school mate Ryan Gilligan in action for Northampton.

Every kid says they want to be a footballer, and for someone you know to actually succeed in the game is pretty pleasing. Ryan was always several steps ahead of anyone else when it came to football at school. When we were about 13 I remember lining up in central midfield alongside him once, playing the Makelele role with aplomb, allowing Ryan the freedom to grab a hat-trick in a 4-3 defeat. At least that's how I remember it. I was probably shite.

I arrived at Sixfields; a stadium often described as being 'tidy'. It is indeed a tidy ground, positioned at the bottom of a steep hill, lying in the centre of bowl-like greenery. It looks, erm, tidy but also spectacularly unspectacular.

A group of Huddersfield fans were making the most of the simple pleasures you can get from a big steep hill. Obviously a bit drunk, some were rolling down it, and one man jumped in a trolley and got pushed down it. It was like a Yorkshire version of *Jackass*. A couple of Northampton stewards were treating this way too seriously.

"Yes this is Frank. We have some Huddersfield fans at the top of the hill in a trolley. What action do you suggest? Over," one young, humourless, weaselly steward said into his walkie-talkie.

The previous two times I had seen Huddersfield play had treated me to 15 goals, but it was clear from the off that this would not be such an occasion. Nothing much happened in the first half, except a crucial clearance off the line from Ryan. Well done mate! Roundwood Park school clearly taught you all you know. It was a poor half, and the Northampton fans were all very quietly polite. Maybe it was too cold for them to take their mouths out of their scarves, but there was little noise.

The half-time pie was a mixed affair. On the plus side it warmed me up stupendously; I was huddling around it like a freezing boy scout around a camp fire. On the down side, with my tonsils still making me look like a frog I couldn't really swallow without wincing with pain. Chunks of meat and potato were barging into my tonsils selfishly.

Take That's *Relight My Fire* was playing as I was struggling to swallow my half-time pie. It had been played before the match too. "This must be a piss take," the bloke next to me said, pointing at the imaginary PA in the sky, "*Relight My Fire* on the coldest bloody day of the year!"

The match was ridiculous really. The pitch looked absolutely rock solid, the icy frost shining up on the surface as 4.45pm approached. Huddersfield had taken the lead through a brilliant long-range free-kick, but despite a hugely unfair red card Northampton kept pressing until the final whistle. The ball was bouncing all over the place with no scientific logic, not dissimilar to a rugby ball. The fans were given something to cheer about at the death when a series of odd bounces saw the ball land t the feet of Adebayo Akinfenwa, who equalised for the Cobblers deep into injury time. The fans weren't exactly jubilant; more pleased in a reserved and polite middle-England way.

Northampton were inoffensive (apart from the extortionate ticket price), but therefore just get added to the long list of clubs that are pretty forgettable to me, disregarding the fact that an old mate now plays for them, and seems to be doing a decent job. He could have done with me to provide him with some defensive midfield stability though. Maybe it's not too late! Once my tonsils have gone down I'll give Stuart Gray a call and recommend myself for the Northampton number 4 shirt...

NORTHAMPTON TOWN 1 (Akinfenwa 90)
HUDDERSFIELD TOWN 1 (Jevons 65)
Attendance 5,110

GAME 53
NORWICH CITY v Charlton Athletic
FA Cup Third Round Replay

Tuesday 13th January 2009, 7.45pm, Carrow Road, Norwich

Alan Partridge, Delia Smith, yellow canaries and incestual farmers. Norwich was my next port of call, a club that I have always admired, whose fans had always struck me as a decent bunch.

Seeing the team flounder in the bottom regions of the Championship (or, the 'arse' of the Championship if you prefer) isn't right. After all, this is the club that was winning the inaugural Premiership for long periods back in 1993, ending up a respectable third. The same year they eliminated Bayern Munich from the UEFA Cup; the first (and still the only) English team to beat Bayern on their own turf in Europe.

The stadium certainly looks top-flight class from the outside. It is positioned on the bank of a river in a recently developed area full of swish looking modern flats. Built into the stadium there's a restaurant called 'Delia's', which was unfortunately closed. I popped into the 'Yellow's' bar, which was bustling, and also noted there was a Holiday Inn and a Ladbrokes merged into the ground. It had everything!

Resisting booking a night at the Holiday Inn (but not resisting Ladbrokes unfortunately), I went into the ground and straight to the pie counter. Along with the pies you would expect there was the 'Pie of the day'.

Pie of the day!

This was brilliant! Actual original, brand-free, home-cooked pies! I wonder if Delia made them herself before the match? I think she definitely did; in a kitchen somewhere behind the scenes, putting her culinary knowhow into some first class pies (apparently cuisine such as 'beef in red wine gravy pie' is common). I looked to see what 'pie of the day' was. Cauliflower cheese! Well that was....unique.

"One cauliflower cheese pie please!" I said to the lady, smiling like a man who has had 52 pies this season, but none with cauliflower cheese in them. The pie was pretty good, despite the fact I don't actually *like* cauliflower cheese.

During my cheesy Delia pie encounter I noticed a load of large posters of former Norwich greats scattered around. This 'Norwich heroes' celebration brought a snigger to my lips. The heroes in question were the likes of Ruel Fox, Craig Fleming and (oh yes) Gary Megson. Not quite Man Utd's Best Law and Charlton tribute is it? I took my seat wondering if anyone in this struggling Canaries team would join Lord Megson in the legends section. Probably not.

I had liked Carrow Road on first impressions, but I was aching for a good football match tonight. It had been a dismal start to the year for me, but surely the standard of Norwich v Charlton (a top flight encounter a mere four years ago) would improve my mood?

It didn't. The match was diabolical. It could have been so different with Darren Ambrose smashing Charlton ahead after only 6 minutes. I thought it would be a midweek FA Cup goal-athon! I was very wrong.

I could tell things weren't quite right at Carrow Road. I was sitting next to a smooth looking bloke in a leather jacket.

"I hope we lose today so Roeder can get the sack tomorrow!" he said.

Judging by the football on show I could quickly see the guy's point.

Despite going 1-0 down in the 6th minute, Norwich had 2 shots for the remaining 84 minutes. The match was painfully low on quality. Norwich's best player was the ginger Pele, the lumping Gary Doherty who was floating the ball around, trying to dictate play from the back. He was even put up front for the second half. This said a lot about the quality of the other 10 players out there.

The Norwich team were wearing a special plain yellow kit, numbered 1 to 11, celebrating 50 years since they reached the semi-finals of the FA Cup. The players seemed uninspired by this though. You got the impression that the team full of loan signings and journeymen don't feel it to be an honour to play for Norwich City FC, and already have an eye on their next move.

Having already had my strange pie, I chatted to this suave bloke next to me during half-time.

"Yeah, I used to play for Stockport County in the 90s actually," he told me, "I played in the same side as Brett Angell. He was on a couple of grand a week, but I got barely anything! One Christmas I got a £20 bonus!"

I'm not sure whether he was full of bullshit, but it would be an odd thing to lie about!

Apart from my smooth Stockport friend the rest of the crowd around me were young simpletons shouting abuse at their players. In the words of the pie queen Delia, the team needed a 12th man today. Where were we? Where were we? Let's be having us!!

The only real noise made was when Charlton's goal scorer Darren Ambrose was replaced by Matty Holland; the noise in question being massive boos for the two former Ipswich Town players. The Ipswich/Norwich rivalry is certainly a biggie; the two teams contesting the 'Old Farm derby' with true venom most seasons.

"You know what mate, I think this might be the worst match I've ever seen," my ex-Stockport chum said.

"I've been to a couple worse I think," I replied, thinking of both the times I've seen Nottingham Forest this season.

Charlton had won 1-0, leaving me having watched Norwich for 270 minutes this year without scoring and losing three times to lower-ranked teams. This was Charlton's first win in a whopping 19 matches, giving some perspective of how much better Norwich should have been.

The murmurings of discontent for Glenn Roeder had turned into mass demanding. "We want Roeder out, we want Roeder out!" was echoing around Carrow Road from 14,000 East Anglians.

I woke up the next morning (after the seemingly never-ending drive back from Norfolk) and found that the main sports headline was that Glenn Roeder had been sacked as Norwich manager. City legend Bryan Gunn took over temporary charge, and 4 days later they thrashed Barnsley 4-0, apparently playing wonderful, fluid, confident football. It's a funny old game isn't it?

NORWICH CITY **0**
CHARLTON ATHLETIC **1** (Ambrose 6)
Attendance 13,997

GAME 54
COLCHESTER UNITED v Cheltenham Town
League One

Saturday 17th January 2009, 3.00pm, Weston Homes Community Stadium, Colchester

Right, so 2009 had been *rubbish* on the football front so far. It was time for another 5 games in 5 days adventure, taking in pretty much every side of English football imaginable with West Ham, Yeovil, Man United and Burnley. But first I would have to venture into a place where only the bravest men may delve. Essex.

Colchester United v Cheltenham Town wasn't making my mouth water quite as much as the four games which would follow. At least Colchester were playing in a brand spanking new stadium (in which this was only the 15th game to take place). Perhaps this would spice up the occasion?

I set off in the car towards Colchester (the highlight of the drive was passing a road called *Turkey Cock Lane!!!!* The hilarity!) and became increasingly agitated with the lack of signs for the new ground. *TomTom* was clueless, and driving around the town aimlessly for an hour made me resent Colchester United FC before even visiting them.

Finally I found a sign, and followed it in blind optimism into the deserted wasteland. This long single car-free road was like a journey into the abyss, the horizon too misty for me to tell whether there is a football stadium in the near distance.

This 'cuckoo farm' area of North Colchester is just barren marshland, a completely flat open planned zone of nothingness. Eventually I reached the catchily titled 'Weston Homes Colchester Community Stadium', thankful that a weird lonesome hitchhiker had not murdered me in the marshy mist.

The £5 stadium car park was full of puddles, despite it not raining. There were occasional trees dispersed between the cars, recently planted in the pebbly wet ground. Unfortunately not one of these trees had sprouted a leaf, and just looked like skeletal eyesores.

More of my money was flushed away with the £20 match ticket. Ugh. For Colchester v Cheltenham? Bloody hell. The ground itself looked like the majority of other new & small lower-league stadiums constructed in the past decade. In particular it is so similar to Shrewsbury's equally uninspiring New Meadow that I am struggling to remember which one was which.

It was just all so familiar. Get to the £5 car park of the new out-of-town stadium scattered with empty seats and little atmosphere, 7/10 balti pie in hand, the PA blurting Dario G, Fatboy Slim and Tina Turner in quick succession.

I was living in Groundhog Day. I was Bill bloody Murray, but instead of partaking in heart-warming romantic comedy situations I was living the same bollocks football day again, and again, and again, and again, and again. I thought about livening up the pre-match by shouting some abuse at a Cheltenham player. *Do* I tell Elvis Hammond that I shagged his Mum? I decided against it.

Everything that was wrong with the 'Weston Homes Colchester Community Stadium' came down to a lack of originality. I'd seen it all before and I was getting irritated. Why not do something a bit different with the quite astonishing £14 million it cost to build?! Like the Galpharm in Huddersfield?

Just when I thought things couldn't get any less exciting I sat through 45 minutes of dross football. Fortunately it went by quite quickly because I nodded off on at least three different occasions. Was 2009 to be a curse of the useless football matches? I sure hoped not with another 38 to go after this.

"This is boring!" A large man sitting near me bellowed accurately.

"Is that little Alan Wright at left-back for Cheltenham Matt?" his mate asked him.

"Wow little Alan Wright! He must be about 100."

"He played for England once didn't he?"

Little Alan Wright spooned a ball out for a throw-in.

"But then again so did Chris Powell and Michael Ricketts, hahaha!"

The first half had been awful. The pitch was so marshy the bounce on the ball was pathetic. The midfielders for Colchester couldn't take control of the game at all, Kemal 'brother of Muzzy' Izzet in particular. The Cheltenham fans were making more noise than the home support, despite there only being about ten of them there. The stewards told these fans of minimal representation to sit down, despite having no one else anywhere near them. Ridiculous.

I was on the verge of losing all hope in 92 Pies and packing it all in when suddenly, out of nowhere, the second half produced a genuinely entertaining 45 minutes. Four goals, one red card, some decent football, BAM. A 3-1 victory for Colchester, the fans go home happy.

To save Colchester from an absolutely scathing review I must note that the staff I encountered; the ticket office people, the programme sellers, the stewards (at least in the home end) were all really friendly, and made for a good family feel to the club.

Nevertheless though, I would certainly not recommend a trip to the Weston Homes bloody Community Centre Stadium or whatever it's called.   The fans were scattered around the half-empty (NOT half-full) ugly new ground of four identical dreary stands, devoid of any atmosphere or originality. And this isn't necessarily the fans fault; yes there should perhaps be more there but in a big out-of-town dull-hole like this who can blame them for not coming?

You can't suddenly make a ground a fortress or force chants and atmosphere when you've been at a home for less than a year. It is not completely inconceivable that one day the Community Stadium might be a fearsome hub of wonderful home support, a Ninian Park or Elland Road for the South East, a dragons lair that makes away teams dread the day the fixture list takes them to Colchester. I just very much doubt it.

COLCHESTER UNITED   3 (Hammond 62, Gillespie 77, Yeates 88)
CHELTENHAM TOWN   1 (Westwood 57)
Attendance 4,183

GAME 55
WEST HAM UNITED v Fulham
Premier League
Sunday 18ᵗʰ January 2009, 1.30pm, Upton Park, Newham, East London

Feeling slightly apprehensive, I sat on the tube absolutely surrounded by West Ham fans. Stella was the drink of choice, shaven head the most common hairstyle, and either a West Ham kit or Ted Baker checked-shirt the most suitable attire. The atmosphere was rowdy but pretty non-threatening until a lady train conductor came and told every one of these large Hammers fans to give her their beers. This ridiculously brave, and possibly very stupid, woman was actually confiscating the Stellas from 15 boisterous East London football supporters.

She raged the beasts, a couple of cans were thrown, meaty 5.2% lager spraying around the cramped tube carriages. The odd cry of "fat bitch!" and other such insults were flown around. It wasn't exactly where I wanted to be right now. Fortunately the tube stopped at Upton Park station quickly after the ticket lady decided she had massive courage, so I jumped off and escaped the awkward situation.

With the winter sun shining I stepped out into Green Street and got a much finer impression of West Ham. Multi-cultural market stalls, busy bustling afternoon people-traffic, the smiling faces of families on the way to match-day. This was more like it. I guess West Ham fans are more agreeable out in the open rather than on a packed train having their alcohol taken from them. One thing I did notice though was a fair few fans with scars across their faces. All part of the Chelsea-smile lifestyle or a series of unfortunate shaving accidents?

I've always liked West Ham; a club who would be far more successful if not for a succession of managers who were garbage in the transfer market. From 'Arry's dodgy foreigners (Marco Boogers or Paulo Futre anyone?) through the Repka years to the present day, where only the best ridiculously injury-prone talent will do. Yes, that's you messrs Bellamy, Dyer, Ljungberg, Ashton, Parker etc etc. Perhaps the new era under lovely Franco Zola will bring the glory days back to Upton Park. Or at the very least a Carling Cup final eventually.

I was going to the match with my mate Sexton, recently relocated to a flat 2 minutes away from Upton Park, who thought he might as well get a West Ham game in (despite being a Chelsea fan, the odd boy).

After finding the ticket office I went through the biggest fiasco I think I have ever experienced in picking up pre-booked tickets. I could go into a lengthy explanation behind what an absolute ball-ache of an hour I had, but that would be boring to read, and infuriating to write. So instead I will just draw a smiley face and pretend everything went fine. ☺

Tickets (finally) in hand I waited for Sexton on Green Street, the magnificent Dr Martens Stand straight in front of me. The stand was rebuilt a few years ago and looks first class with the two mock-fortresses in front of the ground displaying the crest and West Ham flags. It truly looks like a top modern European stadium.

"Tommy boy!" said Sexton, slapping me on the back, Stella in hand.

"Wow, you fit in well don't you!" I said, nodding at his can.

"When in Rome!"

"We're not in Rome."

"Okay, when in Plaistow. You get the tickets OK mate?"

"Yeah, no probs," I lied, teeth gritted, fists clenched. English reserve Tom, repress the anger.

We went in, grabbed two delicious lunchtime steak pies and took our seats.

"I went to the West Ham game at Fulham earlier in the season actually," I told Sexton.

"Oh cool, how was it?"

"Yeah good game, West Ham edged it. The most interesting thing though was the difference between the two sets of fans. In fact you almost can't believe they come from the same city."

"Slightly 'earthier' around here I guess?"

"Yeah just a bit." I laughed, looking around at the indeed very earthy Hammers around us.

These fans were in good voice as the teams came out. The fantastic 'I'm Forever Blowing Bubbles' was belted out by 30,000 odd cockneys to great effect. I've always thought the image of the stereotypical tattooed, skinhead West Ham fan with a little pot of bubbles is a great paradox.

My main problem with West Ham fans has always been their bitterness towards former players. I know every team boos certain ex-players but West Ham take it a bit too personally. Frank Lampard's treatment in particular is ridiculous; the guy did brilliantly for West Ham, and his Dad is a legend at the club.

One such player that I feel may receive a Lampard-esque reception in the near future is Craig Bellamy. Bellamy had missed training and demanded a transfer in the last couple of days, with Tottenham and Man City sniffing around him. The West Ham fans did not take this bit of news particularly well;

"FUCK OFF CRAIG BELLAMY! FUCK OFF CRAIG BELLAMY!" the fans chanted about their own player for large portions of the 90 minutes. I was looking forward to the match. Fulham had gone 10 games unbeaten, but West Ham, and Carlton Cole were in great form. The game got off to the start I had hoped for when West Ham quickly took the lead, but the fans were stunned when Fulham's Paul Konchesky scored one of the best goals I've ever seen live. He was about 40 yards from goal when he just smashed the ball, swerving perfectly into the top-left hand corner.

Sexton stood up and began applauding.

"Erm, Sexton, remember it's the earthy West Ham fans we're surrounded by, not the Kensington Fulham elite," I said as a couple of angry glances came our way.

"Don't care mate, I've got to applaud that goal. Sheer class."

Fortunately I think the home fans also agreed it was a sublime goal, albeit one that meant Konchesky received 'fuck offs' for the rest of the game.

The first half fizzled out a bit, and Sexton and I sank a quick beer during half-time. When in Plaistow. For the second half a row of empty seats a couple of rows in front of us suddenly became occupied by a group of hilarious Germans, drunk as Bavarian skunks. These Germans made the second half completely priceless. They spoke to every fan within a couple of rows of them, in front and behind, and their conversations were phenomenal.

"Zese seats are more like ze crappy cinema seats yes?!" one said tugging at the Upton Park seats, making little sense but making me laugh. They swore profusely, either in English or German, the occasional 'Shieße!' Every couple of minutes half of them disappeared, obviously for another beer, and returned play-fighting with each other and tripping over the stairs. The best thing about it all was the reaction of the West Ham fans around us. They absolutely loved the Germans and found them as hilarious as Sexton and I did. No World War references, nothing! Bonus!

The action was great during the second half, with West Ham outclassing Fulham with their snappy passing. Konchesky ruined his earlier great work by giving away a stupid penalty, slotted home by Mark Noble.

"You only sing vhen you're vinning!!!" the Germans bellowed towards the Fulham end. This was just amazing. Soon afterwards the in-form Carlton Cole got his 5th goal in 5 matches, finishing off a great passing move.

"You are not singing anymore!!!!" the Germans continued in their thick accents.

The match finished 3-1 to the little Italian magician and his happy Hammers. As the fans were heading out the Germans shook every one by the hand earnestly.

I think that it's clubs like West Ham that make the Premiership the best league in the world. They're not one of the 'super clubs', indeed they're probably only the fourth or fifth biggest club in London. They haven't won anything in donkey's years, or ever finished higher than 5th in the Premier League. Yet despite all this they are a club that are world-renowned, with a huge and passionate fan base and a completely unique identity. I'm not saying I hope West Ham go on to challenge the top four and win lots of trophies, just that the size and support of this historic club and others like it (Everton, Aston Villa, Newcastle) makes English football very special indeed.

Keep blowing bubbles.

(PS. Craig Bellamy *did* fuck off the next day, to Man City for a ridiculous £14 million. Probably a wise move. Hammers fans never forget...)

WEST HAM UNITED **3** (Di Michele 7, Noble pen 60, Cole 76)
FULHAM **1** (Konchesky 22)
Attendance 31,818

GAME 56
YEOVIL TOWN v Leicester City
League One
Monday 19th January 2009, 7.45pm, Huish Park, Yeovil, Somerset

Now this one was a bit silly. Despite knowing I had to be in Manchester tomorrow, I decided to drive the rather long journey towards Somerset to watch Yeovil on a Monday night. Was this all part of the adventure? Or a stupid waste of time, effort and serious petrol money? Only Yeovil Town's Huish Park would have the answer.

I didn't really realise how far away Yeovil was until I passed Stonehenge and signs for Glastonbury. I was venturing into proper farmer territory. The sun was setting on the long solitary roads and the look in the eyes of the cows was getting sinister. Had all this non-stop driving and football made me paranoid? Was I going insane? Was I *really* travelling in the freezing cold to bloody Yeovil on a Monday night?

Fortunately when I arrived at Huish Park I realised that it was going to be brilliant straight away. Everything you need to know about Yeovil Town can be summed up by their car park. For the bargain of only £2 you park up in what is basically a muddy field, like a mini-forest with trees and puddles and tractors and horses (maybe not the last two). It was everything the Colchester car park 2 days ago wasn't. *Am I getting too hung up on car parks? Is this interesting? AM I LOSING MY MIND?*

Anyway, the car park made me happy, as did the tiny mud-splattered rusty minibus that was parked outside the stadium with 'Yeovil Town Traffic Management' blazed across it. With crowds of happy West Country folk gathering around the muddy, out-in-the-sticks, and extremely tree-ey (I just created a word) Huish Park I popped into a temporary booze marquee.

This marquee, full of farmer-types, had drink after drink after drink being sunk by the Yeovil masses before kick-off. I decided to have a cider to fit in, as I think 90% of drinks being sold were indeed appley (that's definitely a word isn't it?).

A couple of ciders and laughs with the locals later I took my place in the noisy terrace behind the goal. The Yeovil fans were in pretty good voice, as you would expect when playing the League One giants of Leicester City.

For the first five or six minutes the match was crazy. Leicester missed three absolute sitters. I thought it might be a complete humiliation for Yeovil, but to be fair to them they began to hold their own against the runaway league leaders.

I do feel that I've almost mastered the art of casual observations from the back of a football terrace. I observed that the Yeovil Town terraces have a lot of women on them. Not just girls or teenagers, but proper women. Standing next to me were a couple of ladies probably in their mid-fifties (I think I'm flattering them here) called Jo and Ann, who were wearing their Yeovil shirts and shouting for their team as loud as any young lad in the ground was.

"Well we came here when the ground opened back in, when was it Jo? 1991?"

"1990."

"Yes, 1990."

"Oh you'd be too young I think, but did you ever come to the old Huish Park?"

A spontaneous trip to Yeovil when I was under 5? No I can't say I ever made the journey.

"It was hilarious, the slope on the pitch went like this," said Ann, holding her gloved hand out to a ridiculous angle.

"Wow, really?"

"Oooo arr," said Jo in a hilarious piratey Somerset accent, "when a team was kicking uphill the ball sometimes came back to them!"

On their altogether quite flat new pitch Yeovil held out to go in at half-time goalless; a very respectable scoreline against Leicester.

I took a stop to the toilets and was astonished to be welcomed by a bouquet of flowers. Just sitting there, in a vase, in the tiny stinking Gents. As if to say 'Don't worry, you might be in a lower-league football ground bog surrounded by other pissing men, but look at this lovely bouquet! Doesn't that put it all in perspective?!'

As if the flowers weren't just about the greatest thing I've ever seen, it was bettered at the food stall! Queuing up for my pie there was a sign, hand-written in biro, blue-tacked to the wall next to the menu of the typical pies, burgers, drinks etc. The sign said boldly;

'Soup – Past sell by date – clearance 50p'.

This was brilliant. Out of date soup for sale. Openly. Where else in the Football League could this happen? This one aspect of Yeovil Town made them perfect in my eyes.

"One steak pie, and one out-of-date soup please!"I said upon reaching the counter.

"Sorry love, we've just sold out of soup," the lady said pointing at a man walking behind me, sipping some soup from a pot.

"Lucky him! Just the pie then please," I said, a bit gutted I wouldn't be warmed up with some mouldy soup.

Leicester took the lead through their bulky brick shithouse of a centre-forward Steve Howard shortly into the second half, and looked comfortable from then on. Despite initial frustration (Jo and Ann swearing like builders), the Yeovil fans didn't really let this get them down, and kept going with their noise.

The Yeovil chants were top notch. Highlights included;

"Oh I'd rather be a farmer than a chav! Oh I'd rather be a farmer than a chav!"(directed at the Leicester fans).

"We all hate Leeds scum!" (stretching to Yeovil!!!! That's a gap of 250 miles for two teams that have only ever played each other a couple of times! Honestly you get this song everywhere, it's mental! Simply *everyone* hates Leeds scum.)

And my personal favourite towards the crisp-crazy Leicester fans...

"You can shove your fucking Walkers up your arse! You can shove your fucking Walkers up your arse! You can shove your fucking Walkers, shove your fucking Walkers, shove your fucking Walkers up your arse, PRINGLES!! PRINGLES!! PRINGLES!!"

With the increasingly mucky pitch cutting up more and more it became scrappy by the end, with Leicester getting their deserved second as the 90th minute approached.

The fans weren't really too bothered though; Yeovil were looking safe to stay in League One for another season. As far as punching above your weight goes, I solidly approve of Yeovil continuing to do so.

The official Yeovil Town motto is 'Achieve By Unity', which I think is quite apt. Yeovil (the current 'Family club of the year' holders) are clearly a club for the people of their small town, and it's been the unity that has propelled the green army from the Isthmian League South to playing Leicester City in League One. But thank the Lord they've kept the flowers in the bog and out of date soup at the canteen. Remember where you came from...

YEOVIL TOWN   0
LEICESTER CITY   2 (Howard 57, Mattock 88)
Attendance 4,569

GAME 57
MANCHESTER UNITED v Derby County
Carling Cup Semi-Final Second Leg
Tuesday 20th January 2009, 8.00pm, Old Trafford, Manchester

Grimsby Town made me happy. Morecambe charmed me. I had a bloody ball at Dagenham & Redbridge. Yeovil Town made me want to become a farmer. I would happily accept a season ticket at Aldershot or Huddersfield.

But none of this mattered. For tonight I was going to Old Trafford to watch the champions of England, Europe, and the world.

More than any club in England, Manchester United possess this aura of history, achievement and spectacular mythology. They have dominated the Premier League since its conception in 1992, and are the template for success for all the other clubs to follow. United are a global phenomenon; it is estimated that 5% *of the world* support Man United. I don't think 5% of Grimsby support Grimsby Town.

It was the Carling Cup semi-final second leg, with United surprisingly trailing 1-0 to Derby. To spice up the occasion a bit more this would only be Nigel Clough's 2nd match in charge of the Rams.

I met up with my brother Greg and my cousin Bri for a good old fashioned family outing. A family outing absolutely drenched in gin.

"Man U! Bet you're excited," said Greg as we met at his student bar.

"I really am actually. Not as excited as you must be though," I said to Bri, what with it being her first *ever* football match.

"Oh yes." Bri said half-enthusiastically.

"Where were you last night?"

"Yeovil Town."

"Bit different kettle of fish then."

"Yep."

"Where do you think the term kettle of fish came from?" Bri piped up with. "Do you think someone once boiled some fish in a kettle?" I wasn't sure, but it sounded barbaric.

The truth was indeed that I was tremendously excited about seeing Old Trafford. It was already shaping up to be a legendary season for

Man United; they were top of the league, recently crowned world champions, gunning well in all the cup competitions, hell there had been suggestions of this being a 5 trophy season. Surely not?! A grand opportunity for a trophy would be the League Cup though, as long as they could make it past Derby tonight.

United had it all to do in this second leg, and although their line-up was not completely first-choice it was still an impressive mix of youth and experience with faces like Ryan Giggs, Gary Neville, Nani, Anderson and Carlos Tevez in the team. And there was a certain Portuguese world player of the year warming the bench if things ever got a bit sticky.

We had made it to Old Trafford with what seemed like the entire population of Manchester on the train with us. Getting off at Old Trafford's own little train station, you climb some stairs and reach the monstrous stadium, dominating the skyline. Despite being a League Cup game the match was a sell-out, with well over 70,000 people coming.

We had a wander around the stadium, soaking in the atmosphere. It's an overwhelmingly large ground; 'Theatre of Dreams' may be a bit strong, but it does possess a certain sense of awe around it. The statue of the 'holy trinity' of Best, Law and Charlton was superb, and the Munich clock tribute and Matt Busby memorial looming high above were watching carefully over the crowds of fans.

Unsurprisingly we were up with the Gods. The climb up the stairs was bloody knackering, I thought my legs were going to drop off. The pitch was so far away, but I actually quite like this as it allows you to watch the match as a tactical battle. The superstars were out for the warm up, and watching the likes of Ronaldo, Scholes and Nani in the pre-match routine makes you realise how gifted they are, especially in comparison to what the warm ups look like in League One and League Two. Their incredible range of flicks and tricks kept me mesmerised.

United were coming into form at the right time, so I feared for Derby today. They had just replaced Liverpool at the top of the League in the midst of Rafael Benitez's ill advised explosion of nervous frustration. Honestly, don't try to compete with Fergie at mind-games. "Rafa's cracking up, Rafa's Rafa's cracking up!" sang the United fans.

The pie and beer prices weren't quite as expensive as I anticipated, at £3 a beer (albeit a can of 3.5% Boddingtons) it was almost reasonable for a football game. We put our bets on, downed a couple of Boddies, grabbed the pies and were ready to go! The roar from the crowd before kick-off was wonderful. You hear a lot about how the Old Trafford crowd can sometimes be underwhelming, but from the beginning I was impressed with how up for the occasion the fans seemed tonight.

They were given a lot more to cheer about as the match got off to a corker. Nani scored a terrific long range effort to give United the lead, and their fluid football saw them go in to half-time 3-0 up after efforts from John O'Shea and Carlos Tevez, the half caveman, half Tasmanian Devil, half Hunchback of Notre Dame, half wolf.

United's passing was flowing beautifully.

"This is great!" said Bri, her enthusiasm now completely genuine. And it *was* great. There is a reason it costs so much to see a team like United; you get to watch outstanding football.

The crowd settled once it had become comfortable for United. The thing about Old Trafford is that because it's *so* big, the noise gets lost in different parts of the stadium. Sitting in the top of the North Stand we weren't with the loud fans, and each stand is like 4 different atmospheres rather than one big collective noise. You could tell the Derby fans were singing and chanting, but they were so far away you couldn't really hear or feel their experience of the match.

"Wish they sold gin here," Greg said at half-time, as we reflected on an awesome half of top quality football.

"Take it up with the Glazers." I replied, getting another round of the creamy Boddingtons (a worthy silver medal).

The biggest boo of the night was reserved for everyone's favourite pantomime villain Robbie Savage as he came on at half-time. The contrast could not have been greater with the reception Cristiano Ronaldo received when he came on for Giggs in the 58th minute. It got a bit tense when Derby scored a penalty in the 80th minute which sent the travelling support wild. They only needed one more to go through on away goals!! It was (to quote Sir Alex) squeaky bum time, but United won their own penalty as the 90 minutes were up; the preening peacock Ronaldo coolly slotting home.

With the 90 minutes up and United safely through we decided to miss injury time to get to the train station and avoid waiting for an hour in the rain. This is a genuine gripe with United, there were only trains coming out from Old Trafford to Manchester centre every 40 minutes. Not particularly convenient for 70,000 people! But we made it out a bit early, and as if a 4-1 victory at Old Trafford wasn't good enough, I had only bloody won my bet! £5 on a 4-1 victory at 12-1 odds, I made that £65! Awooga!

"£65!! I'm practically a millionaire." I said to Greg. "Think of what I can do with that! Drinks are on me tonight!"

As we walked down about the 20th flight of stairs a muted announcement came from the sound system.

"Goal scorer for Derby County, number 18, Giles Barnes."

I looked at Greg and Bri with horror. There were no cheers or groans to be heard. Surely I misheard that?

"There were only 2 minutes of stoppage time, Derby can't have scored can they?!" I panicked. Unfortunately they could. It turned out that it was a beautifully struck free kick from Barnes. The absolute selfish bastard. How dare he? I had been cheated out of £65. I was distraught.

"I can't believe it. I'm going to write to Giles Barnes personally and ask him for £65."

"Never mind T, back to the student bar, I'll get the cheap gins in," Greg said as we left Old Trafford.

Man United are a club from a different planet. The statues of messrs Best, Law and Charlton outside the ground remind you of their rich history, which is being rewritten today with the great teams Sir Alex has consistently moulded for the last 20 years. Watching players that immensely talented makes the experience of going to a football match more like going to a top-class show. The players are the performers, directed by Ferguson, with the crowd the audience, waiting to be entertained.

No United fan begrudgingly follows their team through thick and thin; they have never had to bother. Does that make them worse fans than 'long-suffering' supporters of Luton or Rochdale? I'm not sure it does.

To label the fans as quiet, prawn sandwich eating glory-hunters from outside Manchester in unfair. United fans come in all varieties, and amongst the prawn-munchers the rest of the majority are genuine football fans just like everyone else.

In two days I had two of the most different football experiences possible. Yeovil Town had a hand-written A4 sign selling out-of-date soup. Man United had massive revolving advertising boards printed in Chinese. And yet these two clubs can coexist in the 92, a mere two divisions apart.   If this doesn't sum up the brilliance of English football I don't know what does...

MANCHESTER UNITED **4** (Nani 16, O'Shea 22, Tevez 34, Ronaldo pen 89)
DERBY COUNTY **2** (Barnes pen 80, 90)
(Manchester United win 4-3 on aggregate)
Attendance 73,374

GAME 58
BURNLEY v Tottenham Hotspur
Carling Cup Semi-Final Second Leg
Wednesday 21ˢᵗ January 2008, 7.45pm, Turf Moor, Burnley

If last night's Carling Cup semi-final went explosively, I feared tonights would fizzle out with a whimper. I booked myself and Robbie tickets for this second leg tie between Burnley and Tottenham before the first leg had been played, hoping that Burnley would leave White Hart Lane with a respectable result to make this game interesting. They lost 4-1. Game over surely?

"Yid Army! Yid Army! We're the famous Tottenham Hotspur and we're going to Wemberley WEMBERLEY! WEMBERLEY!" sang Robbie, graciously, as we drove from Leeds to Burnley.

"Don't you think it's possible that Burnley might overturn the three goal deficit mate?"

"Not a chance. We're not exactly going to lose 3-0 are we?"

It was a disgusting night in Burnley. The rain was lurking in the air, not pouring, just floating like a damp wet spirit. It wasn't soothing my nerves that my windscreen wipers weren't really working. We were a bit late and the fans were packing the streets, making it impossible to drive, let alone find anywhere to park.

"Park there!" said Robbie, pointing at a private garage with a huge 'NO PARKING' sign in front of it.

I finally found somewhere and we reached Turf Moor; a ground that looks a bit plain and ordinarily mid-sized, with the grim weather not doing anything for the view. A man had braved the rain to sell scarves underneath a big umbrella. Always one for a bargain, Robbie's eyes lit up at the half Burnley half Spurs scarves for five pounds.

"Look at this T! Going to be a souvenir of the road to our second successive Carling Cup!" he said, tying his new scarf around his wet neck.

Despite being 4-1 down, Burnley fans were treating this game with a bit of a carnival atmosphere. It's not every day you play a semi-final, and inside Turf Moor there were flags, cheerleaders, fireworks, and processions all led by their mascot Bertie Bee.

The teams came out to more fireworks, wild ones flying around the air amidst the rain.

No qualms about health and safety here at Burnley! We were behind the goal two rows from the front, getting up and close to the soggy grass. Robbie had his Tottenham shirt well and truly covered by his coat, probably best not to anger several thousand large men from Burnley.

"Burnerley, Burnerley, Burnerley!" sang the fans, fitting in an extra syllable that didn't really sound right. I didn't point this out to them though.

Burnley needed three goals, and after an impressive first half went in 1-0 up. With Robbie feeling a bit despondent we nipped out to grab a pie and a pint. There was a neat A4 sign up next to the food stall, friendlily stating '*In the event that all pies sell out, season ticket vouchers will be valid next home game*' alongside a picture of some meat and pastry goodness. How kind of Burnley! In fact Burnley are sponsored by Holland's Pies, so it's appropriate that they show great concern for those who may not get pie'd up at half-time.

Fortunately they hadn't sold out so Robbie and I were warmed up nicely with our meat and potato pies and pints of creamy bitter.

"You worried yet?" I asked.

"Well we're playing like shit! Bentley isn't with the pace."

"The fans have been giving him crap all game though, booing his every touch."

"He should be big enough to rise over it." Robbie said, speaking some sense.

Spurs came out a bit stronger in the second half and missed a couple of absolute sitters. Pavlyuchenko in particular was very guilty of not putting the tie out of sight. In the 73rd minute a bit of absolute magic put Burnley two up, with the ageless Robbie Blake beating three players with a mazy dribble, and crossing to Chris McCann who slotted home.

Robbie was biting his tongue as the celebrations went on around us. Could Burnley actually do this?

Yes they bloody well could!

With two minutes to go substitute Jay Rodriguez (who is born and bred in Burnley believe it or not) volleyed home after more useless defending from Woodgate and Dawson.

Burnley were 3-0 up. 4-4 on aggregate.

Bertie Bee was celebrating with the 'worm' dance move. The scenes were wild. Fans were kissing me and Robbie, who was showing remarkable restraint.

The atmosphere was incredible, but also one of confusion.

"What's happened? Are we through?!"

"Yeah, away goals count! We're through!!!!"

"No they don't count in the League Cup! It's extra-time!"

I had no idea! Like most people I hadn't really looked into it, not expecting Championship Burnley to get a 3-0 win against Premier League opposition.

Robbie took a deep breath and swallowed.

"It's not over. Away goals do count, but only after extra-time. I read it in the paper this morning. So we've got 30 more minutes." He said calmly to me and all the people surrounding us. I realised that Robbie's Thames estuary accent didn't fit in that well with the thick Burnley drawl.

"'We' meaning Burnley! Come on Burnley!" Robbie then said in a fake Northern accent, causing everyone to cheer him and pat him on the back as the full-time whistle went. Wow. Extra time was here.

"Bloody hell mate, you deserve a medal for your restraint." I muttered.

"I'm bleeding internally I think." Robbie said through his teeth, shaking slightly.

Burnley were pressing and pressing but looked tired, playing their 37th game of a season only in mid-January. I noticed that someone had collapsed in the stand next to us, just a few feet over away from the corner flag. The paramedics were treating the person lying on the floor. People looked a bit concerned.

Despite this unwelcome incident off the pitch, on the pitch it was all happening! Burnley 'keeper Brian 'Beast' Jensen was playing like a man possessed! He produced a series of heroic saves in extra time to keep Burnley in it. "Beeeeeaaaasssssstttt!" Turf Moor sang at their hero.

Robbie had bought a Bovril to calm him down.

"There's always time for Bovril," he said sombrely, "it's just like drinking gravy. Delicious."

Half-time came and went, and Burnley had one foot in the final.

Football however is, ultimately, a cruel cruel game.

In the 118th minute, with two minutes left until Burnley were in the final, Roman Pavlyuchenko smashed home a wonder-goal for Tottenham.

Heartbreak.

Absolute silence greeted Turf Moor except for at the opposite end of the stadium, where a couple of thousand thankful North-Londoners went wild.

Robbie squeezed my hand so hard I thought it would burst.

Burnley kicked off, clearly deflated, and gave the ball straight to Jermain Defoe who scored Tottenham's undeserved second, just before the full-time whistle went.

The Burnley fans were absolutely devastated, but stayed until long after the final whistle, applauding their heroic team off. 2 minutes away from the final! That's why football is so, so cruel.

This was the end of my fantastic 5 games in 5 days, but all the others put together hadn't provided the excitement of this astonishing match. Burnley are a great old club; Football League founders and stalwarts of the lower-leagues. The fans were passionate, supportive, out in their numbers on a miserable evening, and deserved to reach the final. Both the players and supporters were dignified in defeat; clapping both teams off, accepting they were unlucky, and looking to move on.

"Fuck me!" Robbie shouted, clenching his fist and banging the dashboard as we got back into the blissful warmth of the car. "Thank Christ for that!!"

"It's okay mate, let it all out." I smiled.

"What the hell happened there?!?!" he screamed, half laughing and half crying.

"Unbelievable. Well at least you're in the final."

Robbie's reaction suddenly went from despair to elation.

"Oh yeah! Yid army! Super 'arry! This is our season mate!" he chuckled, patting my rain-sodden leg as I drove off, annoyed at myself for laughing with him.

·•·

The next day in the newspaper I saw the awful news that the fan who had collapsed, lifelong Burnley fanatic 68-year-old Kenneth Hartley, had died from a heart attack. It made me feel a bit weird. Despite there being the most dramatic game of the season going on, something actually important in real life was happening a few feet away from us. I suppose at least Kenneth's last thought would have been that his team were on their way to their first major cup final since 1962.

BURNLEY   **3** (Blake 34, McCann 73, Rodriguez 88)
TOTTENHAM HOTSPUR   **2** (Pavlyuchenko 118, Defoe 120)
(After Extra Time) (Tottenham win 6-4 on aggregate)
Attendance 19,533

GAME 59
GILLINGHAM v Exeter City
League Two
Saturday 24th January 2009, 3.00pm, Priestfield Stadium, Gillingham

I had found on t'internet a list from *The Observer* about the crappest stadiums in the Football League. The top 10 was littered with ones I certainly agree with (Kenilworth Road, Withdean Stadium) and ones I would argue against until blue in the face (Blundell Park, Fratton Park). Number One in the poll however, surprisingly edging out my personal nomination of Luton, was Gillingham's Priestfield Stadium, officially the most unpleasant match-day experience in English football.

I wanted to be proved wrong about Gillingham, a club whose tenacity I admire for how they kept themselves in the 2nd tier between 2000-2005. However much I tried to go in with an open mind however, Gillingham FC and I certainly got off on the wrong foot. Way back in the hazy naive days of 11th October I set off to Gillingham to see their home fixture against Morecambe.
A mere one stop around the M25 however my car began spluttering and shaking, and more worrying for me the brakes weren't really working very well. I managed to get to the hard shoulder and let the nice RAC man drag me home. I thought about asking him to drag me to Priestfield, waiting for 90 minutes then dragging me home, but that may have been a tad cheeky. The match was a thrilling 5-0 win for Gillingham. Of course.
I then went to extreme measures to try and get a ticket for the Gills 3rd-round FA Cup tie against Premiership top-four-infiltrators Aston Villa. I was *determined* to go to this match, but it sold out and Gillingham powers that be decided they didn't care about my book and thus wouldn't give me a ticket.
THIS time I would get to the #1 shittiest ground in England without a hitch. Third time lucky? Another abandoned attempt may drive

me to leaving out Gillingham and calling the book 91 Pies instead. As if by magic the car, right on cue, began making funny noises on the M25. Again! What on earth did my 206 have against Gillingham FC?

I ploughed through and shuddered my way to the ground, pleasingly avoiding death. Although death may possibly have been a more desirable option than Gillingham on first glance. The town itself is not particularly lovely; a gloomy graffiti-covered zone of misery, and the stadium doesn't add any element of attraction to the place. Priestfield takes up one entire side of a street, looking like a never-ending stretch of perfectly straight office-blocks.

I popped into the 'Blues Rock Cafe Bar' for a quick drink but then left again immediately after finding it closely resembling hell on earth. Much better was the club shop, which using the best of my impeccable club-shop knowledge was certainly the biggest I had seen in League Two. You could fit about 15 of the Chester City club shops into this one.

I didn't fancy a Gillingham FC teddy bear though so I entered my turnstile, ravenous for my pie. Of course this being Gillingham, the cause of so much pain and misery to me, the food stall had a frosty handwritten sign attached stating <u>NO PIES.</u> <u>NO BURGERS.</u> <u>NO CHIPS.</u> <u>NO SEASON TICKET OFFER.</u> Not quite as friendly as the pie-sign I saw at Burnley three days ago

I did manage to find a pie eventually after visiting about 3 different kiosks, and I took my seat next to a man who looked remarkably like the moustachioed Sky Sports reporter Nick Collins.

Once inside Priestfield I confess the ground had some ramshackle charm, in particular the Brian Moore Stand; an ugly provisional clunk of temporary scaffolding. The PA was broken so the announcer sounded like a stuttering inaudible robot.

The game had started, and it wasn't very good, with the Gills looking woefully short on ideas. Surely I deserved a corker? I had cruelly missed two cracking games at Priestfield earlier in the season. Would this game not deliver? Of course it wouldn't.

I had been treated with a week of glorious football from the likes of Man Utd, Burnley and West Ham, so I suppose a piss-poor return to League Two, was unavoidable.

The people surrounding me were keeping me entertained during the shite on the pitch, mainly because they were all very drunk. It was a large gaggle of drunkards, two of whom I heard saying how they haven't ever watched the Gills without drinking 7 pints first. From this showing I could understand why.

It was a bit of a dysfunctional family situation. One of the two blokes was flirting with a young woman who I think was a friend of his daughter. Creepy. Very creepy. She was asking him if they could link arms and he said 'no fucking problem luv'.

I looked the other way, finding it all a bit unsettling. This man next to me really did look a lot like Nick Collins. Actually....on second glance, it *was* Nick Collins!

"Excuse me, I'm sorry to disturb but are you Nick Collins the Sky reporter?" I boldly asked.

He looked at me, thick moustache twitching.

"Yes I am," he kindly replied.

"Oh right!" my curiosity was satisfied. "I worked at Sky Sports News for the summer actually, I met you a couple of times." I continued, thoroughly un-coolly seeing as he obviously had no recollection of our two incredibly brief conversations.

"Oh yes I remember!" lied Nick Collins politely, before continuing to watch the match with his son. I like the idea that the chief football reporter with Sky Sports, a man who reports on the England national team and has unrivalled access to any worldwide football match chooses to spend his spare time watching a club like Gillingham with his family. It's a bit mad, but a wonderful example of the lure the lower-leagues can bizarrely possess.

The game ended 1-0 after a scrappy goal from Adam Miller, leaving me cursing the fact I missed those other two matches. I left Priestfield thinking that it wasn't a particularly special day out, but equally was probably not the ultimate *worst* in the country either. On the main road near the stadium two kids were tearing down the image from a huge advertising billboard, ripping away like

Neanderthal cave-monkeys hell bent on destruction. All part of the Kent charm I suppose.

GILLINGHAM 1 (Miller 79)
EXETER CITY   0
Attendance 5,638

GAME 60
BURY v Bradford City
League Two
Tuesday 27th January 2009, 7.45pm, Gigg Lane, Bury

I was back up in the North-West, and back on my brother Greg's sticky University Halls floor. Bits of old food, toenails, crusty beer spillages, the odd suspect curly hair. This was my sleeping area. But I couldn't afford a hotel or anything extravagant like that, so it would have to do.

Fortunately the benefit of staying in student halls was that there are always people with little to do, and a massive new instalment of their student loan to do it with.

"So how do we get to Bury?" A gin-drinking, hoodie-clad Greg asked, flanked by his mates Haz and Fred, who both came to Man City with me earlier in the year.

"You have to get the Metrolink from Piccadilly. It's the tram service." All three of their eyes lit up.

"A tram?! Wow!"

"I've never been on a tram!"

"Me neither!"

The way they were talking so excitedly you would think the tram was a spaceship, a magic carpet or the Hogwarts Express.

The tram didn't turn out to be very exotic, just like a non-steering bus full of chavs drinking tinnies, wearing their tracksuits and swearing loudly. Although in retrospect we were doing most of those things as well. The highlight of the journey came when we passed a tram stop called 'Besses o'th'Barn' (apostrophes all accurate).

"That's the most Northern thing I've ever seen," said Greg, in awe of the sign.

Bury are situated only four miles out of Manchester city centre, but are obviously far less decorated than their big city colleagues. In fact the only bit of silverware to hit the town of Bury recently was

1st place in the National Black Pudding Throwing Championship in 2005. Not exactly the FA Cup is it?
My expectations were high however when reading the 'Find Us' section on the Bury FC website;

Rolling moorland, pretty wooded river valleys, industrial activity, even its own vintage steam line, Bury without doubt is a centre of almost unique contrast and variety.

We came in on the smelly tram, and stood out onto the grey dual carriageway, greeted by the sight of a tramp with no trousers on. Pretty wooded river valleys this wasn't.

Whilst the website wasn't exactly accurate, the walk up to the ground was actually fairly nice. There are two great looking pubs just off the main road, and if you pass them you walk up old cobbled streets to reach Gigg Lane.

There was a good vibe all around the stadium, possibly due to the status of the match against Bradford, a 3rd vs. 4th tie, with a War of the Roses subplot. Being slightly inebriated already we were annoyed to find Bury weren't selling booze today, which would have been more of a disaster if not for my full hipflask.

This nearly went wrong upon entering Gigg Lane however, when a phenomenally ugly steward who looked exactly like Earthworm Jim asked to frisk me. I put out my arms and let his wormy hands fondle me, including patting my back pocket and feeling my metal hipflask. Fortunately he clearly had no brain inside his earthworm head, because he let me in. Result!
The Bury faithful were in a buoyant mood. They came up with one of my favourite chants I've heard so far.
"We're all swearing in the family stand! BOLLOCKS!"

The first half was a fairly standard, mid-week, cold-night, low-on-quality League Two encounter. The mascot, 'Robbie the Bobby' was clearly at a loss of things to do. He came into the crowd and was trying to have some jokes with a group of kids who just couldn't be arsed with him. He came up to us and shook all of our hands.

"Why won't he leave?" I whispered to Greg, Bobby still lurking around us.

"I don't know. Nobody wants him here. He's not funny..." Greg muttered. Finally Bobby realised no one wanted to be his friend, and he trundled off miserably, his big head gazing solemnly at his feet.

After a goalless first half I grabbed my very welcome meat pie. I could have definitely done with a lovely beer alongside it instead of a disgusting hipflask 'Sainsbury basics' gin though.

The student-thirst of Fred and Haz was clearly getting the better of them.

"Mate would you mind if we popped out to the club bar downstairs and then come back in for the second half?" Fred asked a very ugly, slightly inbred looking steward.

"You would be ejected and not allowed back in," he said in a threatening manner.

"OK well maybe we won't then," Haz said, looking a bit bedazzled.

Still booze-less, the second half was thankfully a much better affair. Bradford really should have scored several goals. Their bald number 9 Barry Conlon (whose shiny white head resembles a cue ball) missed an absolute sitter.

Bradford paid for all their missed chances when Bury's veteran striker Andy Morrell slotted home with 14 minutes to go, sending Gigg Lane wild! It turned out to be the winner, helping Bury leapfrog Bradford into the automatic promotion positions.

Fortunately we managed to find a great, friendly little pub nearby after the match, where we made friends with a deaf Bury fan. Being a little local pub, I advised the three smelly students not to order their usual tipple of Snakebite and instead get a pint of bitter.

Thankfully they agreed.

Despite Bury's one character fault (that they hate my dear Bolton) I loved going to see them, I loved the fans, the atmosphere and pretty much everything else about Gigg Lane.

"Back on the tram lads! Wahey!" I laughed, as closing time arrived.

It wasn't exactly situated in rolling moorland or pretty wooded river valleys, but Bury was nevertheless about as good and honest a club as you can find in the lower-leagues. Up the Shakers!

BURY   **1** (Morrell 76)
BRADFORD CITY   **0**
Attendance 4,112

GAME 61
BLACKBURN ROVERS v Bolton Wanderers
Premier League
Wednesday 28th January 2009, 8.00pm, Ewood Park, Blackburn

It was time for a full-blooded derby. Blackburn v Bolton. A Lancashire hotpot.

Wanting even *more* mid-week football Greg's mate Haz drove us to Ewood Park, situated just outside Blackburn town centre, and surrounded by a nice area of greenery, attractive old houses and cobble-styled brick walls. I felt like I was in Wallace and Gromit's town.

It's unbelievable to think that a mere fourteen years and just three different champions ago this team was top of the Premier League. There is the common accusation that Jack Walker's millions bought the title for Blackburn, but the fact is that the Shearer-led team had amazing English tenacity and deserved to be champions that year. A team like Blackburn as champions! It wouldn't happen now would it?

The crowd were building up outside, and despite the massive police presence there was a great match-night atmosphere. Plus, I actually liked Ewood Park quite a lot. Perhaps it's not Premier League champion-worthy, but a good example of a top flight stadium nonetheless.

Blackburn v Bolton is one of the oldest fixtures in English football. Two of the Football League founders, fierce Lancashire rivals of similar size with only 13 miles between the two. Heck, Ewood Park is even on the Bolton Road! There were also the additional elements that both teams needed some points to drift away from the dreaded drop zone, oh, and the Big Sam factor as well.

True, neither Blackburn nor Bolton are particularly known for their sexy football but I was still really looking forward to a footy feast. There was one thing that I hadn't prepared for though.

The Blackburn fans.

Now I don't mean that in an intimidating way or anything like that. Exactly the opposite. Despite all the factors to this fixture that should surely have gee'd the supporters up for this evening, the Blackburn fans were some of the quietest and disappointing I have been with during the 92.

To make it even worse, the Bolton fans were in some of the best form I've ever seen them in. I longed to be sat with them, but I had to make do with the miserable, silent Blackburn fans instead.

Of course Blackburn immediately had a lot more to be miserable about than Bolton. Matty Taylor put the Trotters ahead in the 15th minute and Kevin Davies made it 2-0 soon after. I was biting my lip watching the Bolton fans go mental.

Blackburn were awful. Benni McCarthy looked incredibly disinterested every time a ball from one of the back four was punted up towards him. He went down like a sack of spuds, challenged by Kevin Davies.
"Is that a head injury?" I wondered, as McCarthy received treatment.
"Nope," said Greg, squinting his eyes, "it's his bollocks."
The Bolton fans were getting even livelier, singing 'You only play long ball! You only play long ball!' towards us in the home end, the irony certainly not being lost on them.
Despite being 2-0 up at half-time, whilst eating my fairly run-of-the-mill half-time pie I was under no illusions that this lead was going to be safe.

I also wasn't particularly happy with the negative reaction of the Blackburn fans towards Big Sam. True, they were 2-0 down at half-time, but this was his 7th game in charge, with Blackburn still undefeated under his leadership. I love the man, getting Bolton to finish between 6th-8th four seasons in a row was phenomenal.
As if I haven't kissed Big Sam's arse enough already (not literally, what an absolutely horrendous mental image...) I now state that the game turned with an inspired double substitution by Blackburn,

bringing on the '£20million rated' (?!) Roque Santa Cruz and fan favourite Tugay with half an hour to go.

Bolton were looking uncomfortable, and Blackburn were now playing with renewed vigour. It was inevitable that they would score, and they did through Stephen Warnock (a bloody left back! Come on Bolton!) with their first shot on target.

The Blackburn fans were, for the first time, making more noise than a mouse, which increased further when they won a penalty in the 75th minute. Oh God. This was too much for me to take. I looked a couple of rows in front of me at a man with silver hair who it was all too much for as well. Everyone was standing up for the pen, but he sat down, couldn't watch, and just had a crafty fag instead. 'Strictly no smoking' didn't apply here. When I couldn't have been more tense, Benni McCarthy's penalty was superbly saved by Lord Jussi of Jaaskelainen.

"This is so painful," I said to Greg through gritted teeth, as not to upset the suddenly slightly animated Blackburn fans.

"Why are we so shit?" Greg said, also through his teeth.

"Megson. Megson mate." I said, realising the letter 'M' was tricky to say without opening your mouth.

"Do you think people think we're a bit weird talking like this?" enquired Greg.

"Probably. Probably." I said, realising the letter 'P' was equally as tricky to say without opening your mouth.

Blackburn were missing chance after chance. Tugay, the 73-year-old Turkish midfielder was now running the show, and sure enough the inevitable happened, when with three minutes to go the otherwise shite Benni McCarthy slotted home the equaliser from close range.

Plenty of the younger Blackburn fans ran towards the Bolton fans and began taunting them. I felt their pain. A few fans were ejected for their over-zealous celebrations, but with only three minutes to go I'm sure they didn't mind, and the match finished a fair 2-2.

Generally speaking it's easier to like Blackburn as a club once you're there; but the smart stadium, rich history and loveable (ahem) manager were all compromised by a set of supporters who barely mustered a whisper for at least the first 65 minutes. It was shocking. The thing I learnt today more than anything else though? Well, it's a game of two halves.

BLACKBURN ROVERS **2** (Warnock 66, McCarthy 87)
BOLTON WANDERERS **2** (Taylor 15, Davies 35)
Attendance 25,205

GAME 62
ROTHERHAM UNITED v Macclesfield Town
League Two
Saturday 31st January 2009, 3.00pm, Don Valley Stadium, Sheffield

92 Pies has made me unreliable. I confess. Especially when it comes to attending various parties and social occasions, I have often had to utter the words "I can't come I'm afraid, it's the Johnstone's Paint Trophy mid-week matches and I'm needed in Walsall" or something along those lines.

However, my brother Ali's 21st birthday in Leeds was one I couldn't really miss. It was on a Saturday night. Now what fixtures were falling on this Saturday near Leeds? On inspecting the list a fantastic little fixture couplet jumped out. Both Rotherham AND Sheffield Wednesday playing on the same day? Rotherham at 3pm, giving me very little, yet *just* enough, time to pop across Sheffield to see Wednesday play at 5.20pm? Let's do it!

Three morning coffees later I had reached Rotherham's stadium and realised that this was going to be a different kind of match-day experience. Rotherham were kicked out of their ground Millmoor at the beginning of the season and had to relocate to Sheffield, and the rather unconventional Don Valley Athletics Stadium (which is incidentally the biggest athletics stadium in the country).
You can see that times are bad at the club; as well as being removed from their ground they have entered administration twice in the last two seasons, and had a total of 37 points deducted in the past 3 years. The circus surrounding Rotherham and their financial problems is reflected in their desperate use of the Don Valley.

As soon as you get to the stadium you realise how peculiar and unsuitable it is. The outside stadium area is a vast and bizarrely designed zone, with oddly positioned spiral staircases and smoky funnels scattered on the exterior and a 'V.I.P. lift' feature attached to the ground. How many V.I.P.s visit Rotherham United?

Don Valley Stadium is clearly *not* designed for football. Once you step out into the arena you are greeted by the athletics track surrounding a cut-up pitch full of sand and dying grass. One main stand is covered with a jagged yellow canopy creating a low-rent gazebo effect, and the other stands are completely uncovered but with odd bits of poles and scaffolding. There were five massive floodlights, but all on one side of the ground. The scoreboard looked like it was from a 1980s Soviet arena. And to complete the athletics vibe there were two rows of hurdles forming the players tunnel.

A club in the first year of a tenancy at a new stadium will never have much of their character imposed on their new home yet, but Rotherham have this problem more than most. Rather than pictures of former players and trophy wins decorating the back-area there are pictures of Jon Bon Jovi and Tina Turner. I bet it was *them* who needed the V.I.P. lift! Problem solved.

Nothing seemed right, even the toilets didn't suggest football; rows and rows of immaculate cubicles, shining and clean without any skanky urinals to speak of. Can I really complain about the toilets being *too* clean?!?! It seems that I can!

I took my seat next to two friendly old fellas who were pure Yorkshire.

"Can tell you're not from around here lad. What you doing here?" one said, much warmer than it sounds in print. I told them about 92 Pies to which they both raised their eyebrows.

"What do you want to do that for? Have to come to bloody awful places like this!"

"Should have done it last season, got to see Millmoor."

"I've been going to Millmoor for 60 years. Now we've got the bloody athletics track ruining the view!"

Watching the match wasn't much fun, even with the amusing old men for company. Before the match there was a PA announcement 'Anyone caught throwing objects on the pitch will be ejected and banned for life'. This was simply ridiculous. Who on earth could throw far enough to reach the pitch? It was miles away! You would need a javelin. I'm sure they probably had plenty spare javelins backstage.

I didn't really like it. Football is not meant to be watched this far away, especially with lower-league matches where part of the joy is getting close up into the players faces, hearing the on-field speak and feeling a part of the action yourself (which I am sure Millmoor had much of). I could just about tell however that the first Rotherham goal was a product of a very well crafted move. This clearly was not your typical Rotherham United goal.

"Bloody brilliant that!"

"Best goal I've seen here without a doubt!"

The locals (well...almost locals, Rotherham is only a few miles away) were astounded by this goal that was not particularly mind-blowing. Rotherham played quite well in general, showing the form that meant they would be challenging for the play-offs if it wasn't for the 17-point deduction. Their winger Alex Rhodes was having a nightmare though, with a series of poor passes and sluggish runs.

"Such a talented lad that Rhodes. But he's just so *lazy*." One of the old guys said.

"Exactly like Deon Burton a few seasons ago." The other one replied.

"Yep and Marc Joseph as well."

"And what do they have in common?"

I pre-empted what he was going to say and cringed at the thought. Surely he can't?

"They're all *black!*"

My cringing began.

"I mean I know it's not on to say that kind of thing nowadays, but these lads are so naturally talented...but too lazy!"

This clearly inaccurate racial stereotype isn't the kind of thing you want to hear at a football match, but these men were *old*. Certainly late 70s, possibly in their 80s. So different generations and all that, I just about let them off. I admit their lack of political correctness made me chuckle. Blunt Yorkeshiremen and all that.

Rotherham got another one (through the thoroughly industrious and hard working black striker Reuben Reid) and comfortably won 2-0. It was a satisfying beginning to my football-fest Saturday! Walking back to my car I decided I felt sorry for Rotherham United. The team actually played okay, better than a lot I had seen in League

Two, and the fans were an extremely friendly (if occasionally casually racist) bunch.

Rotherham are doing their best to turn this athletics arena into something that can pass for a football ground, but Don Valley isn't right for them, the atmosphere is nonexistent. I hoped the club would manage to move on sooner rather than later and not be stuck like Brighton are in their athletics stadium.

Gosh, the thought made me rather sombre! I jumped in my car and whacked on the radio before zooming the 4 ½ miles to Hillsborough. Local radio. It was only bloody Bon Jovi! The legend of the Don Valley Stadium himself. 'Must be big in these parts', I thought as I put my foot down and zoomed off...

ROTHERHAM UNITED   2 (Hudson 12, Reid 76)
MACCLESFIELD TOWN   0
Attendance 2,945

GAME 63
SHEFFIELD WEDNESDAY v Birmingham City
The Championship
Saturday 31st January 2009, 5.20pm, Hillsborough, Sheffield

COME ON MATCH-DAY BLOODY TRAFFIC! I had left the Don Valley
five minutes before the end but apparently I wasn't the only one to
have had that idea. I was almost definitely the only one who *needed*
to be at Hillsborough in the next few minutes though! *TomTom* was
failing me. He wasn't picking up any satellite. For God's sake! There
were no flipping signs for Hillsborough! How on earth were there
about 20 times more signs for Rotherham United than for Sheffield
Wednesday?
I was stuck behind a blue-rinsed old lady who had clearly forgotten
what second gear was. Finally I navigated myself to what looked
like a massive blue warehouse. It was Hillsborough.

The stadium was in a nice green area near a park, an antithesis to
Sheffield United's Bramall Lane which is very much a city centre
ground. You can tell the ground is *old* as you enter through the tiny
rickety turnstiles, up a huge grassy mount towards the arena.
Only 5 minutes late (result!) I took my seat in the cheap Kop area
next to a group of intimidating looking blokes. It wasn't exactly
luxurious; there was a giant pole blocking my vision of both
goalmouths, and the leg room was about as little as my previous
worst at Q.P.R. and Luton. Still, at £9 a ticket I couldn't complain!
The blokes I was sitting with made the first half pretty awkward for
me. They were talking about all the fights they've been in lately,
their shagging conquests and how they hate Southerners. Hmmmm.
I kept my mouth shut anyway. I gathered that one of them was a
train conductor, a ridiculously skinny bloke with a thin ginger
moustache.
"The other day on the train to London I checked this prick's ticket,
he hadn't got the right one so he got all lippy with me. I told him, I
told him 'if you're such a brave fucker then I'll meet you outside the

station after my shift and we'll have it fucking out!' Well he just shat himself!" he boasted (clearly lying).

Being squeezed next to this charmer wasn't ideal, but I lived with it through the very dull first half. Entertainment was hard to come by. Where was the fat topless Tango Man? Where was the infamous brass band? Where were the 40,000 passionate Wednesday fans screaming at the top of their lungs? Where was Kevin Pressman in net and David Hirst up front? Where was *Andy bloody Hinchcliffe? Or PAOLO DI CANIO?!*

Whilst there was little to inspire me, I could still see the wonderful character Hillsborough possesses as a stadium. It is certainly showing its age, and you can tell there has been relatively little renovation compared to lots of other old grounds. My favourite aspect is the famous clock on top of the south side grandstand; a brilliant old relic of a time gone by.

Half-time arrived, along with a pie that I was genuinely dreading. Being an always-reliable Shire pie I knew it wouldn't be rank. I just really didn't want it. I had foolishly had a full cooked breakfast before I left home, and of course a pie a mere 2 hours ago at Rotherham.

I looked into the orange chicken balti pie and my stomach churned. I decided to eat it quickly. I was so full. Oh God I hoped I wasn't sick on the ginger train worker in the second half. He'd obviously chin me.

Whilst my half-time was horrible, Wednesday manager Brian Laws must have had a more productive 15 minutes, because they came out with vigour in the second half, and quickly went ahead through new signing Lewis Buxton.

Oh no, the bloke was hugging me and shaking me.

"Get in mate! Fucking quality!" he said, his stick-thin freckled arms around me, his body odour now invading my nostrils for the first time. I felt so sick. Don't be sick Tom, try to concentrate on replying in a believable accent.

"Yeah! Get in!" I said in the most abysmal fake-Sheffield accent ever. I was trying to think of any accent I could copy (The Full Monty? Arctic Monkeys?) but just came out sounding Indian, as usual.

Fortunately he didn't notice that I was Southern, and from this point on Wednesday got their act together against a very poor Birmingham side. This made it even harsher when the Brummies got their undeserved injury time equaliser, inevitably coming through Kevin Phillips to secure a lucky point.

I let the crowd die down a bit before leaving and then did something I had meant to do before kick-off but was too delayed.

I went over to the other side of the stadium, the Leppings Lane End. The place where one of the biggest football tragedies of all time occurred back in 1989.

What always strikes me first about the Hillsborough disaster isn't the fallout against *The Sun,* the Taylor Report and subsequent changes to stadia forever, or the Justice for the 96 campaign still ongoing today. It's the fact that it was unique in uniting all football fans, from Liverpool, Nottingham, Sheffield and beyond, into grieving about what was, and is, the most pointless waste of life you could ever imagine.

I saw the Hillsborough memorial and felt a bit weird. Looking at all the crowds pile down Leppings Lane to get back to their cars, moaning about today's result. I thought about what the horrific scene in this exact spot would have been, 20 years ago in April.

Seeing the site humbled me a bit, so I headed back to my car and pondered instead my opinion about Sheffield Wednesday, concluding that the main problem with the experience was the attendance. Even though 18,000 is very respectable for the Championship, the 40,000 capacity Hillsborough deserves better; the empty seats made more statement and noise than the full ones did. Hillsborough is a forgotten gem of the English game; a charming relic of a bygone era, one that oozes history out of its pores, both good and bad, yet remains a ground all should visit. And a ground that I hope will one day be sold out again to recreate the terrific atmospheres it surely used to hold.

In the car, slightly worn out from my long football day, I called birthday-boy Ali.

"Going to be a bit late getting to Leeds brother, I'm stuck in traffic." I said as the queues out of Hillsborough seemed never ending.

"Yeahhhh, what's the phlenba? Oi! No bleeeauhh!" said Ali, so pissed he was incomprehensible. I looked at my watch, it was 7.35pm.
"Wow! Good going! Going to be a short night then I guess." I laughed, hanging up, looking forward to a well deserved drink after two rather testing games in the same day.

SHEFFIELD WEDNESDAY 1 (Buxton 57)
BIRMINGHAM CITY **1** (Phillips 90)
Attendance 18,409

GAME 64
AFC BOURNEMOUTH v Shrewsbury Town
League Two
Saturday 7th February 2009, 3.00pm, Fitness First Stadium, Bournemouth

Oh the weather outside is frightful, but the fire is so delightful, and since we've no place to go, Let it snow! Let it snow! Let it snow! – Let it snow, Sammy Cahn.

Well I respectively disagree with you Sammy Cahn. Bollocks to snow! *Bollocks* to it!

After celebrating Ali's birthday I had stayed up in Yorkshire for two full extra days for the Bradford v Darlington Monday night match. I *needed* to get this one in. I was falling behind on my fixtures. So I spent two days Ali's tiny stinking house, in its damp-walled, dry-rotted spare attic room waiting for the night match.

And then on Sunday night/Monday morning the snow came. An absolute shed load of snow. The biggest single snow fall in six years. The Bradford game was cancelled and I had been bumming around the dry-rot room in Leeds for no reason. I drove home on the treacherously icy M1, more pissed off than I'd been this year.

The snow continued all week, with every single mid-week match called off. My morale was at a new low. Would I even complete 92 Pies?

There had been no signs of the snow letting up, but as I woke early on Saturday morning, I looked out of the window to see the sun beaming down. It was a gorgeous day. Surely some games would survive today?

Most of Leagues One and Two matches had been called off, but I came across a promising lead on the endearing AFC Bournemouth website. It said that supporters had met at Dean Court yesterday twice to clear snow from the pitch, and all looked OK for the match against Shrewsbury to go ahead! I thought that the phrase 'all looks

OK' was confirmation enough to justify the 250-mile round trip to Bournemouth.

I put on my red and black stripy shirt which looked a bit like the Bournemouth kit and headed for the door. To make the occasion that extra bit more exciting, my Mum had decided to come along with me for her first match of the 92. The last free day she could have come was when I went to the New Den, but I think Bournemouth is a bit more mummy-friendly than Millwall.

"So are they a good team Bournemouth? Doing well in the league?" asked Mum hopefully.

"Well..." I replied, "last season they had a 10-point deduction, got relegated, and came close to complete liquidation."

"Oh no!"

"And this season they started with a 17-point deduction, have gone through 3 different managers and needed to prove to the Football League that they have enough financial stability to compete in League Two under threat of expulsion."

"Oh poor them!"

"But they're doing OK at the moment under this new young manager; they're starting to sort themselves out and might actually not get relegated now!"

"Oh thank goodness!"

"He's only 31!"

"That's too young to be managing a team surely?"

"Just 'cause it's a generation younger than you," I teased my greying mother.

"Bugger off! I just thought all football managers were Alex Ferguson's age. Or at least mine and Jose Mourinho's age..." said Mum dreamily.

"You're not the same age as Jose Mourinho!!" I laughed.

"I bloody well am! Nearly..."

We reached the charming three-sided Dean Court (or the 'Fitness First Stadium as one should technically refer to it as), driving up a lovely scenic thin road in the middle of a sprawling green park. Dean Court is (or was) an old ground until it was almost completely rebuilt in 2001. The pitch was rotated 90°, which logistically boggles my mind.

"Darren Anderton!! I remember him! You told me I wouldn't know any of the players!" said Mum excitedly as we approached the charming club shop, adorned with a huge image of Dazza Sicknote himself.

"Unfortunately he retired two months ago," I said.

Good old Dazza. I saw him score for Bournemouth in Grimsby back in November, but he decided those rickety old legs had had their day, so made the match against Chester in December his last ever. As if Roy-of-the-Rovers had written the script himself, Dazza popped up with the 90th minute winner. Legend.

The club shop was unfortunately clearly feeling the post-Anderton credit crunch pinch, with lots of Dazza merchandise in bargain bins, alongside unsold calendars and autograph books.

Dean Court was pretty busy on this gorgeous but freezing Saturday afternoon and the atmosphere was great. The remains of the snow were all over the sides of the pitch, with the mascot Cherry Bear allowing kids to lob snowballs at his massive face.

"Come on lads!! You're playing for your jobs!" a fan around us shouted to a few giggles. It was true though. More reports in the papers suggested that Bournemouth needed a buyer, and fast.

The linesman was wearing a cap. *Linesman wearing a cap?!?!* It wasn't *that* sunny! Prima Donna.

The beginning of the game was held up by an injury to the Bournemouth player Joel Ward.

"Get up! You're fine!" Mum laughed. She felt a bit guilty 6 minutes later when he was still down injured and had to get stretchered off.

"I hope you feel bad about yourself Mother." I said sternly.

"I thought he was faking it! Like that tosser at Chelsea always does!"

"Drogba?"

"Yeah him."

Shortly after the injury Bournemouth went triumphantly ahead through Brett Pitman, who scored directly from a corner! The crowd went mad! If they could win this game they'd finally climb out of the relegation zone for the first time since August.

I got our very satisfying pies in the second half as the crowd was beginning to feel some nerves. Could they hold on against a superior Shrewsbury side? Bournemouth's best player by a country mile was the 36-year-old legendary striker Steve Fletcher. 'Fletch' was back at Bournemouth to do his old mate, manager Eddie Howe, a favour, and his bulky forward style was unsettling the Shrewsbury defence. "I've just realised you can see our car from these seats!" said Mum, looking through the trees behind the empty stand.

"Hahaha, oh yeah. At least we know it hasn't been nicked."

A clearly frustrated Shrewsbury went down to 10 men and ended up losing 1-0. It was a richly deserved win for a plucky Bournemouth side for whom I wish great things.

I read somewhere recently that Bournemouth is statistically the happiest town in the UK, despite the football team probably being the league's most financially troubled. There's a famous story that back in 1997 Bournemouth were apparently 15 minutes away from closing down for ever, until a last minute buyer came in. From what I understand they're in almost as bad a situation now, despite the young manager Eddie Howe working miracles on the pitch.

If anything like karma or fate exists then Bournemouth will be fine. The club has a great set of fans, and the vibe around the stadium is terrific. Whilst perhaps karma did indeed bite Luton Town where they deserved it, I've got a feeling everything might work out for Bournemouth. With or without Darren Anderton.

The fire is slowly dying, and my dear we're still good-byeing, but as long as you love me so, Let it snow! Let it snow! Let it snow!

3 days later, and it was about 3pm on the Tuesday. I had spontaneously decided to drive up to Gresty Road to see Crewe v Bristol Rovers. It hadn't snowed in days. What should take about 2 ½ hours took nearer 4 ½ hours with a massive traffic back-jam on the M6. "Come on! Come on!" I shouted to myself, looking at my watch. Kick-off was fast approaching. *5 Live* was on the radio discussing the merits of Liverpool using Steven Gerrard as a supporting striker.

It was 7pm and I was still on the motorway. COME ON! Finally I managed to get off and sped towards Crewe. 7.35pm. 10 minutes to go! I had reached Crewe! There were signs for the station, wasn't the ground right next to the station? Not many people around.

7.43pm. Brilliant, if I could find somewhere to park easily then I'd actually make kick-off. But where are all the people? 7.44pm.
5 Live informs the listeners that the Crewe v Bristol Rovers match has been cancelled.
I slam on my breaks as I pull up literally right next to the stadium. I wind down my window and speak to a pissed off looking bloke in a replica Crewe shirt.
"What the hell's happened mate?"
"Ref called it off about a half hour ago pal. Frozen pitch apparently, would be 'dangerous' for the players."
I sat in my car absolutely devastated. 4 ½ hours. A full tank of petrol. What the hell am I doing here? This isn't a proper way to spend your life. What exactly am I trying to prove, and to who? Fucking ridiculous. I looked at Gresty Road and thumped my steering wheel with force. And turned back towards the M6 to drive back home.

BOURNEMOUTH   **1** (Pitman 23)
SHREWSBURY TOWN   **0**
Attendance 4,187

GAME 65
SWANSEA CITY v Fulham
FA Cup Fifth Round

Saturday 14th February 2009, 12.45pm, Liberty Stadium, Swansea

Crewe fecking Alexandra. Frozen pitch? It wasn't even cold! I was still furious. 92 Pies? I thought about packing it in. What's the point? The next fixture was in bloody Swansea. What if I drove there and *that* was cancelled? I don't know how my soul would recover.

But I didn't. I ploughed on. Because going to 64 football matches for no reason over the course of half a year would be ridiculous. I could do it. I knew I could do it.

My alarm went off. 5.50am. On *a Saturday morning*. I felt low. I rolled over to the empty other half of my bed.

5.51am snooze.

5.52am snooze.

Never has a minute gone so quickly. It was a grim, freezing cold Valentine's Day. At 5.55am I finally got up. Alone. And drove to Wales.

Yep. It was Valentine's Day but the only romance on the agenda for me was the potential romance of an FA Cup 5th Round upset over 200 miles away in a different country. Annabel wasn't speaking to me. I had officially chosen football over my girlfriend, and it felt horrible.

I had invited her to come to the match! Of course. I even (rather gentlemanly) offered to pay for her ticket. The response was greeted with expletives.

Feeling quite bad about myself I made the arduous journey to Wales and arrived at the remarkably spanking white Liberty Stadium. The ground opened in 2005 and gleams from miles away, looking like a grounded UFO that has passed the Daz doorstep challenge. It's a clean, modern, if slightly unspectacular new ground that must be a world away from the rough and tumble of the old Vetch Field.

There's even a hairdresser built into the stadium; the unusually tanned ladies of South Wales getting a 'do before the footy.

Although I was at a personal low for several reasons, I was actually really looking forward to this match. Swansea were in great form, as were Fulham, and this had all the makings of a good cup tie. I took my place next to a couple holding hands. My stomach sank, they were having a lovely Valentine's Day afternoon. So what if both were over 20 stone, and not particularly pleasing on the eye. Love conquers all boundaries no?

"Fuck off back to England!" the bloke shouted at the Fulham fans taking their seats. "Yeah fuck you you fucking wankers!" the girl followed, giving the pleasant Fulham family fans the V-sign. How romantic.

The teams came out to thunderous noise from the home faithful, which continued throughout the first half.

Everything about Roberto Martinez's Swansea team was first-class. The short passes were a joy to watch, and Nathan Dyer was causing Fulham defenders all kinds of problems on the right wing. Fulham's Brede Hangeland fouled Dyer in the centre circle.

"Fuck off you English twat!" my fat neighbour bellowed at Hangeland. Which didn't really work seeing as a) Hangeland isn't English, and b) Dyer *is* English.

The fans were standing for the entire game; only the second time I'd been at a match where the home fans do so, the other being Leeds at Elland Road. There was vicious swearing directed at the Fulham fans and players throughout the game, but it sounded kind of funny in a thick Welsh accent rather than threatening. The support showed a great mixture of wit and passion, my chant of choice being "We like fluffy sheep, we like fluffy sheep!"

Swansea weren't taking their chances, and sure enough were made to pay when their captain Garry Monk (who I saw sent off at Charlton on the opening day of the season) scored an own goal to unfairly give Fulham the lead against the run of play. He must dread me coming to watch him.

My ravishing appetite would need to be cured to help sooth this disappointment. Stepping back out into the arena after fetching my much needed half-time pie I was greeted with quite a unique sight.

A man *dressed as the FA Cup* (in what looked like the most uncomfortable costume ever designed) was taking a penalty against Cyril the Swan. To be fair to the FA Cup he took a decent penalty, but Cyril made a miraculous save with his left wing. Sign him up!

The pies were a new brand I hadn't tried before, *Lewis's,* and I wish I hadn't bothered. First time in a while I'd actually longed for a *Pukka* effort. What was wrong with me? I had hoped Swansea might sell 'oggies', a massive Welsh pasty and the best thing to come out of Wales since Tom Jones, Shirley Bassey and Neville Southall.

Swansea came out in the second half with all the vigour they showed in the first period, and equalised through a fantastic strike from Jason Scotland; his 12th goal in 12 games. The fans went absolutely crazy, I was kissed by both the fat man and his fat girlfriend. I felt loved on Valentine's Day; big sloppy Welsh snogs.

"If you hate Cardiff do a bop!" sang the fans, the entire Liberty Stadium bopping up and down as the match finished as a spectacularly entertaining 1-1 draw.

In 2005 Swansea were languishing without any money in League Two, but now they are showing true Premier League potential. They are on an incredible run under Martinez, with this match being their 16th game without defeat. Fulham's Simon Davies compared Swansea's playing style to that of Barcelona after the match. Not sure about that Simon, but they were pretty darn good.

The sad truth for me was that I bloody enjoyed the match, the English-Welsh banter, the atmosphere, everything. I was questioning what kind of human being I was becoming; was I genuinely *obsessed* with football now?

I went to Oxford on the way home to make it up to Annabel. Via a petrol station for some £3.99 flowers...

SWANSEA CITY 1 (Scotland 52)
FULHAM 1 (Monk O.G. 44)
Attendance 16,573

GAME 66
BRISTOL ROVERS v Yeovil Town
League One
Tuesday 17th February 2009, 7.45pm, Memorial Stadium, Bristol.

The snow had almost completely disappeared and my mood was improving. I had just about got over my aborted matches at Bradford and Crewe, and Annabel had just about got over me standing her up on Valentine's Day. Almost. But what use was pondering the past when I had a full set of Tuesday night fixtures to hand pick a game from?!

Bristol Rovers seemed the only feasible choice, so backed up again by my Mum, we set off for a footballing treat. My little mother, a Year One teacher, had been bitten by the football bug at Bournemouth a week ago. It was her half-term, so we decided for a mini family day out in Bristol, culminating in a bit of (possibly) high-quality League One football.

It was my first time in Bristol, and I thought it was great. Everything about it appealed to me, even the new wave of teenagers who hilariously dress in straw hats and fluorescent trousers, thinking they might get spotted for the new series of *Skins*.

After a foot-numbingly long wander of Bristol centre we popped over to the Horfield suburb and the Memorial Stadium. Now this is a weird ground. It used to be just a rugby stadium, but the main stand is a dominating bit of cricket-pavilion style architecture and the rest of the ground is an off-key mishmash of oddly sized stands and unusual concourses.

The music choice was winding me up, the club DJ clearly having a severe case of ADD, changing each song after about 30 seconds of it. At one point the pre-football music standards of *Place Your Hands* by Reef and *Sweet Child O Mine* by Guns N Roses were actually overlapping each other to make an uneasy version of 'Place your hands on the sweet child of mine'.

Kick-off between Rovers and Yeovil was approaching and a group of pirates were parading their cutlasses around the pitch. Mum was excited by the pirates, but concerned by the people selling fanzines. "Black Arab! The Black Arab fanzine! Read all about the Black Arabs!" bellowed a bearded man drinking cider.

"Read all about the Black Arabs?" Mum whispered to me, looking a bit aghast. "I don't understand! That sounds a bit oddly raci..."

"No no, the Black Arabs is the name of an early incarnation of Bristol Rovers. It's like a nickname for the team now." I explained.

"Oh OK. But you said earlier that their nickname was the 'gasheads'..."

"Yeah, because they used to be placed next to a gas station or something."

"And Black Arabs because???? I assume in the 19th Century their team wasn't made up of..."

"No. I don't know why."

"So where do the pirates come in to it?"

"I think it's their third nickname!"

"Three nicknames? Greedy," laughed Mum, as a man in a pirate costume came up to us and said 'OOO ARRR!' waving his cutlass around.

The match kicked off and the first 20 minutes were terrible, but out of the blue Bristol Rovers scored two goals in quick succession which effectively killed the game.

Neither set of fans were in good form tonight, despite the fact that the local paper was building up the fixture as a fierce local derby (of sorts). Yeovil had just oddly sacked their manager Russell Slade after 4 consecutive wins, but this failed to add much spice to a muted atmosphere. Occasionally a Rovers fan would bellow 'Wanggkkerr' at the Yeovil support which made Mum giggle every time. The word 'wanker' does sound hilarious in a West Country accent.

Rovers have been at the Memorial Stadium since 1996, but it didn't feel like a natural home for a football club to me. Nothing is quite right although I liked the variation in refreshments; a cider bar instead of a beer bar and piles of Cornish pasties on sale next to the pies.

Mum was tucking into a pasty, while I obviously had to go for yet another bloody pie.

"A *chicken balti* pie? Well I've never heard of that!" said Mum.

"Yep they're quite popular, do you want a bite?"

"Oh no. Curry in a pie? Sounds weird."

The second half was petering out, Rovers were comfortable and Yeovil looked lost without a manager. Mum was yawning emphatically, and trying (and failing) to hide it.

Fortunately the second half provided one moment of magic through Rickie Lambert. Lambert had been scoring goals for fun this season, and despite carrying a knock came off the bench to score an absolute screamer of a free-kick from 30 yards.

I think Mum's feet were about to cave in from all the walking and standing so we trotted back to the car for a well-earned feet-up (well, for *her,* I had to drive back 150 miles). It might have been a bit of a lame 'derby', but a day in out Bristol is something I would recommend to anyone. Just perhaps don't link it in with a trip to a dilapidated old rugby ground to see the Black Arabs, the pirates, the gasheads or even plain old Bristol Rovers.

BRISTOL ROVERS 3 (Pipe 19, Duffy 30, Lambert 86)
YEOVIL TOWN 0
Attendance 8,049

GAME 67
PORT VALE v Lincoln City
League Two

Friday 20ᵗʰ February 2009, 7.45pm, Vale Park, Burslem, Staffordshire.

My travel-rucksack was packed. My tyres were pumped and my tank was full (my car's tank I mean, not mine. Not my tyres either).
I was about to hit the road for 7 games in 7 days.
This was make-or-break.
If I could do this then I would have every chance of finishing 92 Pies. If I had a nervous breakdown, serious injury or severe football fatigue then it might be the end of me. My destinations screamed glamour and excitement; Blackpool, Wolverhampton, Wycombe, Oldham, Macclesfield, Hull. But to start them all off? Port Vale. Let's go!
On a chilly Friday night I parked up and made my way to Vale Park, very begrudgingly purchasing my £19 ticket. I entered the huge Port Vale club shop, heaving with supporters due to the free programmes being handed out. "Too bloody right I get a free programme, spending £19 on a ticket!" I muttered to myself, slightly insanely.
There were some bona fide bargains in the shop too. Last season's home kit for £4.99! Wow. I texted Collo and Paul; 'Would either of you guys like an old Port Vale home shirt for £4.99?' Collo quickly replied 'Yes! I'd be a fool *not* to get one!' so I spent a fiver on a well-earned Vale shirt. I thought about buying a Port Vale time capsule too! Wow. I don't know what you'd put in it though; a signed photo of the goalkeeper or Robbie Williams's *Rudebox* album perhaps?
Oh yes. Robbie Williams. Mr. majority shareholder. You can't escape his name when visiting Vale Park. In the match programme there was even a bit about him today, the headline news being that he had actually watched Vale for the first time in several years away at Brentford last week.

The last (and only) time I saw Port Vale was away at Huddersfield where they produced the most amazing comeback in the best game

I've seen to win 4-3. Would today also give me a 7 goal thriller? The answer was a resounding....

No.

The match was dull dull dull, and Vale Park is about as mediocre a ground as you can find. Not horrible enough to be interesting, not nice enough to be desirable, just mediocre. A bit like Walsall.

I think the whole night was doomed the moment I took my seat and the Thunderbirds theme music began counting down, before 'Who Let the Dogs Out' pumped out and Vale's mascot Boomer the Dog (shirt number 'K9') ran on the pitch to zero applause.

Things went from bad to worse the moment the players stepped out on the pitch, both teams wearing white kits, with slightly different sleeves, but not quite enough to significantly tell them apart. This was going to be a *long* night.

If this wasn't bad enough I had bought a meat and potato pie with the stodgy consistency of a scotch egg. It looked and smelled like cat food. Things weren't going well, but little was I to know though that the worst was yet to come with the useless match. Lincoln took the lead in the 12th minute with a hilariously scrappy goal; the ball hitting the post, smacking the 'keeper in the face and bouncing off Dany N'Guessan's testicles into the net. But nothing else happened for the remaining 78 minutes.

Nothing.

Well nothing except the constant moaning from the Vale fans, particularly at their manager (and former Vale playing legend) Dean Glover.

The fans absolutely *hated* Glover, a man clearly lacking the ability to inspire. He seemed like the managerial equivalent of a damp flannel; not quite wet enough to properly wash your face. If that's a publish-worthy metaphor (which it obviously *is*).

I noticed something weird going on in Burslem; there were lots of attractive young(ish) girls there with their much older, gimpy, ugly boyfriends. About 5 or 6 different couples around me were like this. Ugly balding fellas, piece of advice; if you want a sexy girlfriend out of your league, head to Port Vale and pick one up.[1]

[1] 'Dear Deidre' eat ya heart out. Future career as relationship adviser here I come.

The match was coming to a close and the atmosphere was still very depressing. I overheard a conversation between two blokes behind me.

"Had to sign on yesterday Ron. On the dole for the first time in my life."

"Come to that has it?"

"Yep. Wish Vale would be less shit to make me feel better about all the other crap going on."

"We're awful. Who'd be your man of the match?"

"Boomer the dog. For giving out sweets to the kids at half-time."

"We need Glover out ASAP. The man's about as inspiring as a carrot." (come on, my metaphor was better than that wasn't it?)

Poor Dean Glover. Although, being a fair judge, I suppose the Vale fans did have a point at the bemusement of taking a striker and bringing on a defender when they were 1-0 down with 25 minutes left. COME ON DEAN! You're not helping yourself now are you?

If I'm talking about feeling sorry for Dean Glover, then I have equal amounts of sympathy for Danny Glover. Not the 62-year-old black Lethal Weapon actor. I don't feel sorry for him whatsoever. But Danny Glover, the skinny ginger 19-year-old goal-shy Port Vale forward and son of the manager Dean Glover.

So the fans hate Dean, but they hate Dean so much that their hate transcends to Danny too. He seemed OK, playing solidly without setting the pitch alight. He wasn't worse than any of the other 10 though. Being the manager's son must be difficult at the best of times, but when you're the son of the most unpopular manager your club has ever had it must be a million times harder.

The polar-opposite differences between Dean Glover and the brilliant Lincoln manager Peter Jackson can be summed up by one single act. Whenever a Port Vale player got substituted Glover would subtly shake their hand as they made their way to the dugout. When a Lincoln player came off, Jackson would grab them by the face, hold their neck and shout spitty words in their ear, kiss them and slap their arse.

For the third time this year I'd been transfixed by Jackson. He was again looking dapper, this time in a long white coat like a pimp Batman. At one point he flobbed out his chewing gum onto the pitch; a piece about the size of a golf ball! Bloody hell man, you must have had two packs of Orbit in there! I suppose there's every chance Jackson's a *Hubba Bubba* man though.

The final whistle thankfully eventually arrived, and Lincoln had won 1-0 despite missing numerous late chances to make the scoreline even more embarrassing for Port Vale.

The piercing boooooos and 'Glover out' chants greeted the final whistle; Port Vales's 9th defeat in the last 16 home matches. I felt depressed. This wasn't much fun, and I had 6 more games in the next 6 days.

Poor game, poor atmosphere, poor fans, poor stadium, poor poor *poor* Dean Glover. Pour me a drink, I'm off to Liverpool for a richly-deserved night out.

PORT VALE   0
LINCOLN CITY 1 (N'Guessan 12)
Attendance 5,097

GAME 68
BLACKPOOL v Watford
The Championship
Saturday 21st February 2009, 3.00pm, Bloomfield Road, Blackpool

My richly-deserved night out in Liverpool was followed by the sad inevitability of driving to another dodgy ground with a blinding hangover. Today it was the turn of Blackpool; the town that made the phrase 'tacky crap' what it is today.

People say Blackpool is a bit like Marmite; you love it or you hate it. I fall firmly in the latter. For those of you that haven't spent a Friday night around Blackpool pier I thoroughly recommend most diseases ahead of it. With a blinding hangover, I eventually managed to park in a residential area a few roads down from a massive derelict burnt out old multi-storey car park. Inside this huge ruined building I heard smashing and loud laughing, but decided not to head in to investigate.

Passing the world's most depressing looking *Travelodge* I reached Bloomfield Road, a ground that isn't exactly pleasing on the eye. With a majestic statue of Stan Mortensen situated in front of the famous Blackpool Tower I should have felt a stronger sense of history than I did. One possible explanation for this is the unbearably grim industrial wasteland surrounding this otherwise iconic image.

Dismal surroundings and crumbling stands are sometimes all part of the charm with a football ground, but I just wasn't feeling warmth of any kind at Blackpool. I decided to give the club itself a chance when I went up to get my ticket.

"Hi there, what's your cheapest ticket?" I asked the lady at the kiosk, deciding to be slightly cautious given my rather expensive alcohol adventures out in Liverpool last night.

"£28."

"£28?!?" I stated with an equally large number of question and exclamation marks.

"That's right sir."

"What about any discount? Under 21? Student?" I squawked, despite not being either under 21 nor a student.

"No we don't do concession tickets except for over-65s."

I thought about asking for an over-65 ticket but I'm not sure whether I looked that old. I rudely slammed down my £28 on the ticket desk, paying for most of the final pound in coppers. That'll show them! I took my extortionate seat next to Blackpool's finest football fans, who were actually the best thing about the whole day. They were a funny and pleasant and occasionally loud bunch, putting up with a poor team in an even worse stadium.

Oh yes, the stadium. Bloomfield Road essentially only has two proper stands; the third stand (for the away lot) is temporary scaffolding seating that looked like it was going to blow over.

The poor away fans definitely don't get their £28 worth; sitting on tiny, crappy seats, completely exposed to the most bitter of bitter North-West winds in one of the most dingy grounds of the 92. Oh and of course I forgot about the fourth stand! Well, there isn't a fourth stand. Behind the goal there is nothing except for the rows of terraced houses and advertising boards.

Okay, so things weren't going very well, but at least I had a football match to look forward to yes? No. Blackpool v Watford first half was 45 minutes without incident, excitement, passion, quality, joy or talent. Even the seagulls who were watching the beginning intently got impatient and flew off.

I needed some half-time food to soak up my mixture of booze and resentment. The wallet-raping ticket price was slightly softened by the ultra cheap pie. For the credit-crunching £1.30, the Holland's cheese & onion effort was worth every penny (and I don't necessarily mean that as a compliment).

Oh God I felt awful. Everything was ghastly. Eating my cheap costing, cheap tasting pie, I popped over to the newly built 'Blackpool corridor of fame'. Unfortunately despite the good intentions behind this expensive new addition to Bloomfield Road, it was essentially a long orange walkway with some photos of many mediocre footballers on the wall.

Along with the Matthews/Mortensens of Blackpool's chequered history there were some more questionable recent additions. The two Bolton managers of recent memory (*Elle* magazine number 1 and 2 'sexiest managers in English football messrs Megson and Allardyce) were both at one point in charge of Blackpool, and had their places on the corridor of fame.

Enough of me patronising the recent history of an esteemed football club. Fortunately the second half was, whilst not being brilliant, a great improvement on the first period. Blackpool looked a better team, but Watford were more clinical and ended up winning 2-0. The Seasiders had struggled since the recent departure of Simon Grayson to Leeds, and were jeered off by their passionate fans at the final whistle.

So despite a slightly improved second period I've still moaned about the parking, the town of Blackpool, the match, the facilities, the stands and the ticket prices, but am I done? Gosh no. Let's see what else I've got up my sleeve....

The pitch! Oh my. It was like the mud-drenched Glastonbury fields after 5 days of downpour. The sandy, bobbly monstrosity didn't help the quality of the football.

The police presence! There were almost more police there than people. Blackpool isn't the calmest, most trouble-free town in England obviously, but for a mediocre Championship fixture against a club like Watford the ridiculously large police presence just made the atmosphere unnecessarily edgy.

I could go on but the whole day was just majorly disappointing. The overriding gripe though was still the price of the ticket; I had spent a hell of a lot of money already but parting with the dosh for this one felt awful. For £28 I could have gone to a couple of concerts, I could have taken my girlfriend out for a romantic meal she richly deserves but seldom gets, I could have bought 2800 penny sweets.

Walking back to my car I passed a group of four girls in their late teens wearing black. Two were pushing babies in prams, the other two were smoking joints. I was losing faith in humanity, and faith in my project. 2 games in 2 days had already made me feel truly down. I had 5 more in the next 5 days. I prayed things would get better than Blackpool.

BLACKPOOL 0
WATFORD   **2** (M.Williamson 54, Priskin 85)
Attendance 7,451

GAME 69
WOLVERHAMPTON WANDERERS v Cardiff City
The Championship
Sunday 22nd February 2009, 1pm, Molineux, Wolverhampton

I've always had a bit of a pre-ordained irritation towards Wolverhampton Wanderers, but this was accentuated when back in November I actually bought a ticket for Wolves v Barnsley. With my car in the garage I turned up at Milton Keynes train station to find out that because of the rain (heavy drizzle rather than monsoon) all trains had been cancelled. I had no way of getting to Wolverhampton in time for kick-off. And Wolves didn't refund my unused ticket. Bastards.

Other than this I didn't really know *why* I didn't like Wolves. I had no beef, or indeed pork, with any Wolves fans. Indeed the only Wolves fan I know, my brother's friend Fred, is in fact a very agreeable and pleasant human being. Hopefully today I could make a more informed and sensible opinion of the club.

Arriving in Wolverhampton at midday there was a lazy Sunday lunchtime sense of positivity around the place, with the orange-clad masses heading down the hill from the town centre to the modern looking fortress of Molineux. It looked fantastic in the sunshine.

I fancied popping into the club-shop quickly.

"Sorry moite, no food or drink allowed in the club shop," a burly Black Country doorman said, putting his hand to my sternum. I was eating a KitKat.

"What harm can my KitKat do?" I replied.

"Get chocolate on the shirts or something. Club policy moite, out you go," he said, pushing me away.

Except for this ridiculous jobsworth, everyone else I spoke to at Wolves was a thoroughly good egg; a bunch of funny, clean-cut, friendly folk. Especially the people that dealt with me being a bit of a fool concerning finding my seats...

I did something silly. I entered the wrong stand. I partly blame the turnstile operator for letting me in the wrong gate, but summing up the laid-back attitude of people from Wolverhampton he just didn't realise. I was clueless to my perilous situation as I approached row M seat 204 and politely told the gentleman that he was in my seat. "Don't think so pal! This is my seat! Season ticket," he said, flashing me his season ticket pass.

"Oh. But my ticket..." I protested to the man.

"Moite you've got it properly wrong! Haha!" he said, patting my back friendlily. They like personal contact these Wolves fans. "You're over therrrrre," he continued, pointing at the Steve Bull stand far away and directly opposite.

I thanked the man and apologised for trying to chuck him out of his beloved season seat. Approaching a steward with my dilemma he was equally as unhelpful.

"No free seats on this stand! It's packed today! Big promotion game against Cardiff. You're going to have to go out and try and re-enter the opposite stand," the little old steward informed me.

So I had to leave the arena and try and re-enter?? But what if they didn't let me in?! I would have to come back to Wolves for a match another day!!! Buy my third bloody Wolves ticket of the season!

No, this wouldn't do. I decided to go to the furthest entry point in this block to see if there were any free seats. There were absolutely loads. This whole area was practically empty. No free seats eh?

In terms of stadium design, Molineux is one of my favourites. It's a very smart ground that looks brand new. The attractive design has the stands set apart from the pitch with zig-zagging straight lines, looking like a pentagon.

"And it's Hi! Ho! Wolverhampton!" the fans were singing as the teams emerged in the beautiful late-winter sunshine.

Wolves were still topping the Championship, but 1 win in 9 matches was causing some concern. Early on in the match you could see the team's problem, with Ebanks-Blake and Keogh both missing stone-wall sitters in the first 10 minutes. I was delighted at the reaction of the Wolves fans to these missed chances though; instead of moaning the supporters were getting behind their team, applauding their efforts and encouraging them to do better. This actually worked in spurring the team on, because the terrific Ebanks-Blake put Wolves ahead with a header a minute later. Maybe it was time for a turnaround in fortune?

Cardiff were in good form though, and Chopra equalised for the Welshmen after a half-hour. The fans went insane, all sprinting over to the nearest home support and roundly mocking them in true Cardiff-fan fashion!

A terrific half of Championship action in my new seat later it was half-time, so I went for my pie. I sat back down in my fairly isolated area with the sun beaming on my face. Lunchtime bliss! My always satisfying chicken balti pie was going down a treat as I observed an odd half-time event; two large cars doing a full circuit of the pitch. How did they get in there?!

Cardiff went ahead early in the second half and Mick McCarthy was looking nervous in his tiny managerial dugout resembling a little plastic golf buggy. He made three subs in quick succession and Wolves soon found an equaliser. McCarthy, you tactical genius!

Well not quite. The goal was a tame cross heading straight towards the Cardiff's debutant keeper Dimitrios Konstantopoulos's (I challenge you to spell that correctly) hands, who dropped the unchallenged cross into his own net, sending the Wolves fans crazy. It was the ultimate head-in-the-sand moment.

2-2 was a fair final result for struggling Wolves. Football is a game as much in the mind as in the feet, and in the last 10 games these players have forgotten how to win.

Despite the comedy football and seating fiasco I had really enjoyed being at Molineux. Wolverhampton have a top class stadium for a top class club, with a terrific crowd supporting their team rather than moaning about them. Optimistic West-Midlanders? Now I've literally seen everything.

WOLVERHAMPTON WANDERERS 2 (EbanksBlake 11, Konstantopoulos OG 81)
CARDIFF CITY **2** (Chopra 31, Johnson 48)
Attendance 22,093

GAME 70
WYCOMBE WANDERERS v Rotherham United
League Two

Monday 23rd February 2009, 7.45pm, Adams Park, High Wycombe

I was nearly halfway through my mammoth 7 games in 7 days, and it was time to drop back down south, and drop back down to League Two. Wycombe v Rotherham wasn't going to watch itself now was it?

Being the only fixture on this Monday I thought it was (just about) worth heading all the way back south to watch it. My pal Harry is a Wycombe supporting native so I called on him before the game and dragged him to Adams Park.

"How's it going mate?" I greeted Harry, met with his famously firm handshake. "Last time I saw you you were..."

"Making copper wire?"

"Yeah! That's it. What you up to now?"

"Making copper wire." Harry's big round face dropped.

"Oh cool. How is it?"

"Exhilarating. How's watching football?" he asked with a slight sense of irritation in his voice.

"Getting a bit hard now, did Port Vale and Blackpool in the space of 24 hours, made me nearly want to kill myse..." I stopped myself before finishing that sentence, seeing the copper wire-plated envy in Harry's eyes about to burst.

The area approaching Adams Park is mainly a rather un-scenic industrial estate, but once you actually reach the ground it's quite attractive, with lots of surrounding trees and greenery.

We reached the gates and were greeted by a large friendly man.

"Hello folks. Hi there. Thanks for coming. Thanks for not being an armchair fan and actually turning up. Ta everyone. Hi there..." the man said, greeting every individual walking towards the stadium. A bit bitter about the reduced attendances on Monday night televised matches perhaps. Still, at least it was more polite than the song we heard at Elland Road "If you're watching on Setanta you're a c**t," being sang so loud that it was actually picked up on Setanta.

One of the first things you notice upon arriving at Adams Park is how much evidence of Wasps there is. The rugby club, not the insect. The club shop is half devoted to Wasps and half to Wycombe. It's weird to think that a London club play out here in the Home Counties sticks. Especially with a club featuring internationals like Sackey, Cipriani, Worsley and Vickery (see! I know some rugger players! Not just football eh?)[1] sharing a ground with League Two Wycombe.

The official club car park, full of the Mercedes and Bentleys you still find in League Two, is situated right next to the smallest stand.

"Surely all these flash cars are exposed to flying footballs going over the ground?" I laughed.

"Yeah, once a ball went over and from inside the stadium we heard a smash and a car alarm start! Was the highlight of the match if I remember rightly," replied Harry.

"Watching Wycombe that good is it?"

"Just you wait..." promised Harry with the world-weary sigh of a League Two regular.

On entering the ground I was struck by how huge the one massive stand was, dwarfing the other three. Harry claimed it was the biggest stand in League Two, but I suspect Valley Parade (or Meadow Lane too?) would have something to say about that.

My mouth was watering for my meat and potato *Peters Pie,* which unfortunately did absolutely no favours in satisfying my appetite. It wasn't a good one, and was the start of a pretty poor evening.

Munching our mediocre pies, we were laughing at the creepy Wycombe mascot roaming the sides of the pitch. He was in a costume of a creepy ginger man with seedy red lips being sucked in to look like he's sucking an ultra sour sweet. I don't know how else to describe him without resorting to the claim that he looks like a paedophile.

He put out his hand to shake mine and I returned the compliment, despite feeling a bit weird about touching him. He did the same to Harry, only to pull his hand away when Harry outstretched his and

---

[1] Not really, I had to look them up.

do a *nerr nerr ne nerr nerr* gesture with his hand on his nose. I've never seen such outrageous rudeness from a mascot before. Harry was devastated, mortified, humiliated.

"You got school-boyed. Merked. Are you OK?" I warmly asked my friend.

"Not really. That hurt."

"Why would he do such a thing?"

The trauma of the mascot encounter still smarting, we observed the players warming up. They looked pretty dire. It always amuses me when footballers even look crap in a warm up. One player was practising shots against the goalkeeper and blazed the ball over the bar.

"That's why you're on the bench! That's why you're on the bench!" sang the Wycombe fans at their own player in jest, but with an undercurrent of disappointing truth.

The wasteful sub couldn't have done much worse than the players on the pitch. Top-of-the-league Wycombe were out of form; their passing in the final third was often nervous and ineffective, and the fans were loudly criticising the team throughout the match. The quality was poor enough for plenty of balls to fly over the stand into the car park. I feared for those cars!

The game finished 0-0 without much incident or much cause for me not to drift to sleep. I looked up at the away stand opposite our terrace and saw an advert for 'dreams bed specialist zzzzzzzzz' which I thought was an unfortunate coincidence.

"Well that wasn't great was it?" moaned Harry.

"Not the best no, but you did warn me about watching Wycombe."

"I thought I told you it was like watching Brazil on a bumpy pitch? Never mind. I guess you must have seen loads of 0-0s anyway."

"Errr. No that's my second out of 70 actually. And the first in which I've taken someone else with me." I said apologetically.

Harry looked devastated. "Great. That's great. Back to the wire-making tomorrow on the back of a rare nil nil."

We passed the car park and saw a BMW with a football-shaped dent in its bonnet. "Well it could be worse I guess, at least I'm not that guy!" Harry laughed, pointing at the car.

WYCOMBE WANDERERS 0
ROTHERHAM UNITED   0
Attendance 3,739

GAME 71
OLDHAM ATHLETIC v Bristol Rovers
League One
Tuesday 24th February 2009, 7.45pm, Boundary Park, Oldham

I begrudgingly turned my car engine off. I didn't want the battery to go and leave me stranded in Oldham on a night as flipping cold as this. 6 layers and I was still shaking. I looked around the pub car park as it was slowly filling up with Oldham fans. 'Do not leave any valuables in your car, there have been thefts from this car park recently' stated a sign. My laptop was in the boot.

Anxiety was surrounding me. Back in October I had seen Oldham fans cause a near riot away at Stockport, resulting in bloody faced fans being led across the goalmouth as the players watched on.

The fans around the car park seemed like a good friendly bunch though, so I braved the arctic conditions and headed towards the small stadium around the corner. It was really dark in the thin road next to Boundary Park. I saw the club shop and hoped it would protect me from the chill. Oh yes! Bliss. And it smelt oddly like coconut!

Amongst the usual club shop items, novelty t-shirts featuring Boundary Park legends were apparently selling like hot cakes. I noticed one with Earl Barrett's face on it, and another with Gunnar Halle's Norwegian grin smiling back at me. How wonderful of a club like Oldham to celebrate heroic early-Premier League mediocre full backs like Barrett and Halle!

I texted Collo 'Do you want either a £10 Earl Barrett or Gunnar Halle t-shirt from the Oldham club shop in addition to that £5 Port Vale kit I got you last week?' Collo quickly replied saying he would edge towards the Earl Barrett one if push came to shove.

I didn't get one though, my wallet was becoming dangerously thin. Lots of football was taking its toll.

"Do you do any discounts? Concessions or anything?" I asked the lady on the turnstile.

"Only under 16s, which you most certainly are not," she said sternly, "we're not that rich up here you know!!"

Slightly terrified at her attitude and concerned that she had recognised me as an Oldham infiltrator so easily, I meekly asked for one £19 adult and entered the ground.

It is odd to think that Oldham were playing the likes of Man United and Arsenal in the 1990s considering that Boundary Park isn't exactly 'state-of-the-art'. I did quite like the ground though; the design of the famous 'Chaddy End' impressed me, and the old fashioned floodlights added some rustic charm.

Something Oldham do better than any club out of the 92 is the mascot. After the distain I had towards Wycombe's poor effort yesterday, Chaddy the Owl (two time winner of the 'mascot grand national') was a breath of fresh air. He's certainly one of the 'edgier' mascots in the league, getting in fights at Doncaster and Blackpool, being in trouble for mooning Cardiff fans and being accidentally flagged offside against Peterborough. I had seen Chaddy wipe his owly-arse with a Stockport County scarf earlier in the year, and today he was in just as good form winding up the Bristol Rovers fans.

Laughing at Chaddy in the warm-up were Oldham's lethal front pair; Lee Hughes and Dean Windass. On a night when Man Utd were playing in the Champions League it was not Rooney and Ronaldo on everyone's lips, but Hughes and Windass. They were winding up Chaddy by kicking balls at him. If I were a centre-back I would not want to be facing either of them; two big bulky bruiser centre-forwards, one of whom has spent several years in prison, the other has a forehead made of brick.

Oldham were in a fairly secure play-off position, but they looked dire for the first half-hour, the only real chance coming from a missed penalty by Hughes.

"Come on lads, it's a European night!" a fan bellowed at the Oldham players. "We're missing United for this shite!!!"

My teeth were literally chattering as the half-time whistle went, and to make it worse there wasn't any inside area to go and warm up in. I compensated and sat in the toilets for 10 minutes, complete with leaky ceiling and prehistoric urinals. This was a new low. At least my good ol' reliable *Pukka* warmed me up slightly.

Bristol Rovers looked the better team in the second half and ended up winning 2-0, but despite this disappointing home performance the Oldham fans were in fairly good spirit. No bloody-faces being led across goalmouths this time.

They were mostly funny and jolly, except for one bloke who was (to put it politely) a *massive twat*. He thought he was being funny shouting and swearing at his own fans, mostly families, for being too quiet.

A fan left 5 minutes before the end with the game stagnating at 0-2 and got an absolute tirade of abuse from this guy for leaving early. A steward told him to calm down and stop swearing. The fan tapped me on the shoulder.

"Hey who the fock does that focking steward think he is pal? Eh? He looks like Mr Bean! WHERE'S YOUR AUTHORITY YOU FOCKING NOBHEAD! I'm going to chin the bastard on the way out! Hahaha!" he laughed, poking me firmly in the shoulder.

"Yeah, good one mate," I said in the worst fake-Lancashire accent ever. I sounded like a Zulu. The final whistle went and I made a run for it to escape my horrible new friend.

It was a cold and shit night of football but I came out of the experience quite fond of Oldham Athletic. The ground had a lot of charm about it, but would benefit massively from a 4th stand (due to be rebuilt this year until the evil toothy monster called 'the credit crunch' came and crunched up these plans). And I feel ultra sorry for the poor cameramen perched up on the most rickety of temporary scaffolding. It was moving in the fierce wind, I was genuinely worried for their safety!

Fortunately they didn't die, nor did I, nor were there any bloody faces. Great success! One more down. And my laptop didn't even get nicked! Result.

OLDHAM ATHLETIC 0
BRISTOL ROVERS   2 (Duffy 48, Anthony 63)
Attendance 3,745

GAME 72
MACCLESFIELD TOWN v Port Vale
League Two
Wednesday 25th February 2009, 7.45pm, Moss Rose, Macclesfield

It was another time for two games in one day! Today would feature two mammoth encounters between struggling sides, battling relegation at all costs.

The first was Paul and Collo's 'Modern Languages FC' playing against the Christian Union in the Liverpool University inter-departmental league. The Christians got nailed. 2-1. And very ungracious in defeat they were too, swearing at the ref and causing scuffles all over the pitch! That's not very holy is it?

It was (fake) champagne time after this vital 2-1 win, all but ensuring survival for another season, but I had to cut the party short as a trip to Macclesfield was imminent.

"You up for it fellas?" I asked Paul and Collo, both looking grizzly in their unforgivably-tiny sports shorts.

"Moss Rose! I'd be a fool not to go!" Collo gleamed, swigging from his bottle.

"Don't think so mate, I'm going to continue celebrating here rather than watching some rubbish League Two," grumbled Paul in his floorboard-vibratingly low voice. Sky Sports News was on in the background. The story was about how Marlon King, who had just beaten up a woman in a club (or something like that), was being represented in court by the same lawyer who represented Michael Barrymore and Gary Glitter.

"Wow, Glitter and Barrymore. The only way's up for Marlon King's public reputation then!" laughed Paul.

"So just me and you then Collo?"

"Let's roll."

We set off in my car, with Collo opening the 2nd bottle of £3.99 'champagne' from ASDA for the journey.

"I've always like Macclesfield," I said to an increasingly tipsy Collo, "their name connotes everything a bit charmingly rubbish with the

lower-leagues. Before Accrington Stanley came back on the scene I always thought of Maccy as the most triumphantly low of the lot."
"Aye la," replied Collo, "I liked them since Paul Ince clawed back a 30-point deficit or whatever it was to keep 'em in the league. He should still be there really, wouldn't have humiliated himself at Blackburn!"
In the leafy suburbs of south Macclesfield we found the stadium, tiny and hidden amongst the residential streets.
There is a bold sign on the main stand of Moss Rose saying 'Real football for real fans at real prices'. Often when reading between the lines the term 'real football' can be substituted for 'rubbish football'. Reading in between the lines even further, the Maccy website describes Moss Rose as an 'intimate ground full of character', which of course could be fancy-talk for 'an unacceptably small ground with shite facilities'.
But that's just me being cynical and miserable, because Moss Rose actually *was* an intimate ground full of character; feeling very non-league, but in a good way.
  The first smack of charm Collo and I received to the chops was on the gates, the elderly gent making a tally chart of those who enter through his turnstile. I peeked at his A4 sheet and noticed the headline CONCESSIONS with 2 tallies underneath it, and ADULTS with a mighty 3 tallies.

One thing Macclesfield definitely didn't do well was the mascot. I had been on an interesting 3 day run, with Wycombe's weirdo and Oldham's heroic owl. But Macclesfield's was just *pathetic*. 'Roary the Lion' had severe problems with his head. He regularly had to lift his lion head up to breathe properly. The facade of a mascot is smashed when you realise it's a small fat bald bloke with asthma inside the powerful king of the jungle.
The ball boys around the crap mascot (or 'crapscot' as I think he should be referred) were showing some awesome skills.
"Look at that kid Collo! His touch is top notch."
"Careful, you sound like a paedo there mate. Wearing your glasses and watching lots of football alone in your big coat."
"Oh thanks. I'll watch out then..."

"At least you would know which lawyer to represent you! Just give Marlon King's lawyer a bell!" Thankfully the players had emerged so Collo shut himself up from his frenzy of paedophile jokes.

This was my 6th match in the last 6 days, and it became immediately clear that it would be the 5th awful one out of the 6 (thank the Lord for Wolves v Cardiff). The quality on show was non-existent, as was the home-crowd noise. At least Collo and I were in great spirits, finding almost everything around us funny.

The Vale fans on the other hand were in great voice. They were a pretty rough, sweary bunch, but I'd prefer that to the 'I'd rather be anywhere else than watching my own club' OAP misery-guts that we were surrounded by.

"We should be with the Vale fans la. It would give me a chance to wear my £5 Vale shirt!" Collo pointed out. Of course, I forgot I had bought him that at Vale Park last week!

"You had a chance to wear that yet?" I asked.

"Yeah, wore it to Mod Lang FC training at the weekend. Went down a treat with the lads. You should have seen them; all green with envy they were."

We were standing right by the dugouts, positioned in between the cool, calm and collected Macclesfield manager Keith Alexander and Port Vale's under-fire boss Dean Glover. I had witnessed some horrendous abuse directed at Deano last week at Vale.

"Look at him," I murmured to Collo, "he's a vision of repressed anger and distress isn't he?"

"Should we taunt him?" urged Collo.

"Better not. He might suddenly explode and do a Cantona kung-fu kick on us."

Glover was trying to shout instructions to his Vale players but none of them were listening. In fact, Glover's voice was getting huskier by the minute, and therefore ignored even further. Poor bloke.

Half-time came with some horrendous mid-90s techno Europop on the PA, which must have gone down a treat with the ancient Macclesfield crowd. With our lovely steak pies the second half began with the Port Vale fans unveiling a massive banner proclaiming 'GLOVER OUT, V2001 OUT, PVFC FOR SALE.'

The Vale protests were overshadowing a very poor game. Macclesfield had nothing going forward. I noticed Wayne Rooney's younger brother John was on the Macclesfield bench, maybe he would have livened things up a bit?

With the Vale fans screaming for Glover's head they looked a bit sheepish when they took the lead with five minutes to go. It was a massive error from the Macclesfield 'keeper, letting a tame shot slip through him into the net. Shaken from this late mistake, Maccy conceded again in injury time, rounding off a limp and lifeless performance.

Despite Vale deservedly winning their fans were persistent with their 'GLOVER OUT, GLOVER OUT' chants.

"Glover out? Glover *in* more like based on that spirited display!" said Collo.

"Poor bloke," I said, looking at a forlorn Dean Glover, "let's go talk to him..." I said with a rush of blood to the head, dragging Collo over to the winning manager.

"Well done today mate," I said to Dean Glover, "and don't listen to the Vale fans! From what I can tell you're doing a great job," I lied.

"Cheers lads. Try telling it to that lot though," said Glover with a strong undercurrent of sadness.

"Yeah you're, erm, great!"said Collo, clearly massively star-struck.

"Can we have an autograph?" I asked.

"You want *my* autograph?!" Glover said, taken aback by the request, "You got a pen and paper?"

Collo rummaged around in his bag. "Yeah I've got some notes from my German lecture earlier!"

So Dean Glover signed Collo's German homework and shook our hands with a firm, managerial handshake.

Back in the car we were still laughing about the incident.

"He loved getting asked for an autograph didn't he! Poor bloke," Collo laughed, opening his final beer, "Mr Glover Glover...a Glover hmmmm!" he sang to the tune of Shaggy's Mr Bombastic.

"Glove will tear us apart!" I hit back.

"Some Glovers do have 'em."

"Roy of the Glovers!"

"Rubbish!"

"Can you feel the Glove tonight?"
"Better...

So with a Glover-pun contest to entertain us, I drove home happy to have Macclesfield Town ticked off my list. Real football for real fans, played at an intimate stadium full of character. Just about.

MACCLESFIELD TOWN **0**
PORT VALE **2** (Ahmed 85, Dodds 90)
Attendance 2,267

GAME 73
HULL CITY v Sheffield United
FA Cup Fifth Round Replay
Thursday 26th February 2009, 7.45pm, KC Stadium, Kingston-Upon-Hull

I had nearly finished my 7 games in 7 days. Wow. I was feeling rather pleased with myself, but I still had the massive task of travelling many miles towards the city of dreams; Hull. Or more precisely drive from Liverpool to Manchester to Hull to Hertfordshire. Yikes.

I said a fond farewell to Collo and Paul and set off to Manchester to pick up Greg, who was coming home from uni for a half-term break. Via Hull! Only I hadn't told him yet.

"Cheers so much for coming to get me bro," said Greg gratefully.

"Errr yeah no problem!"

"So are we going straight home? Or do you fancy spending the day around Manchester?"

"Well neither actually....we're going to Hull."

"Hull?"

"Yeah, there's a rearranged FA Cup 5th Round replay against Sheffield United which I thought would be criminal to miss! It's *pretty much* on the way home too."

It wasn't even remotely on the way home, but fortunately Greg's geography of the UK was poor enough for me to get away with it.

"Oh and you owe me money for the ticket."

I struggled to get away with that.

Honestly though I couldn't have missed this. Hull, still in their honeymoon period of top-flight luxury, were selling out every home match. It would take a Thursday night FA Cup replay for me to even be able to get hold of a ticket, so this fixture was a welcome addition.

A couple of hours later we parked up and popped in a nearby pub, Parkers, for a drink.

"See who needs to be home eh G? This is what it's about." I said, cheersing his pint of bitter with mine. The atmospheric pub was awash with bright orange shirts, both on the punters and on the walls as memorabilia.

Hull had had a miraculous start to the season but the bubble had definitely burst, with Phil Brown (or 'sunbed Phil' as the Bolton fans call him) doing most of the bursting himself. He floated the idea around the media of the possibility of Hull reaching Europe, and after that and his infamous on-pitch half-time team talk at Man City the bubble was not so much burst as mauled by rabid rottweilers .

Hull still looked good to avoid the drop though, and certainly have a ground fit for a top-flight club. The KC Stadium (or Kingston Communications Stadium if I were to be doing the sponsors a favour) is a visually arresting bowl, and one of the more interesting of the new stadiums built in the last decade.

From the inside the design is quite odd, with vast grey blocks looking a bit like the Death Star from Star Wars. With the fluorescent blue gleams peeking from the sides of the ground it is very much a 21st Century design. Even the lights are futuristic, little lamps rather than floodlights that gave the game an indoor glow, and were absolutely blinding.

The stadium wasn't quite full, but the home support were in great form as the match kicked off. Hull took the lead in the 25th minute through one of the most bizarre goals I've ever seen. A cross came in towards the Sheffield penalty area and their defender Kyle Naughton powered a header towards his own goal, bouncing on the crossbar and over the line.

"One for the bloopers DVD! Nick Hancock's Football Nightmares volume 7 or something!" laughed Greg as we celebrated with the Hull fans.

The big screen directly above the goalmouth immediately showed a replay of the hilarious own goal.

This was a bad decision.

The replay showed that the ball, after hitting the crossbar, in fact did *not* fully cross the line. It wasn't even close! The Sheff Utd fans were absolutely furious, while the Hull fans were laughing and celebrating, starting chants of 'the referee's a tiger!'

It was a farcical situation. Only 30 seconds after a goal was given, the referee, the linesmen, the players, managers and 17,000 fans knew it shouldn't have been a goal. But nothing can be done about it! It's like video evidence being in place but not in a facility where the ref can actually change a decision!

Fortunately United equalised very quickly to even things up. The atmosphere was getting testy between both between the fans and the players. Wee Nicky Barmby slid in with a crunching, but fair tackle on United's hard-arse Chris Morgan.

"Barmby's having one hell of a game," I said to Greg.

"He sure is. We should start a chant, Nick Barmby's barmy army."

"Or... Nick Barmby's *barmby* army..."

"That's good! Might catch on."

"Nicky Barmby's barmby army!" I began singing.

"Please don't," my younger brother said, looking mortified.

Half-time came, and we queued up for our drinks and pies.

"Look at that lad," Greg whispered, pointing to a boy of about 9 or 10 drinking a beer.

"That must be his Dad's beer?" I said, slightly outraged, slightly impressed.

"Nah look, his Dad's got his own beer."

"Wow they start them young in Hull don't they!"

With unsatisfying chicken and mushroom pies in hand (they'd run out of all the good ones) we took our seats again. Not for the first time this season there was a marriage proposal on the big screen at half-time. The 'will you marry me' beaming up was greeted by the sadly predictable 'You don't know what you're doing!' chant. Oh dear. The big screen was becoming more trouble than it's worth today!

It was clear in the second half that Hull were the only team going to win this match, the evergreen Barmby providing the cross for the eventual winner from Halmosi. The match ended with furious reaction from the Sheffield camp, but Hull didn't mind. Regardless of any arguments about video technology Hull didn't care; they were in the FA Cup quarter-final!

"So how near are we to home?" Greg asked as we got in the car.

"Hour or so?"

"Errrm...not exactly. Triple that. And that's without traffic."

Greg looked at me with disdain.

"And would you mind driving G? I'm pretty sleepy." I asked. Greg very reluctantly got in the driver's seat. However much I push my luck, the older brother status will win through in the end. Plus I needed to put my feet up after 7 games in 7 days! Bliss.

HULL CITY   **2** (Naughton OG 25, Halmosi 56)
SHEFFIELD UNITED **1** (Sharp 32)
Attendance – 17,239

GAME 74
CHELSEA v Wigan Athletic
Premier League
Saturday 28th February 2009, 3pm, Stamford Bridge, West London

I was tired. Friday night had ceased to be the party climax to the week it once was. I was slumped on the sofa watching Jonathan Ross, staring at the fixtures list (me, not Jonathan). I didn't want to go to a game tomorrow. This week had been *long*. Hull had been good yesterday but it was a big old trip, and 7 games in 7 days had tested me.

Could I miss a Saturday match-day? I looked at Wossy's guests. David Attenborough, Clive Owen and U2. What would *they* do with this dilemma? Attenborough looked at me with his wise eyes, nodding at me to do the right thing. Bono shrugged at me, patronising the ridiculous thought of me missing a match, the self-righteous bastard. Bloody guilt-trip. I looked at the fixtures and decided it would have to be Hereford United. A 300-mile round trip. I was resigned to my fate. That was, until I got a phone call from my old chum Liam.

"Hello mate. Fancy coming to Chelsea tomorrow?"

The word "YES!!" came out of my mouth before he had even finished the sentence.

It was a nice afternoon; sunny enough for Liam to justify wearing sunglasses walking through London.

"Almost shorts weather isn't it?!" I laughed.

"I thought about wearing sun-cream," said Liam.

We met up with Liam's dad Mark, and uncle Paul at a great little pub around South Kensington, called the Anglesea Arms. With a wide selection of ales, a fireplace for the chilly and outside terrace for the warm, I would recommend the Anglesea Arms to anyone fancying a quieter pre-match Chelsea drink. *AND* it's posh enough for the sign to be for the 'loos' rather than 'toilets'.

Mark is a great big friendly cockney bear of a man, a season-ticket holder at Chelsea who very kindly had sorted me out today. I hadn't met Paul before but he seemed pretty interested in what I was doing, he himself being a seasoned lower-league veteran having been to 'about 60' of the 92! Liam and Mark looked on with bewilderment as Paul and I shared tales of Morecambe and Colchester.

"So what kind of review you giving Luton then?" Paul, (a Luton fan) asked.

"Errrmmm....Well I feel sorry for the fans mainly," I replied, sugar-coating what I had really written.

"It's a shit-hole though the Road isn't it!"

"Haha well, yes."

"But it's *our* shit-hole..." said Paul loyally, perhaps a sentence that was oddly the most poignant I had heard a football fan say this year.

"So what we think about today then lads?" said Mark, bringing yet another round of beers to the table.

"Terry to score first is always a good bet, and Chelsea to narrowly win," I Mystic-Megged, hoping we would see a bookies on the way for me to cement it.

"Yeah I reckon a good performance today, apparently Abramovich is here for the first time in about half a year," said Mark.

"Seeing how the crucial battle for 2nd place is shaping up?" teased Paul.

"Haha! Like you're seeing how the Conference is shaping up next year?" Mark laughed.

A few more beers on the terrace (pretending it was summer) later we set off to the ground, passing through the unfathomably wealthy streets, all very dignified surroundings for one of the world's richest football clubs. The Stamford Bridge area is just as grand nowadays, with the old Chelsea Village, club hotels and hospitality zones all integrated into the busy streets.

Despite not always possessing a great atmosphere, Stamford Bridge certainly has character about it. The seats are right next to the pitch; those by the corner flag can almost reach out and touch it.

Chelsea supporters are a diverse bunch, historically a mixture of the affluent Kensington-types and people from the more working-class Battersea area. They probably have the most varied support in London; the monocle-wearing butlers, the 'shine-ya-shoes-guv' cockney scamps, and everyone in between. The class boundary within Stamford Bridge is noticeable in the stands too, with Mark and Paul behind the goal in the more honest and atmospheric Shed End, and Liam and I in the magnificent glass-roofed West Stand with the toffy Knightsbridge-elite.

A noticeable lack of noise from my fellow fake-Chelsea fans didn't damper my day out however. A Premiership game was absolute joy. I was being spoiled by the likes of Lampard, Ballack, Drogba, Anelka and the rest on show. Aaaaahhhh. It was an odd time at Chelsea; Scolari had been sacked a few weeks earlier, and the old Dutch devil Guus Hiddink was taking charge of his first home match.

Wigan came out the better team, and had shots cleared off the line from both John Terry and Ashley Cole. Chelsea being Chelsea though, they came back strong from this early pressure and went ahead through a sublime left-footed volley from Terry.

"What a goallll!" cheered Liam. I wasn't so happy; I *knew* I should have put money on Terry to score first!

It was a really good game, with Wigan matching Chelsea in every department. The crowd, who had started the match in quite good voice, had began muttering to each other rather than singing. They were becoming increasingly restless towards certain players; Kalou and the lumbering Ballack in particular.

"It's exactly like this every time I come here," said Liam, "if it gets to about 60 or 70 minutes and we haven't put the game out of sight then the crowd get really impatient. Most the people here expect a thrashing against Wigan, and when it doesn't happen they get all anxious and irritated."

Michael Ballack thoughtlessly misplaced a pass.

"Pah! Although sometimes it's all justified." Liam groaned before standing up and bellowing some constructive criticism at Ballack; "WHY DON'T YOU CONCENTRATE BALLACK YOU LAZY GERMAN SHIT-HEAD!"

"Do you mind!" said a small lady.

"Less of that language here," a different bloke said, telling Liam off. Liam looked a bit shell-shocked and sat down, apologising timidly.

"Unlucky mate." I whispered to Liam. "This is my 74th game this season and the first time I've heard someone told off for swearing!"

"That's Chelsea," he grumbled.

"You made a good point as well. He *is* a lazy German shit-head."

"Thanks mate."

If Liam's mildly offensive language shocked the fans, they were further taken aback by Wigan's equaliser in the 82nd minute. It was a fully deserved goal from a decent Wigan side, whose man-of-the-match was unquestionably Titus Bramble; he had one of those occasional first-class displays at the back (before he inevitably makes a crucial error next week).

The masses were leaving Stamford Bridge as the game went into injury time.

"What's the point?" moaned Liam, "These people paid ridiculous money for their tickets and they leave now? Anything could happen in the next 4 minutes."

And indeed it did!

Frank Lampard, Chelsea's best player on the day (as he is on most days), scored a looping header in the 93rd minute, sending those who stayed at the Bridge wild. Tremendous scenes of jubilation from everyone in the stadium except for the 200 or so Wigan fans, and Guus Hiddink, who remained seated, looking as stern and composed as ever. The man is class.

A buzzing Liam and I met back up with Mark and Paul at the pub again, grins etched on both their faces.

"Great wasn't it?" said Mark.

"Even better news, Luton won 3-1 at Vale!" grinned Paul.

"This man had his i-phone out all match keeping up with the Luton score!" Mark laughed.

Brilliant that; you can be at a packed Stamford Bridge watching the former League-Champions and not be able to think of anything other than Port Vale v Luton, a largely irrelevant League Two clash.

It had been a top day out, and a really good match, and whilst I didn't feel much warmth towards Chelsea (as I knew I wouldn't) I certainly felt warmth towards the experience of the Premiership again. The beers flowed as England lost to Ireland in the rugger-bugger on the big screen TV, and I pondered how the day would have panned out if I had gone to Hereford. I will defend lower-league football to anyone that will listen, but sometimes you do just need a bit of the style, quality, money and glamour of the Premier League.

CHELSEA   **2** (Terry 25, Lampard 90)
WIGAN ATHLETIC **1** (Kapo 82)
Attendance 40,714

GAME 75
SHEFFIELD UNITED v Birmingham City
The Championship
Sunday 1st March 2009, 12.15pm, Bramall Lane, Sheffield

My head was hurting, my stomach was hurting, my soul was hurting, it was an ungodly hour in the morning and I had to leave for Sheffield. I was killing two birds with one stone, taking Liam back to uni in Yorkshire and catching the Blades v Birmingham; a top-of-the-Championship encounter that admittedly didn't seem very appealing at the time.

My head.

I had stayed with Liam at his parents' house in the little village of Kimpton; a Wicker-Man like community of maypole dancing and interbreeding. Liam looked rough, his normally well-coiffured hair resembling a haystack.

"Alright Tom."

"Meh."

"How do you feel?"

"Feel not that up for driving to Sheffield and back. Your Dad and uncle know how to drink don't they."

"They've got lengthy experience in the field."

A not entirely pain-free journey later we arrived in Sheffield in time for the lunchtime kick-off. I don't know if it was due to mine and Liam's collective drunk lethargy or not, but the Sheffield United vibe was brilliantly relaxed. It was a sunny lunchtime, a hint of Spring in the South-Yorkshire air, and the crowd were mainly groups of families having just woken up. It reminded me a bit of the equally pleasant lunchtime feel of Wolves exactly a week ago. I loved it!

Now here's the problem with Sheffield United; they are obviously a great historical club with a tremendous fan base and consistent top two-tier pedigree, but the club have won *nothing* since 1925. A long old haul for those poor United fans, of which 25,000 were here for the televised lunchtime Sunday kickoff.

"Imagine coming for over 80 years without winning anything." I said as a very old man trotted passed us. What if I go the next 60 years with Bolton still having won nothing?! At least we have the 1989 Sherpa Vans trophy to fall back on.

Outside the club shop there was a plaque with an inspirational quote on it. Could it be Gandhi? No. Mandela? No. Churchill? No. It was Brian Deane, with the nugget 'Arriving at Bramall Lane felt like coming home. It was good to be back.'

Located a stone's throw from the city centre, Bramall Lane is believed to be the oldest ground in the world still to be hosting professional football, and today it manages to maintain this traditional sense of history alongside some brilliant aesthetic modernisation. There are state-of-the art new club hotels at the front of the stadium but grassy mounds, rickety scaffolding and wonky construction on the other side. It's a wonderful mixture of styles.

From the inside though, Bramall Lane is all very modern. The sharp red seats were glimmering from the sunlight and there was a brilliant chilled-out atmosphere. The players came out as the fans began to sing their famous 'Greasy Chip Butty' song. As far as football songs go it's an original one, the lyrics far more complex than one might expect:

You fill up my senses!
Like a gallon of Magnet!
Like a packet of Woodbines!
Like a good pinch of snuff!
Like a night out in Sheffield!
Like a greasy chip butty!
Like Sheffield United!
Come thrill me again!
Na Na Na Naaaaa oooo!

It set up the game perfectly.

"This is great!" Liam smiled, pulling out his sunglasses and basking in the fresh Spring rays. "None of the stress of Chelsea, but the West

London sun has come to Yorkshire!" All was good as we tucked into our very welcome (almost) hangover-curing steak pies.

United went in at half-time a deserved goal up, but struggled to find a second as the game went on.

"They'll regret it, missing all these chances," I wisely said to Liam. "Birmingham are fluky bastards, they'll snatch an undeserved equaliser." I thought back to seeing the other Sheffield team have their win cruelly snatched away by Birmingham a few weeks ago.

Indeed my prediction came true as Birmingham equalised with 15 minutes to go, another own goal from Sheff Utd (after seeing the hilarious and cruel 'own goal that shouldn't have been' against Hull a mere 3 days ago!')

"Bloody hell, look at the managers," laughed Liam as Blackwell and McLeish were both furiously gesticulating with their arms. You could see how much it meant to them, a world away from cool calm collected Guus yesterday.

United finally got their deserved winner when Jamie Ward (a new signing who I saw score a hat-trick for Chesterfield in game 25! called his potential...) won a fortuitous penalty, slotted home by Cotterill. The fans gave the players a standing ovation as they walked off, and Liam and I obliged.

Everything about Sheffield United was classy; the fans (loud and passionate yet laid-back and friendly), the smart stadium, and indeed the performance of the players.

My only criticism would be the heavy-handed stewards. When Birmingham scored the stewards were too aggressive with some of the Blues fans, leading a guy out of the stadium for over-celebrating, the meat-head steward twisting the poor Brummie's arms behind his back so he was wincing with pain, his screaming girlfriend in tears running after him being violently led out.

We nipped to a city centre pub to watch the Carling Cup final. "A thoroughly enjoyable two days of football old boy," Liam toasted, his beer smelling much less appealing than my lemonade.

"Indeed," I cheersed back, "hopefully Spurs can lose this final to round it off nicely."

"Why do you want Spurs to lose?"

"I saw both United and Spurs's semi-finals didn't I! And Spurs beating Burnley was one of the most heartbreaking things I've seen. Poor Burnley."

As the goalless final reached extra time it had become clear that pretty much no one was watching the big screens. Instead the whole pub was transfixed on what was happening on the bit of green outside.

Bang in the city centre, in broad daylight, there were 2 sets of tramps couples *having sex.*

I'm certain that all 4, the two dreadlocked women in particular, were having an acid trip because they had no idea what was going on. It was revolting, yet you couldn't peel your eyes from it. Like a car crash. It rendered the 30 minutes of extra time unwatchable.

After the homeless copulating, one of the gentlemen approached the pub and (please stop reading if you are eating anything) pulled down his trousers, preparing himself for a, ahem, *number two.*

It was at this point he got stopped by some policemen. They didn't mind the shagging I guess, it was just the mucking of the streets they had a problems with.

Anyway, it was an intriguing first ever visit to Sheffield city centre. A good first impression I'm sure you'll agree. Not quite as classy as Bramall Lane and indeed everything associated with Sheffield United; a truly first rate football club.

SHEFFIELD UNITED   **2** (Webber 44, Cotterill pen 83)
BIRMINGHAM   **1** (Morgan OG 74)
Attendance 24,232

GAME 76
STOKE CITY v Bolton Wanderers
Premier League
Wednesday 4ᵗʰ March 2009, 7.45pm, Britannia Stadium, Stoke-On-Trent

Turn into Stanley Matthews Way, pass George Eastham Avenue on your right reach Gordon Banks Drive and you're parked.

Why it must be Stoke City![1]

A cold night didn't deter me from making the long trip to the Britannia Stadium to see Stoke play my much-loved but currently rubbish Bolton.

It had been a good season for Stoke City, back in the top flight for the first time in 24 years and presently lurking 18ᵗʰ, but a victory away from 14ᵗʰ, reflecting the topsy-turvy nature of this Premier League campaign. Despite no away wins this season, Stoke's home form had been very impressive. I had a feeling it wouldn't be a good day at the office for Bolton as I parked up in Gordon Banks Drive and saw the Britannia Stadium a few hundred yards away.

The Britannia Stadium is pretty standard new out-of-town ground; too far from any community to feel special. The Britannia is especially exposed however; taking its place on top of a windy hill with nothing nearby whatsoever for the early-bird fan to appreciate other than to admire the streets named after legendary players.

It is also, for a new stadium, rather *ugly* and a bit underwhelming. It is very square, four individual stands with very exposed corners. I mean, the Britannia opened the same year as the Reebok, but aesthetically they're on different levels (I'm biased, true – but it's a fair point. Perhaps the Britannia has a better atmosphere though....). Even a lovely statue memorial area to Stanley Matthews is plonked in the middle of a car park rather than outside the ground, which I struggled to comprehend.

---

[1] There will be a 'Rory Delap Rise' next if his long throws keep Stoke in the Premiership...

On entering the stadium early the main thing I noticed was how the open sides of the ground left the interior extremely vulnerable to wind. In other words – it was bloody windy. It was also hard to get away from what was occurring on the big screen; an extreme close-up of Rory Delap's face (not exactly eye-candy) making a plea about child abuse, reading an autocue without an awful lot of natural flair.

As the match started I regret to say that it was clear from the off that only one team were going to win this match, and fair play to Stoke and Tony Pulis for coming out so strong and positively.

Less than 3 months ago I saw James Beattie playing for Sheffield Utd against Forest, and looking like a fat imitation of his former self. Now at Stoke, Beattie looks trim, and leads the frontline with aplomb, the Bolton centre backs couldn't deal with him as he ran through them and slotted home in the 14th minute, his 5th goal in 7 games for Stoke.

Something weird was happening now, it can't be can it? Yes it was! It was snowing!!! I know the weather's been weird this year, and yes it is bollock-freezing, but *snow?!* There had been a sudden drop in temperature, and of course that's not what you want at the Britannia Stadium, when sitting right in a corner. The most famously windy ground of the 92 was now blowing windy snow in my face, which slightly hampered my enjoyment of proceedings.

It didn't bother Tony Pulis though, who was kicking every ball from the sidelines, wearing his trademark cap and looking a thoroughly more inspirational touchline figure than Mr Megson. Bolton fans were singing Owen Coyle chants following rumours he was being lined up for the job this summer. Stoke fans meanwhile were oddly quiet.

I'd heard a lot about the Britannia being a cauldron of noise, but I saw little evidence of this. The first 5 minutes the fans were on storming form, the atmosphere dropping a bit only to explode again when Beattie scored. As the dull second half meandered, the crowd were very quiet. I could hear myself cough a bit too loudly. I had to chew my pie quietly as to not upset the hairy Stoke fan next to me (a Wrights balti pie, predictably too crusty and crumbly at the bottom of the pastry producing an almost shortbread-ish texture AS USUAL!)

Stoke finally scored the second goal they deserved, through their main man Ricardo Fuller. Fuller was just returning from a suspension after slapping his captain Andy Griffin and smashed in from 12 yards after yet more poor Bolton defending.

The supposedly infamous Stoke fans, and 'cauldron' of the Briannia Stadium, I must admit, disappointed me a wee bit, although maybe Bolton on a Wednesday night wasn't the most enthralling of matches. Don't get me wrong, the atmosphere was *good,* but not exactly buzzing. The thing about Stoke fans is that they don't maintain the noise for the whole match; when they are loud they are very very loud, but when they are quiet they are, erm, quiet.

Where was my car again? Oh yes on Gordon Banks Drive. Not Rory Delap Rise. Actually his throw-ins weren't very effective today maybe he won't get that road named after him after all. A lengthy scrape of snow off my windscreen later I was in the long queue to escape this isolated square of Stoke-On-Trent, a tad underwhelmed by the whole experience despite a great Stoke performance, (and not through my bitterness at Bolton losing, honestly.)

STOKE CITY   **2** (Beattie 14, Fuller 73)
BOLTON WANDERERS 0
Attendance 26,319

GAME 77
BRADFORD CITY v Aldershot Town
League Two
Saturday 7ᵗʰ March 2009, 3pm, Valley Parade, Bradford

I was in good spirits driving through the labyrinth of Bradford's one-way system with my brother Ali, Valley Parade sitting like a fortress above the city centre, the huge main stand dominating the skyline.

"Are my eyes playing tricks on me," I said, "or is that stand almost vertical?"

"No, it is a bit vertical," Ali reassured me, looking up at the unmissable stadium.

Bradford City are a club with a turbulent recent history; from their Premier League exploits at the turn of the Millennium to two recent administrations and subsequent relegations. The ups and downs of Bradford however are all firmly in perspective with the horrible tragedy of the 1985 fire.

Bradford had won Division 3 and paraded the trophy around the pitch before their match with Lincoln. As half-time approached, the main stand began going up in flames, thought to be caused by a cigarette butt alighting flammable rubbish collected under the wooden terraces. Just imagine that now. With no fire extinguishers, and the terraces closed for exit, 56 people perished in a tragedy that was at the time (before Hillsborough) unparalleled.

The stadium had intensive building work over the next few years, and as a result is as marvellous, confusing, but uniquely charismatic a ground as you will find in the entire Football League.

Everything about Valley Parade is from another planet. It is situated on a former quarry site and built on a very steep hill, defying the laws of physics in the process. The structure is mind-boggling; from the outside the ground seems to actually climb down the hill. There are bits hanging over old brown-bricked Yorkshire walls and residential streets, with the stadium being supported by a giant maroon spider-like structure holding it together.

Dodging the advances of some very friendly ticket touts, (they wer
EVERYWHERE! More here than at United or Chelsea!) Ali and
bought our tickets and were directed to the other end of th
stadium. To reach this, we had to leave the stadium area, go dow
a residential road, dodge some kids playing on bikes, climb down
wall, run down a grassy mount, and turn back on ourselves. It wa
a wonderful confusing mishmash maze of a ground.

Confusing enough for us to accidently reach the turnstiles for th
away end.

"You away fans then lads?" the bulky Yorkshireman asked.

"Erm, no, we're neutral!" I replied shiftily, rather than explain th
concept of 92 Pies to him.

"Neutral??? Not many neutrals at Bradford v Aldershot usually
Hmmm. Can I check your bags please?"

"Actually, we'll go in the home end! Thanks anyway."

Ali and I walked back to try and find a home turnstile, obvious
aware that by claiming to be neutrals, and leaving before a successf
bag-search we were portraying ourselves as pretty dodgy.

Finally, both panting from going up, down, up and back down th
hill, we managed to get in just in time for kick-off. If Valley Parad
is odd from the outside, the trend continues from the inside. Th
main stand does indeed look vertical, and the other 3 stands are
wonderful mix of shapes and sizes, including a tiny space of concret
terracing that only a few workmen were standing on.

As the match had started we were thankful we hadn't farted aroun
with the bulky steward for any longer, because as soon as we too
our seats Bradford took the lead, and soon went 2 up through
smashing Dean Furman volley.

"This is great!" said Ali, begrudgingly coming with me to get a fre
lift down south, (free except for the £20 Bradford ticket price).

I looked at my brother and turned up my nose. He smelt of egg.

"Why do you smell of egg?"

"It's these," he said, producing a packet of Walkers 'Builder
Breakfast' crisps from his pocket and continuing to munch them
"They're pretty much just egg flavoured. Revolting."

"Not revolting enough to stop eating though?"

"Not quite."

It was an easy match for Bradford and the atmosphere was lovely, a real family feel, with tons of kids wearing Bradford scarves making them look like young Hogwarts students cheering their team on.

Despite being a huge ground for the 4th tier, it actually felt rather full, and the attendance of over 12,000 was remarkable for League Two.

My stomach was growling as half-time arrived.

"How about the 'Fans Feast' deal Ali? Two bottles of Carlsberg and 2 meat and potato pies for £10?"

Ali looked unimpressed. "They use the word 'feast' a bit generously don't they? No thanks, the pies look horrible. Besides, I'm full from my eggy crisps."

Eating my horrible meat pie at half-time I was watching a group of young Asian kids playing with the chicken mascot. In fact, for the first time on this long journey of endless football grounds I noticed that a city with a large Asian population actually has a fair amount of Asians attending the football team.

Clubs like Leicester, Luton and Leyton Orient (something about the letter L?) are positioned in areas with a strong Asian community, yet the crowds don't culturally represent the area. It is a trend that I had noticed with most multi-cultural areas in the country; British-Asians often don't seem to attend football matches. The number of professional British-Asian footballers is shockingly disproportionate too, with Bradford's Zesh Reshman being one of very few.

Reshman went over to a group of kids at half-time to applaud their Pakistan flag; receiving a hero-reception. There have obviously been massive problems with racial segregation in Bradford, with the 2001 riots taking place a stone's through (pardon the choice of words) from Valley Parade. It seems the city is making positive strides against this though, and a group of happy singing Asian youngsters at the footy can only be a good thing.

Whilst I was deep in thought over complex racial-debates, the players re-emerged out of a house-like brick dugout to the unusually morbid musical choice of Nirvana's 'Come As You Are'.

Just when I thought things couldn't get much weirder, a fat man in a bowler hat stepped out from the crowd onto the pitch behind the goal, and began initiating chants with the crowd.

"How is this allowed?! He's wearing the same shirt as the players, surely that's distracting!" I laughed to Ali, as the police and stewards ignored him.

"It's the City Gent!" said the bloke sitting next to me.

"The City Gent?!" I enquired, "Sorry for being naive, we're, erm, neutral!"

"Haha, no problem! Well the city gent is like a mascot for adults. He eats pies, drinks pints, and is like a representation of a typical Bradford fan. It's always this same bloke, he's based on a cartoon character that was in fanzines in the 1960s."

"Wow. Thanks mate." I said, pleased to be sitting next to the fountain of Bradford City knowledge.

Bradford walked the second half like a training match, albeit a very entertaining training match. After going 3-0 up the crowd were soaking in the (relative) glory, and the second half was predominately spent doing Mexican waves! That's right, Mexican waves. In Bradford.

Bradford soon scored their 4th and 5th, with Aldershot's defending quite simply the worst I've seen this year. I had now seen them lose 4 times. Poor Aldershot boys.

Bradford had won 5-0 though, and they thoroughly deserved it. They need promotion badly, and I really hope they get it. Whilst still financially unstable, the club have a foundation to grow with a great coaching staff of Football League legends; the likes of David Wetherall, Nigel Martyn, and of course Stuart McCall, a true Bradford City hero who knows what the club is all about having played on the fateful day in 1985 where the fire broke out.

I loved Valley Parade and Bradford. It was chaotic, unconventional and a bit weird; but these are all things that should be applauded, and make up a tremendous match-day experience.

BRADFORD CITY   **5** (Thorne 2, 54, Furman 15, Conlon 88 Day OG 90)
ALDERSHOT TOWN 0
Attendance 12,465

GAME 78
EXETER CITY v Bradford City
League Two
Saturday 14th March 2009, 3.00pm, St James Park, Exeter

The final stretch had officially begun. A weekend away in Exeter and Bristol would bring me to 79. Cor. Devon was the first port of call for myself and Annabel, a long overdue weekend away together that *coincidently* linked in with two football matches.

After a long old drive to Exeter, and a night out in the lovely town centre, a sunny Saturday of football arrived! Annabel and I found a pub to watch the Man Utd v Liverpool game (4-1 to Liverpool! Maybe the title race isn't all over yet....) which was packed with both Bradford and Exeter supporters, enjoying some good friendly banter[1].

A policeman came into the pub, with the Bradford fans blaring out a 'Who are ya! Who are ya!' chant. The policeman looked at the fans sternly but then began to grin.

"Don't you mean 'You fat bastard! You fat bastard'?!" he laughed, getting his chubby belly out and wobbling it around to the delight of the Bradford faithful.

From Utd v Liverpool to an equally important, if slightly less glamorous game in Exeter v Bradford. The teams were poised beautifully in 7th and 8th place in League Two, teetering on the edge of the play-off places, and a win today would do wonders for either side's League One credentials. There was a man selling homemade carrot cake outside the ground. Get that at Old Trafford? I thought not.

"This is so cute!" said Annabel, devouring her recently-purchased carrot cake. St James Park is a splendidly amateurish little ground, perfect for a friendly club like Exeter City. Surrounded by plenty of pretty pubs and terraced houses and situated on top of a grassy

---

[1] Including a wacky Bradford fan dressed up..... AS A BANANA!!!!! Those Yorkshire lunatics eh?!

muddy mound above a minor train line, the stadium looks rickety and run-down, but somehow in a beautiful way. St James Park was built on a rural site for fattening pigs at the turn of the 20th Century. In 1904 the ground had a lease stipulating 'no menageries, shows, circuses or steam roundabouts' allowed on the premises, which I assume is still relevant today.

As you enter St James Park you go through tiny red turnstiles manned by a wispy white-haired OAP (referring to a handwritten price-list bluetacked to the wall) you can scarcely believe you're entering a professional football arena.

Going up some jagged wooden stairs, we reached the open arena, the sun beaming down on the happy Devonites. Sitting on the front row, delicious steak pie in hand, close enough to smell the grass, there was a glorious atmosphere at Exeter. There was a big net at one corner of the ground, presumably to stop stray balls from flying onto the train tracks. It didn't really work though; 4 balls went over in the first 20 minutes.

"How many balls do you think they actually *bring* to a match? What if they run out?" asked Annabel, a question to which I had no answer.

"Oooo-arrr! We are Exe-tarrr!" sang the fans in their best West Country accents as the teams kicked off to a good crowd of well over 5,000.

Exeter took the lead through a deflected long-cross from the talented winger Dean Moxey, a complete fluke that Bradford boss McCall called the 'weirdest goal he has ever seen'. The match was a good solid, (albeit League Two-standard) battle for the most part. The atmosphere was a PG-rated family feel-good romp. Although we *were* sitting in the family end I suppose. No swearing was audible, except for one incredibly hairy bloke standing up and bellowing "Yorkshire?! It's full of cow shit that is!" at the Bradford fans, much to the blistering amusement of everyone else. The teenagers behind us were boasting to each other about how many detentions they had received this term, and the man sitting next to Annabel had a big *Domino's Pizza* that he was sharing with his kids. "How on earth did he smuggle a *Domino's Pizza* in here?!" I said, slightly befuddled by the situation, "I got an apple confiscated from me at Sheffield Wednesday!"

Half-time came, and I ventured back-stage to find the toilet. The whole back-area at Exeter is like a rundown dungeon, with steel walls, rogue pipes and uneven cold concrete floors. The toilets were awful, but not in a disgusting way, although they are small enough so that you are almost rubbing up against the man peeing next to you, (which is always a tad awkward).

Escaping from this bit we found a little door, leading to a small carpeted corridor and what looked like someone's front room, but was actually just an extra part of the ground selling food and drink. We ordered two hot chocolates, complete with flakes and a mountain of whipped cream for only £2.40, which in football ground terms is a Bobby Dazzler of a bargain.[1]

"This is the busiest I've ever seen it in here!" a very old man said to the lady serving the pies.

"Oh yes it is! I'm afraid we're out of your usual Harry. We've got a chicken tikka slice left if you'd like one though..."

"Chicken tikka?! No thanks. Spicy food doesn't agree with my bowels," he said, adjusting his hearing aid. A couple of very serious St John's ambulance workers came squeezing through the busy room, looking worried. Oh dear, perhaps someone had fainted at the thought of a £1.20 hot chocolate! Or a brawl had broken out over the last tikka slice? It turned out that they were seeing to a crying boy with a tiny graze on his elbow. Not a particularly *edgy* club Exeter City.

Sinking our creamy flakey hot chocolates far too quickly (and burning my tongue in the process) on the way back to our seats we found a new food stall. An exciting food stall.

Unbelievably, flabbergastedly, outstandingly, there was a *Dominos Pizza* stall IN THE GROUND. This was big news. Now I'm not a particularly big *Dominos Pizza* fan by any means, but at game number 78 this was the first proper chain food outlet I have ever seen at a football ground. What's next? McDonalds at Aldershot? KFC at Bury?

"Well it explains how that guy had 'smuggled' the pizza in doesn't it," said Annabel.

---

[1] I'm not related to David Dickinson. Honestly.

"Yep! Mystery solved." I lingered my gaze at the pizza seller for a moment. "You want a bit?"

"Tom, you've just had an indulgent hot chocolate, a pie, and way more than your allotted 'bite' of a carrot cake. You really want a Dominos Pizza too?"

We only got a small one. Honestly, the *novelty!*

Chomping on pizza I didn't really want, the second half was underway and with Exeter's one goal lead it was a tense affair. Both teams missed good opportunities, in particular Exeter's Marcus Stewart (that's right...THE former Ipswich legend and 2nd top scorer in the Premier League 2000/2001 Marcus Stewart!).

I quite like watching football on the front row; you're so near the players and the officials it becomes personal.

"Tell the linesman he's got a nice pert arse." I encouraged Annabel.

"No! He doesn't anyway."

"Tell Arnison he's rubbish!" I said, looking at the small Bradford right-back within ear-shot.

Annabel looked nervous by the prospect.

"You're rubbish Arnison!" she whispered excitedly, before going bright red and slumping down in her seat.

The match finished with a narrow Exeter victory, and deservedly so. Exeter are a very small club, but one who spent 83 consecutive years in the Football League before their relegation 6 seasons ago. Now deservedly back in the League they are showing tremendous ambition in challenging for the Play-Offs.

There may be no pig-fattening, menageries or circuses here anymore, but Exeter City's St James Park is about as fun a day out as I've had during my 92 Pies, a bite of a carrot cake, one amazing hot chocolate and a Dominos Pizza. Actually, maybe there is some pig-fattening still going on...

EXETER CITY   1 (Moxey 20)
BRADFORD CITY 0
Attendance 5,253

GAME 79
BRISTOL CITY v Cardiff City
The Championship
Sunday 15th March 2009, 1.15pm, Ashton Gate, Bristol

The sunny Saturday in Exeter turned into an even sunnier Sunday in Bristol. I have decided that football is a game that should be watched on a sunny afternoon. If I was at Bristol City v Cardiff on a wet evening I doubt I would have enjoyed it as much as I did at 1.15pm on a beautiful Sunday lunchtime.

The day was shaped by the optimism and good feeling around Ashton Gate, which I think was fuelled by the weather. Next to the stadium there is a massive park, which despite being circled by a busy duel carriageway was gorgeous in the sunshine. I was delighted with the old style dangerous playground too; climbing-frames that a kid could genuinely break their neck on, the way they *should* be. "All football grounds should be next to a park like this!" said Annabel as we lay on the grass, Strawberry Splits in hand.

There were hundreds of kids in Bristol City shirts kicking balls around, the backdrop of Ashton Gate on one side, and Clifton Suspension Bridge on the other. It was a postcard-perfect scene for football in Bristol.

As kick-off approached we left the park and headed to the ground, where the atmosphere had changed a bit, but was still terrific. Instead of kids playing football and eating ice-creams there were men drinking cans of lager and (of course) cider, eagerly awaiting the big game as the police drove past and laughed along with them. The police can go some way to determining the atmosphere around a football stadium, and bizarrely by letting people drink on the streets there was a much more relaxed feel to the early afternoon. If I had dared to open a tinny outside Chelsea I think I would have been arrested by anti-terrorism police and banned from all future football matches.

Today was a play-off chasing match between Bristol City and rivals Cardiff. Both managers had stated before the game that the game was a MUST win. So the draw was inevitable of course.

"Hey Darren!" we saw a friendly skinhead yell at his friend, "Oi'll meet you boi the pissers mate."

Nothing can ever sound threatening in a thick West Country accent. Throughout the match, whenever a Bristolian shouted some abuse at a player or the ref it just sounds funny and playful, however brutal "I'll fucking kill you ref you fucking twat" looks in print. A young man in front of us was a particular classic case, swearing with every other word but maintaining a sense of unintentional ironic comedy.

"Oi told you moi hair-gel would melt Dave..." he said to his mate, touching his sloppy spiky hair as the sun melted it.

The pre-match vibe was buzzing. Scrumpy the Robin was exciting the crowd, the banner 'Bristol City: We Always Believe' was being presented, and the fans were ultra-excitable. Also, the PA music was of unparalleled excellence. 'We are the cider drinkers' followed by 'One for the Bristol City' by the Wurzels (cutting edge West Country pop) greeted the teams out, as fireworks exploded into the already bright-enough sky.

The Bristol City fans were relentless with their noise from the off, particularly the 'bounce around' chant, where the different stands take it in turns to stand up and bounce around.

A lot of friendly(ish) anti-Welsh banter was predictably going on, probably more than usual what with Bristol spitting distance away from the Welsh border. The common 'England England England' 'Sheep Shaggers' and 'Always shit on the Welsh side of the bridge' chants were out, as well as the 'England bounce around' causing the entire home support to jump around as the Cardiff fans sat firmly on their seats.

I was chatting to the bloke next to me, using my football bluff to perfection by pretending I knew anything about the Bristol City players.

A defender with 'McCombe' on his shirt produced a great last ditch tackle.

"He's great on his day McCombe isn't he?" I said to my friend, despite never having heard of him. The term 'he's great on his day' can apply to pretty much every player ever, from Pele to Titus Bramble.

"Yeah he sure is."

Master of the football bluff.

Cardiff had come closest so far, with the Football League's sternest player Stern John (he's *so* stern) clearing a shot off the line, but Bristol City finally got the goal they deserved; a cracker by Nicky Maynard, causing the crowd to absolutely erupt.

"Wahey!" I cheered, hugging Annabel, with my new mate the other side patting my back.

"What a strike!" he said, "That's some of his transfer fee paid back right there! How much did we pay for him was it?"

Oh no, a solid question..

"Phhhhh! Enough to see a couple more goals like that!" I replied, covering all angles (unless he joined on a free transfer).

The crowd were on such sprightly form. "Johnson! Bounce around! Johnson Johnson bounce around!" they sang at manager Gary Johnson, who brilliantly responded with a little Dad-dance bounce from the sidelines. Even the sloppy-gelled haired youth in front of us was getting a friendly laugh for shouting "Oi Taylor! Taylor! I were screwing your missus last night I was!" at Cardiff 'keeper Stuart Taylor.

The afternoon ended on a slightly sour note though as Cardiff undeservedly equalised with 2 minutes to go, probably hammering the final nail in Bristol City's promotion aspirations. "Cardiff! Bounce around! Cardiff Cardiff bounce around!" sang the jubilant Cardiff fans, rubbing it in to the home support.

Equaliser or no equaliser it had been an amazing day, and indeed an amazing weekend. One aspect of the weekend that was particularly brilliant was that Annabel, for the first time ever, seemed to be really enjoying being at the football. Wow. If 92 Pies had taught me anything it was that a trip to watch Exeter and Bristol City can turn a girl onto football as much as the bigger teams can. Tremendous.

BRISTOL CITY 1 (Maynard 71)
CARDIFF CITY 1 (McCormack 88)
Attendance 17,487

GAME 80
SWINDON TOWN v Southend United
League One
Tuesday 17th March 2009, 7.45pm, County Ground, Swindon

Sacrificing a St Patricks Day night out I set off to Swindon, trying to remain positive about what lay ahead. I had limited energy for this one. Negotiating the quite impossible 'Swindon Magic Roundabout' I narrowly avoided death, parked up and prepared myself for some mediocre League One football.

The County Ground is situated in a nice leafy residential area, with tall trees looking over the stadium and the cricket and athletics grounds nearby. The County Ground itself though is a pretty bland stadium, nothing really noteworthy other than the old rusty pylon-like floodlights that look like they were built in the 19th century.

Shire steak pie in hand (honestly, I've had far too many Shire steak pies) I took my allocated seat, bang right behind a thick pillar, but realised the stand was unlikely to fill up so moved so I could at least see both goals. As far as stadium announcers go, Swindon must have the most discouragingly honest in the League. 5 minutes 'til kick-off and the ground wasn't showing any signs of filling up.

"Oooooh, it looks a bit thin in here, but let's make some noise hey County Ground!" the announcer said, trying to rouse some (any) form of enthusiasm. "Let's hear you Don Rogers Stand!!!!!" There was complete silence.

"Wow that was quiet," he said dejectedly.

The match kicked off and you could tell straight away there would be goals. In the first 10 minutes there were numerous chances for both teams; Southend in particular defending like a pub team. Whilst the action was surprisingly interesting I couldn't take my eyes off a separate incident going on.

A teenage person of indistinguishable gender (I was certain it was a girl at first but I changed my mind halfway through) had somehow got their legs stuck in their chair during the first couple of minutes.

Their back was to the football so they were facing me, legs merging with the old chair seat, and they were in *pain*. They were screaming and crying trying to get their legs out, and once the stewards and St John's ambulance folk came there were about 8 or 9 trying to get him/her out. Finally, after about 10 minutes of pain it turned out his/her legs would not have to be amputated and they were released. The person didn't thank the ambulance staff but turned on an old man near them.

"Fuck off you old fucker! You think this is funny do you?" he/she screamed at the old gent who had been giggling at them. It *was* funny though. The old man just continued to laugh.

Swindon were 2-0 up after 20 minutes which totally killed off the match, but the fans kept fairly lively; singing some good songs of hatred about Oxford United, 'chim chimney chim chimney chim chim cheroo, we hate those bastards in yellow and blue' and the traditional 'wash your mouth out son and fetch your fathers gun' rival songs being the favourites.

I found it interesting that despite Oxford being non-league and Swindon riding (relatively) high in League One there was no big man/small man issue going on, and the Swindon fans still truly hated their old rivals despite the gap in the leagues.

After a trip to the dinosaur-age toilets and food hall at half-time the second period contained little action except Southend's Anthony Grant blocking a fierce Swindon shot with the ball going crushingly into his testicles. A bit like the kid and their legs getting trapped earlier, I couldn't help but snigger on the inside about his pain. Am I sadistic?

An alert came on the PA that sounded like an old train station jingle from the 1960s, played by a sole OAP on an xylophone.

"Could the fans in the Town End please sit down. Thank you." Which of course led to the entire Town End, myself included, rising to their feet and start singing "Stand up! For Swindon Town stand up!" If you want a group of football fans to do something, ask them the opposite.

The crowd-pleasing ref gave Swindon, and the impressive Simon Cox, their second penalty of the night in injury time, ensuring the win for Town.

Despite a good win today, being a Swindon fan can't be much fun. A club that was in the very first season of the Premier League back in 1992/93 is now floating between League One and League Two in front of ever-dwindling crowds.

The fact is that Swindon Town FC does have something very interesting and unique about it, I'm just struggling to figure out what.

SWINDON TOWN   **3** (Robson-Kanu 13, Cox pen 19, pen 90)
SOUTHEND UNITED   **0**
Attendance 6,269

GAME 81
ACCRINGTON STANLEY v Exeter City
League Two

Saturday 21st March 2009, 3pm, Fraser Eagle Stadium, Accrington

"There's only one Accrington Stanley! One Accrington Stanley!" sang the 200 or so supporters known as the 'Stanley Ultras' behind the hugely sloping goalmouth. The words may not perfectly fit the rhyme but there is truth to the sentiment behind it. There is indeed only *one* Accrington Stanley.

I had roped along Collo for some more League Two action, (Macclesfield and Shrewsbury clearly weren't enough for the man) feeling the after-effects of the Wigan beer festival from the night before. That's right. I said the 'Wigan beer festival'. That's the kind of thing we do with our evenings. At teatime Collo had suggested the 10.5% 'Paradox Smokestack' whisky-cask aged stout and it was downhill from there.

I had faith that if anything could make us feel better, it was Accrington Stanley. I had been really looking forward to this one. Stanley are the undisputed minnow of the 92. Accrington is the smallest town in England with a Football League representative, the Crown Ground is the smallest Football League stadium, they are the club with the lowest attendances, lowest turnover, and have only existed in their current form since the 1960s.

The main question in my mind was whether Stanley *were* in fact as tiny and shitty as these facts would suggest, or that they was smothered in small-club charm, lovability and a feel-good football factor.

With me driving like a groggy, probably-still-over-the-'Paradox-Smokestack'-limit, irresponsible moron we parked up in a bit of grassy farmland right next to stadium. The smell of manure lingered strongly in the air, but you felt it could genuinely be natural arable cowpat goodness unlike the similar smell at Chester City which more resembled toxic sewer blockages.

We asked the nice lady running the 'car park' where the nearest cash point was.

"By the postbox," she replied firmly but friendlily, pointing vaguely to the main road. The Accrington main road was rows and rows of similarly distinctive yellowy brown terraced houses, and after about 5 minutes of hawk-eyed searching we found the cash point, indeed right by the postbox.

"Can't be many notable points of interest in Accrington if they refer to the postbox as a reference point," I said.

There were a number of pubs however, including the 'Crown' which actually belongs to Accrington Stanley FC! Collo and I poked our noses in but decided against getting another beer. Never again in fact.

The first thing you notice about the ground is that it is *very very* small. The club shop was beautifully tiny, selling such luminous items as a Stanley brandy glass. The general stadium area was a bit dingy though; there was a small scrap tip next to it and big ugly metal fencing by the turnstiles.

Paying the rather reasonable £8 to get in we prepared for the match with some beautiful piping hot pies (with mushy peas! Result!). The food and toilet area was all outside in the open, the milk for the tea being a two-pint bottle from the *Happy Shopper* with the price tag still on, teetering with the lid off on the edge of a fold-out table.

We were standing with the 'Stanley Ultras' (an ironic nod to the Italian football die-hards) behind the goal. The terrace we were next to was ridiculously small, beyond amateur-size, and the pitch was on the biggest slope I have seen in the league.

"I've played on flatter pitches than this on Sunday mornings!" I said.

"It looks like what happens when a snooker table gets wet and starts caving in the middle doesn't it?" said Collo.

The teams came out and it looked like there were barely 1,000 in the ground, despite a very good showing from the Exeter fans, who were brilliant when I saw them a mere week earlier. There was barely any noise at all, come on Stanley Ultras! Where are you?! There were quite possibly more people in the gymnasium drinking ale at Wigan beer festival last night.

The Accrington team started abysmally, allowing Exeter chance after chance until they went 1-0 up in the 5th minute.

"This could be a thrashing," I wisely said to Collo, proving my vast knowledge of League Two in the process.

I was quite quickly proved wildly wrong, when Stanley suddenly got their act in gear and began playing pretty good football (for lower League Two). The Stanley Ultras erupted (a small ejaculation rather than a volcanic explosion) when Accrington equalised through a sumptuous John Miles volley from outside the area.

At half-time there was little on-pitch entertainment apart from the groundsman talking to his son in the stand about what time dinner would be tonight! Another lad was chatting to his mate watching from his bedroom window behind the terraces. This was some lovely personal small-club charm from Stanley you can't buy at the big boys. Another such feature was the sheer amount of balls that went out. I've talked about this at the likes of Exeter and Wycombe, but Accrington take the award. I reckon 17 or 18 balls were used in this match, with every few minutes a clearance bouncing on the tin roof of the Whiney Hill terrace into someone's garden. I'm surprised the fragile vibrating tin roof hasn't collapsed from consistent ball crushing over the years...

Stanley managed to score a winner and hold out to claim a (not very) vital win to catapult them into lower-mid table, and (hopefully not) stunt Exeter's promotion campaign.

The main question concerning Stanley remains 'where will the fans come from'? There is a sense with the existing fans that they know they have lousy support, many of the actual Accrington citizens supporting the 'big boys' Blackburn or Burnley or the 'gigantic boys' Liverpool or Man United.

Accrington Stanley remain a bit of a running joke; the affectionate loser that the general public root for without knowing much about. Their name is synonymous with lower-league pauperism, which is why I wish I loved them a little bit more. Oh well.

Which means that this chapter can naturally only be concluded in one (milky) way.

Accrington Stanley?
Who are they????
Exactly.

ACCRINGTON STANLEY **2** (Miles 34, Lindfield 64)
EXETER CITY **1** (Stansfield 5)
Attendance 1,169

GAME 82
LIVERPOOL v Aston Villa
Premier League
Sunday 22nd March 2009, 4.00pm, Anfield, Liverpool

On a slightly different level from Accrington Stanley came Liverpool FC. Walk on, walk on, calm down, calm down, 5 times, 5 times, Shankly, Paisley, Daglish, Rush, Keegan, Heysel, Hillsborough, Rafa, Yanks Out, Torres, Carra, Ste Gerrard Gerrard, this....is Anfield.

What with Liverpool home tickets being tantamount to golddust, (and possible matches quickly running out) I had thankfully managed to get a ticket through a friend of a friend who works in the PR section at Anfield. AND for one of the biggest games of the season, against Champions League-chasing Aston Villa.

Now the eagle-eyed readers amongst you may have twigged that Liverpool are not my favourite club. Spending 3 years living in the city introduced me to a different side to Liverpool FC supporters; notably the whingeing and deluded fans (it must be said, often from the south as well as the natives). However, just because I don't necessarily like Liverpool doesn't mean that I'm right.

Liverpool are a magnificent club, and I went to Anfield putting all prejudices aside (it was difficult) and transformed myself into a red for the day.

I had been to Anfield twice before, both for Bolton games, both home wins. The Michael Owen-inspired Liverpool win in 1998 is a great memory; experiencing the Anfield buzz for the first time. Less fabulous was last season's 4-0 win for Liverpool. The ground was silent despite the thrashing, I was absolutely stunned by how quiet it was. At one point a sole Bolton fan stood up and shouted "Greatest fans in the world?! Are you joking!?! You can hear a bloody pin drop in here!!!"

The Anfield atmosphere has a great reputation, but judging by the Bolton game last season I questioned whether it is deserved. I was intrigued to see whether the crowd would be on better form today for the Villa game, or in fact whether they do reserve the noise for those legendary European nights.

I arrived at the ground ridiculously early after another night on Paul and Collo's curry-stained Liverpool sofa, and collected my ticket from the plush Centenary Stand executive suite collection office. I felt like a superstar.

Anfield is located in a fairly run-down suburb of Liverpool, but the zone surrounding the stadium is committed to Liverpool FC associated shops, stalls and pubs. The stadium from the outside is actually quite unremarkable and a bit ugly, it really takes going inside to experience the magic.

Anfield is now a massive tourist attraction; there were people of multiple nationalities soaking in the atmosphere. A group of Polish supporters were posing for photos in front of the Bill Shankly statue with their flag. There were a huge amount of Chinese and Japanese fans revelling in the pre-game vibe. The queue for the club shop was stretching around the corner of the stadium.

There was also great interest around the opposite side of the ground at the lovely Hillsborough tribute area. It is done really tastefully, with the names of those who died engraved on a brown marble memorial, and personal pictures, messages and flowers placed below. Situated below the 'You'll Never Walk Alone' gates, it is all rather moving, and does bring to home how much the disaster affected the club, the city, and indeed football in England in general. Around the corner from the Hillsborough tribute a crowd had gathered to see the struggling Aston Villa team get off their coach. I was excited. Regardless of the outcome of this match it had been an historic couple of weeks for Liverpool FC. The 4-0 humiliation of Real Madrid showed how terrific Liverpool can be, but this was unbelievably bettered by the 4-1 win at Old Trafford 4 days later. Additionally Benitez had just finally signed a long-term contract, and there was the no small matter of the 20th anniversary of Hillsborough coming up in a couple of weeks.

The thing the Scousers were most bothered about was unashamedly gloating about the Man U result. T-shirts had been hastily printed with the 'Man Utd helpline number; 4-1-4-1-4-1' slogan on it. About half the people at the match seemed to be wearing these shirts!

Mediocre chicken balti pie in hand, I took my seat in the Main Stand. The ground seems a lot older than some of the other big ones, the leg room and comfort is a different planet away from the Emirates, but I suppose this adds to the sense of history that Anfield carries. I could do without splinters in my arse from the wooden chairs though.

Pre-match, Sammy Lee had been out on the pitch by himself for about 20 minutes pumping up balls, placing cones out and squirting water bottles. On his own. Sammy no-mates. I had a sudden sense of thanks for Gary Megson. Eventually though the superstars emerged to rapturous applause.

Fernando Torres and Javier Mascherano were playing a game where they would ping balls at each other's faces when they weren't looking, missing by a whisker quite deliberately. The passing accuracy of these two players was unbelievable. The same cannot be said of Andrea Dossena, who had Dan Agger give him a bollocking for frequent over-hit passes in a simple circle-passing warm up. Honestly, it was hilarious how awful he was.

This was probably only the 2nd most bemusing sight before kick-off though, with 4th official Howard Webb signing autographs and posing for photographs with the fans. Know your place Howard. You're not the star, the players are. Don't become a Graham Poll/Jeff Winter figure of fame-seeking arseholedom.

The players came out to 'You'll Never Walk Alone' as always, and it does send a shiver down your spine. What is it about that tune? It's just *perfect* as a football anthem, and not bettered anywhere else in the country. I was sitting in between two sets of people that quite accurately represent Liverpool FC. On my left were a couple of South African dudes, wearing shades and designer gear, bragging of meeting Torres in the players' lounge before kick-off. On my right was a very shrieky Scouse lady and her kid with masses of passion for their club.

"Why you think the players are wearing black armbands?" one South African guy asked the other?

"Jade Goody?!" the other replied laughing (Jade died this morning – a bit soon for jokes?) "Or maybe signalling 'the death of Man United!' hehehe."

It turned out it was for club secretary Bryce Morrison, and an eerily quiet minutes silence preceded kick-off. I always feel uncomfortable during a minutes silence, I always think I might blurt out something in a tourettes-fit. I didn't though thankfully.

Liverpool kicked off and were terrific from the moment go. They quickly went ahead through everyone's favourite 'try-hard' Dutchman Dirk Kuyt ('try-hard' substituting for 'a bit rubbish') and Albert Riera doubled the lead with a thunderous drive straight from a Reina goal kick. Route-one at its most glorious.

Anfield was erupting, it was a bubbling cauldron. Reina made a fantastic save from John Carew later in the first half too, proving his worth in more ways than one. Liverpool won a rather fortunate penalty soon after this, Gerrard slotting home in the calm composed manner in which he wouldn't for England.

"What a half hey!" I said to the lady next to me, my ear ringing from all her shrieking.

"Incredible. It's Jamie's first game too," she said gesticulating at her little son.

"Wow, good for you Jamie! Is he named after Carragher?" I joked to the lady.

"Yeah, he is actually," she said with a serious face. I couldn't tell if she was joking, but it seemed like she wasn't. Wow.

Just when I was settling down with some affection for Liverpool, out came John Aldridge at half-time. My nemesis (see chapter 18). Just my luck. I was on the verge of liking the club and then this moustachioed moron comes out to ruin it all. Well, he *was* coming out to become a patron of the national disabled supporters' charity. Can I still hate him after this? Yeah, I can just about live with myself for that.

It was more of the same in the 2nd half, and everything good Liverpool were doing was through their captain. Steven Gerrard, as he sometimes does, dictated the pace of the game single-handedly from the middle of the park. He was making crucial tackles in his own penalty area, starting moves with probing through balls, and going on mazy runs down the left wing himself. He even nutmegged his old pal Gareth Barry in the 2nd half.

Adding to his goal tally, Gerrard scored a lovely placed free-kick in the 50th minute and completed his hat-trick with another penalty 15 minutes later. Brad Friedel had brought down Torres through on goal and received a straight red card. The Kop gave Friedel a huge round of applause as he trundled off. I suppose it's easy to give a former player a rousing reception if he has conceded 4 goals, conceded a penalty and got sent off.

Gerrard had scored his first ever Premier League hat-trick. Anfield was happy.

Liverpool are a truly multi-national club, a superstar of the global game. People from all over England, from all over Europe and from all over the world love this club and everything they stand for. I do not love Liverpool FC, but I concede that it is a very special club. And it hurts me to admit that.

I think the thing that makes Liverpool so special is the fact that despite the club being a hugely popular global brand it has retained its Scouse identity. Everything about Liverpool is still Scouse; the sheer obsessive passion, the optimism and idolising the supernatural figures of Torres, Gerrard and Benitez, the frequent sense of strong injustice against something; be it the American owners, FA discrimination or *The Sun* and Hillsborough. Liverpool FC helps shape the entire city, second only to 4 musicians from the 1960s, and apart from possibly Newcastle I can't think of another example of a club playing as crucial a role in the town.

LIVERPOOL   **5** (Kuyt 8, Riera 33, Gerrard pen 39, 50, pen 65)
ASTON VILLA 0
Attendance 44,131

GAME 83
CREWE ALEXANDRA v Millwall
League One
Saturday 28th March 2009, 3pm, Alexandra Stadium, Crewe

I never had a problem with Crewe Alexandra. We were cool. Until I drove for 4 ½ hours up a traffic-clogged M6 only to find the game 'frozen off'.

It had been several weeks since this disaster but the resentment had still not gone, the vendetta had been solidified. It technically wasn't Crewe's fault the game was called off, but I still blame them. My new least favourite club. I had to do it though, so I reserved a Saturday for the Millwall match, and especially booked a train so I didn't have to drive up again; a (sort-of) bitter mini-victory for me. Crewe is a town with a famous railway history, with the football team being nicknamed 'The Railwaymen', so I thought I was doing my bit by soaking up the culture of Crewe (the train station). I arrived early and bought my ticket from a surprisingly empty ticket office booth, and went for a grumpy coffee in a nice little cafe on the rain-soaked wind-swept Nantwich Road.

With Millwall just outside the automatic promotion spots and Crewe just outside the relegation zone it was a real League One six pointer! It was bound to be crap. A couple of Burberry-capped Millwall fans came in, pissed out of their heads, and ordered baguettes, ruining the pleasant calm vibe in the process with their booze-drenched swearing. I was glad I wasn't sitting with them today.

I sped-drank my coffee and headed back to Gresty Road. Walking around the ground it has lower-league class to it. The railway lines look bronzed with ancient rust behind one goal, and behind the other amongst the old brown houses there is a lovely cobble-bricked fish and chip shop called 'Fish and Chip Stop'. Just around the corner however this mirage is popped by the recently expanded Main Stand. With a capacity of nearly 7,000 it dominates the rest of the ground, and indeed the whole standing area, it looks like a Premier League stand.

I made my way to the gate and found a *massive* amount of policemen there.

"Can we search your bag sir," one said, going through my rucksack before I had said 'yes'. "Oh. Look what we have here. A bottle of water," he said sarcastically, talking to me as if a bottle of water was a handgun.

He confiscated it and let me through saying "I was allowed through now," as if he was doing me a massive favour. Then it dawned on me that there were actually an awful lot of blue shirts going in around me. And no red shirts. I looked at my ticket; 'Visiting Supporter'.

Arrghh!! I bought a ticket for the bloody Millwall end!!! Thankfully, because I hadn't quite gone through yet I managed to squeeze back through some very hard looking Millwall fans, and past my policeman nemesis back to the ticket office.

"You sold me an away ticket! I wanted a home ticket!" I said to the girl on the counter.

"Oh, sorry," she said, swapping it for a home ticket. This one was red. My old one was blue. I should have guessed! Still, why on earth did she give me an away ticket?! My accent isn't significantly cockney so I am automatically a Millwall fan. I was coming to the end of my tether with Crewe Alexandra...

At least I was until I got chatting to the most lovely steward. She called me 'luvee', recommended the *Pukka* chicken balti pie (I think I needed little help in that field though) and told me to wrap up warmer when it's this windy in future. Sound advice seeing as I had forgotten to bring my big coat. The food area in the main stand was absolutely massive, and decorated with paintings of Gresty Road by local school children, a delightful touch from a club I was annoyingly starting to warm to.

The whole atmosphere was very family-friendly. The PA announcer man was on the pitch with the 4 mascots grilling them on the microphone, Paxman style. "What's your favourite player? Favourite goal? Have you got a girlfriend? What's your opinion on the conflict in the Gaza Strip?" It was relentless.

A quite drunk, but very friendly bloke was sitting next to me.

"Alright mate, are you a Crewe fan?" he asked, peculiarly, his bleary eyes staring at me. Surely I must be a Crewe fan, sitting in the Crewe end at Crewe, watching Crewe play. But I wasn't! How did he know? Was I that obvious?!

"No, actually!" I said, and proceeded to tell him what I was doing. His name was Tom as well! What are the bloomin' chances hey? What a small world!

"I'm from Portsmouth so don't come up much, but I bloody love it when I do! CUMMON YOU REDS!" he bellowed, oozing League One passion (and some beery sweat too).

The match was poor, Crewe did very little going forward and Millwall always looked the better team. Their bleached-blonde centre back Zak Whitbread had the Crewe strikers in his pocket.

"Crewe could do with Calvin Zola today eh?" I said to Tom, pretending I knew about the absent centre-forward.

"Zola?!" he said disgustedly, doing the 'wanker' sign with his right hand. Not at me, about Zola (I hope). "He's a wanker. Say no more," he said viciously, suggesting he had some kind of personal vendetta against him.

"Oi lineo!" a guy in front of us chanted, "you're as shit as that woman last week!"

Tom perked up.

"Was that woman linesman here last week against Leeds?" he asked. "Yeah mate! She was crap! She was standing in front of the Leeds fans and they were intimidating her for the whole match so she gave them absolutely everything."

I wonder if they were just being sexist or whether there is a point about female officials? It's a complex debate anyway (just don't ask Mike Newell).

The game went by slowly and painfully, but at least I had a funny pissed namesake to talk to. I just couldn't shake off my irritation that I actually *liked* Gresty Road despite being fully prepared to slag it off. Just as I was getting up to leave, Millwall scored the only goal of the game through the substitute debutant Jason Price. It was the last kick of the game.

I even felt sorry for Crewe for losing at the last minute! I might as well just piss on my principles and come out of the closet as a Crewe fan. Damn!

CREWE ALEXANDRA 0
MILLWALL   **1** (Price 90)
Attendance 4,680

GAME 84
HEREFORD UNITED v Brighton & Hove Albion
League One

Tuesday 7th April 2009, 7.45pm, Edgar Street, Hereford

84 games in and the Football League still had the power to surprise me. From the outside, Hereford United's Edgar Street is probably the least attractive ground of the 92, and certainly the least modern and progressive. The ground looks like an abandoned maximum security prison, without an inmate for decades.

The huge floodlights can be seen from far away; they are massive intimidating pillars of doom resembling a communist Soviet watchtower, I half expected uniformed guards to be watching over me with rifles. Above the stained creamy-grey brick walls is thick spiralling barbed wire. Everything about it connotes doom and depression.

I wandered a bit further and found a completely isolated man in a cloth cap, lonely and selling programmes, yet no one approached. The petrol station next to the stadium is closed at 7pm. Despite being miles and miles from the coast, seagulls were circling Edgar Street like vultures, waiting to pounce on the prey of the dead, possibly those who tried to scale the unyielding and brutally thick barbed wire.

There was a hand-written small sign for the ticket office that looked like it hadn't been changed since the 1930s. Whether this was a somewhat ironic and nostalgic deliberate move from Hereford or simply something that they've never got round to replacing I don't know.

Most jaw-dropping of all were the turnstiles. For my stand you had to climb an odd little mound of litter-strewn grass to reach them, and upon reaching you realise they look like a medieval torture implement. The man operating the turnstile could well have been a hooded torturer in a previous life, with a thick dirty beard and his bulbous eyes staring me down as I went through.

"Enjoy the game...." he muttered in the unplacable Hereford accent (bit Midlandsy, bit Welshy, bit nothingy), in a friendly way that somehow sounded sinister, like the game in question was Russian Roulette.

This season was Hereford's first ever in the 3rd tier of English football, having meandered in non-league and the 4th division for their entire history. With there being no sign of any fans outside the ghost-ground I wondered if any would be in, and indeed when I entered Edgar Street I suddenly saw a brilliant bustle of smiling football fans. The ground was equally as shabby from the inside as the outside, but now everything felt right, a bit less *shit*. It is a very strange ground, with four unique stands different from each other, but I love that. Behind the goals the terraces curved round, something I've never seen before, resembling a curved grandstand audience watching an orchestra.

One of the pitch-length stands has seating on the 2nd tier and terracing on the 1st, making it look like an 'upstairs downstairs' class division you may have found in the early 20th Century, with the paupers standing while the aristocrats ate swans in their comfy seats. The icing on the unconventional cake was the tiny brick dugouts, looking far too small to fit the manager and all the subs.

Despite finding joy all around me I was dreading this game a little bit. It was 22nd v 23rd in League One and the season was reaching squeaky-bum time. I didn't envisage a classic.

The clocks had gone forward a week earlier so as the match kicked off there was a moody sunset still going on over the horizon. The view was great, with the orange sky and the town's main church and cathedral both visible from my stand.

Brighton had opened the scoring early on and looked the likely winners. Hereford had one shot in the entire first half, and even that was rubbish. The half-time pie didn't improve matters for me; why oh why did I eat a bloody McDonalds an hour earlier?

My favourite moment of the match was when a Hereford defender smashed a hefty clearance in the air onto the top of the Edgar Street Stand and the ball hit a seagull.

Honestly, it hit a bloody seagull!

Being a seagull-despiser myself, I have tried to hit seagulls with all kinds of things in the past; rocks, shoes, knives, but always failed. This player however managed to actually get the bastard in the head! The seagull flew off looking very dazed, zigzagging through the air, looking as if he may keel over and die, plummeting from the air to the pitch at any minute. Whose job would it be to remove the potential bird carcass I wonder? Anyway, the poor gull lived, and slowly escaped to the chorus of "Seagull! Seagull! Seagull!"from the Hereford faithful.

That was a good chant, but the best chant of the night had to be the Hereford fans, singing "You're going down with the Hereford!" to Brighton. At least they have a sense of humour, regardless of how pants their team are.

Amidst the seagull-domination the game was apparently still going on, and Brighton got their second with 15 minutes to go, resulting in some boos ringing around Edgar Street.

A furious looking blonde haired man walked to the front of the terraces in the curved open space behind the goal and bellowed at us all, "WHY DO WE COME? IT'S BLOODY USELESS!" before purposefully striding out. Half the crowd booed him and half cheered him.

Yes, Hereford are bloody useless. But as a small club punching above their weight what do you expect? Half will moan to the heavens and half will support their team through thick and thin. That's what it's all about. Indeed, the fan who stormed off early missed Hereford score an injury time consolation.

The 2-1 defeat had flattered Hereford though. It was possibly the single worst performance I have seen this season, with honorary mentions to Chester, Barnet and Notts Forest. I wondered how on earth this team beat Leeds a few weeks ago. The result meant that

Hereford were, almost definitely, going to return to League Two after a lovely adventure in the third tier.

I can't see Hereford United ever being much more than that team Ronnie Radford scored for to knock Newcastle out of the FA Cup in 1972, but something about their wonderfully rubbish stadium captured my heart and I can safely say that I really did like, nay, love the Hereford and Edgar Street experience. Maybe it was the seagull getting twatted, who knows?

HEREFORD UNITED **1** (Taylor 90)
BRIGHTON AND HOVE ALBION **2** (Fraser 9, Owusu 75)
Attendance 2,033

GAME 85
CARDIFF CITY v Derby County
The Championship
Wednesday 8th April 2009, 7.45pm, Ninian Park, Cardiff

I woke up to the noise of the inexplicably common Hereford seagulls squawking at my B&B window as if to deliberately get their own back for me laughing at one of their friends getting hit with the ball last night.

Still annoyed at the seagulls I set off towards Wales for the dreaded Cardiff City match. As a city I love Cardiff; it's forward-thinking, progressive, modern, friendly, chilled-out, clean and attractive. However, the city's football team and stadium is pretty much the opposite of most of these things.

Cardiff City FC had always struck me as being a bit backwards. The ground was supposed to be a crumbling relic, and the fans could often behave very unpleasantly, as I had witnessed earlier in the season at Reading.

Indeed, a mere 3 days ago it had been the Swansea match, where there were sadly predictable fights outside Ninian Park, and referee Mike Dean had been struck with a coin from the crowd leaving his head bleeding. But I had a suspicion that there was a redeeming element of shoddy brilliance to Cardiff City, and I hoped I would be proved right as I made the short trip from Hereford.

I arrived in the Welsh capital in the early afternoon and parked up near Ninian Park, about a 30 minute walk from the city centre, but one that would complement the lovely sunny day. Walking around Cardiff was great; seeing The Millennium Stadium, and the way it has been effortlessly merged into the city centre, is a particular highlight. I have fond memories of the place (Bolton winning the 2000-2001 play off final) and it looked no less spectacular 8 years later.

After a splendid day out I trotted back to the ground, passing the Ninian Park train station and pub. I considered going in until realising looked a bit intimidating. Any hint of my English accent and I would have been garrotted with a leek.

This is Cardiff's final season in their historic ground, and their new stadium is being built just across the road. It looked like it was coming along very well indeed, not too dissimilar from Swansea's impressive Liberty Stadium (although I certainly wouldn't have told anyone from Cardiff that).

But forget any new modern stadium claptrap because, bar entry to the play-offs, this was the 3rd last game to ever be played at the very special Ninian Park.

I was in the 'Bob Bank Terrace', one of the last remaining terraces existing in a top stadium. It was a glorious evening, the smell of food and the summer grass, the feel of the air and small flies congregating, reminded me of a music festival more than a football match. The moody sunset was as spectacular as yesterday, making Ninian Park glow orange as kick-off approached.

I immediately loved it.

Everything about the ground is just *old*. The outdoor food stalls and toilets, the poles everywhere, the ancient floodlights, the crackly old TV screen that Cardiff bought from Bolton's old ground Burnden Park.

The notoriety of the Cardiff fans, with their 'soul crew' firm and reputation for intimidation and violence certainly made me apprehensive mixing amongst them, particularly in a cramped terrace. The Cardiff fans absolutely hate the fans of each of the other 91 clubs. 90 of them because they're English, and 1 because they're Swansea.

At first I kept my mouth slightly more quiet than I normally would at a new ground. Mainly because my ridiculous fake-Welsh accent sounds Jamaican. After seeing the Cardiff fans in their most mental element at the Madejski, punching policemen and storming the pitch, I thought keeping myself to myself would be wise.

Everything about the Welsh fashion was dinosauric (yep, I created a new word. 'Dinosauric'. Meaning old enough for the dinosaurs to remember.) Pencil-thin moustaches, sideburns, thick gold chains, hoopy earrings, the 'step' haircut, *flares*. The Cardiff fans' fashion sense was as outdated as the ground's facilities.

Despite their questionable fashion senses, today the Cardiff fan
were brilliant. The teams emerged and the terrace came alive.
had obviously been on plenty of standing terraces this season, bu
none at a ground full of nearly 20,000 people. The terrace wa
crammed, I couldn't see one entire third of the pitch, and could onl
see the further away goal if I stood on the absolute tip of my toes
The crowd was buzzing as the teams were read out, with Derb
midfielder Robbie Savage being introduced as 'the former Wels
international Robbie Savage' to ear-splitting boos. Savage bein
Savage applauded the big boos with a massive smile on his smu
face.

The shabby charm of Ninian Park held no boundaries; the slope o
the pitch is incredible and the ground was so uneven that Cardif
knew never to pass back to their 'keeper Stuart Taylor on fear of th
'bobble'.

The highlight of the first half for me was the PA announcing 'Can the
owner of a red Vauxhall Astra registration XXXXXX please go back to
your car, you are blocking the entrance to the allotments and you
car will be towed', followed by a man getting up with his red cheek
glowing, and almost 20,000 fans laughing at him and applauding him
as he went back to his car meekly. Very funny stuff.

Half-time came with Cardiff 1-0 up and things were going well.
hadn't been murdered by Welsh separatists, and I had delicious pie
well worth the long queue. Cardiff, without playing brilliantly, were
ruthless, and after 15 static minutes they let fly on Derby, scoring 2
goals in quick succession.

Whilst the Vauxhall Astra incident was the highlight of the first half
the highlight of the second half was when the ball got cleared out
into our Bob Bank Terrace and was headed by a fan to a massive
cheer. There were then 5 subsequent heads from the folk in our
terrace as the 22 footballers waited annoyed for their ball back,
hands on hips. Brilliant!

Cardiff had mauled Derby, and there was still time for misfit Cardif
striker Eddie Johnson to score a goal in both ends, making the final
score 4-1.

I had lived to tell the tale. More than that, I had loved being at
Cardiff City. Sure, they can be a bit more boisterous than many fans,

but today they were terrific. It would be the last night game ever to be played at Ninian Park, and I was privileged to be there.

You can tell that being at a ground as intimate, personal and traditional as Ninian Park must improve the performance of the players. However good the new stadium is I can't imagine it will be anything like as intimidating for an away player.

This time next year Ninian Park will be a building site for new housing. A thought which saddens me. I'm just thankful that I managed to go there. After all, Pope John Paul II and Bob Marley had both visited the ground, and if it's good enough for them, it's good enough for me.

As I established, Cardiff City and Ninian Park aren't necessarily progressive, modern, friendly, chilled out, clean or attractive like the great city they exist in. But that doesn't mean they aren't bloody brilliant.

CARDIFF CITY   **4** (R.Johnson 16, Rae 61, Bothroyd 63, E.Johnson 79)
DERBY COUNTY **1** (E.Johnson OG 90)
Attendance 18,403

GAME 86
SCUNTHORPE UNITED v Huddersfield Town
League One
Friday 10th April 2009, 7.45pm, Glanford Park, Scunthorpe

Occasionally a club gets laughed off somewhat unfairly due to their name. Scunthorpe United is one such club. A bit like 'Grimsby', 'Scunthorpe' as a word is just a bit harsh, shabby and funny sounding. And of course there is a sweary swear slapped in the middle of it. Even I was dreading a Friday night in Scunthorpe, but realised I know nothing about the place and I was just as bad as everyone else who dismisses it as a shit hole just because of its name.

Of course I got to Scunthorpe and it *was* a shit hole.

Well, this isn't really true, I only really saw Glanford Park; a grey slab outside the town centre, built in 1988, a time where aesthetic pleasure obviously wasn't high on the priority list. It reminded me of Walsall's equally uninspiring Bescot Stadium, built around the same time. In fact the best thing about Glanford Park was the massive car park attached to the stadium, cheap(ish) and accessible to all. That's right; I have got to the stage where I judge a club by its car parks. That's what 92 matches will do to you.

I was waiting for kick-off in my car, the rain slamming on my windscreen. I wasn't feeling sociable. There was a bar attached to the ground, the IRON bar which I decided to give a miss. The two bouncers outside, their faces being prominently monobrow, looked like they may murder me just for being from the south. Being plonked out of town there was the always convenient, never desired, McDonalds, KFC, Tesco, Frankie & Benny's and so on. The grey skies, splattering dismal April showers and disappointing soggy Big Macs didn't create an exotic image of Scunthorpe.

The gloom of the weather had rubbed off on the fans, with dark cloudy expressions hanging on their Humberside faces. Scunthorpe were doing well this season, bouncing back after the disappointment of relegation last year by remaining in the play-off spaces for most of the season.

Five days ago they had lost in the Johnstone's Paint Trophy final against the mighty Luton Town, and the fans had faces like hangdogs being hung tonight. It wasn't just me that wanted to be somewhere else on this pissy Friday evening. To be fair the ground does have more character inside than out, the terraces hold in the atmosphere fairly well and as League One grounds go it is fine, if not spectacularly charismatic.

The fans were singing "Hi Ho Scunthorpe United" (surely too many syllables for the tune there) and the teams emerged to 'Any Old Iron'. The man in front of me was shouting the words to Any Old Iron at the top of his lungs, seemingly inspired by the city's steel and iron history. This man absolutely stank. I mean sewer-smelly. Also his ears were remarkably hairy, like little tufts of blonde fur coating both lugholes.

The match wasn't a belter, Scunthorpe never looked confident after the Luton defeat last weekend, although they did open the scoring with a brilliantly worked goal. Huddersfield equalised shortly after, but I missed the goal because I was staring at the man's ear-hair. Did it muffle his hearing? Was that why he was shouting so loud? Maybe his nostrils (out of my vision) were equally as hairy, explaining why he doesn't notice how bad he smells.

The sole focus of the Scunthorpe crowd (who didn't have hairy ears to entertain them) was Huddersfield's former Scunthorpe midfielder Jim Goodwin. The home fans *hated* their former player. Whenever he came over to take a corner a handful of furious Scunts ploughed towards the corner flag and hurled violent abuse at him, the stewards losing a battle to prevent them from doing so.

At half-time I realised I didn't want my pie. I looked at it, all small and unsatisfying and glutinous. I poked the steak with a fork around the saucy gloop. I didn't want this. I had just spent £2.50 on an item of food I didn't want, and was only eating because I had told myself 8 months ago that I would. Where is the logic in that? I took a bite and loathed myself a little bit inside.

Huddersfield deservedly took the lead early in the second half, and not much else happened except for the rain picking up. When it began raining harder the players got noticeably worse; more laboured, lethargic and sluggish.

This didn't make for an entertaining half, and nor did the referee's contribution. 26 year-old ref Stuart Atwell had had a pretty eventful season (the 'ghost goal' at Watford v Reading the standout) and today's performance was another shocker.

The match finished 2-1 and I ran off to the dry warmth of my car. It wasn't the most enjoyable of nights; a rainy evening in Humberside with mediocre League One football, hairy ears and unwanted pies for company.

I feel my bad mood clouded my judgement of Scunthorpe slightly; but if my biggest compliment to give a club is about their car park management then I must have had a bit of an uninspiring night.

SCUNTHORPE UNITED 1 (Woolford 19)
HUDDERSFIELD TOWN 2 (T.Clarke 26, Roberts 54)
Attendance 5,543

GAME 87
PRESTON NORTH END v Blackpool
The Championship
Saturday 11th April 2009, 1.00pm, Deepdale, Preston

Drenched in rain I had stayed in Leeds at my friend Faye's house ("Scunthorpe? Sounds horrible!") and had a good night sleep in preparation for popping over to Preston for a delicious looking lunchtime kick-off against Blackpool. With Preston battling for a play-off place and Blackpool hanging on against relegation there was a lot at stake, and I was hoping for a thunderous Lancastrian battle. I met my mate Matt, a Preston diehard, and his girlfriend Jodie for a look around Deepdale before kick-off.

"Blood-curdling derby this one! Makes Boca Juniors v River Plate look like a Disney classic," said Matt excitedly.

Preston North End is absolutely rooted in the fabric of English football. They are founder members of the Football League, the first English champions, and Deepdale is thought to be the oldest football venue in the world (Bramall Lane was built earlier, but not used as a football arena until after).

Deepdale is a fantastic stadium. I really liked it. Preston have rejuvenated it over the years rather than being tempted to re-locate, and it has the perfect mix of modern and old; the stadium retaining its wonderful sense of history.

"Fancy a look round the museum mate?"said Matt; lanky, bearded and grungy, looking like the student that he is.

One such slice of history comes from the National Football Museum, which is attached to Deepdale and is probably the best pre-match slice of entertainment you can get anywhere of the 92. The three-floored museum has the Jules Rimet trophy, the 1966 World Cup match-ball, countless old kits and boots, the English football hall of fame, and much more to kill some time before kick-off.

The current special exhibit was a tribute to Sir Tom Finney. If there's one thing that you can't escape when you visit Deepdale, it's the very true fact that Sir Tom Finney is a legend. The museum had great

Sir Tom Finney memorabilia such as (my personal favourite) a cassette tape entitled 'Sir Tom Finney's Preston Christmas', with Sir Tom Finney's personally selected carols for the festive season.

Deepdale (situated on 'Sir Tom Finney Way') has a fantastic statue of Sir Tom Finney outside, with a water feature around it representing a famous picture of Sir Tom Finney performing a tackle with water splashing around him. Inside the stadium an image of Sir Tom Finney's face is painted into the seats. Shortly before kick-off, the PA announcer led a tribute to Sir Tom Finney along with a charming old brassband, culminating in Sir Tom Finney, sitting in his usual seat in the Sir Tom Finney stand, waving to the adoring Preston masses. If ever there was a club devoted to a former legend, it's Preston North End and, whatshisname, Sir Tom Finney.

"Is the mascot on crutches?" I asked, squinting at a duck-type thing. "Yeah I think he had a fall last week," laughed Matt. I had read a news piece this week about Chaddy the Oldham Owl getting stretchered off pre-match at Boundary Park recently. It's obviously dangerous to be a mascot these days!

I took my metaphorical hat off to Preston when it came to the pie. A special deal for pie, peas and gravy for £3 was precisely what I needed. After an unwanted pastry last night at Scunthorpe I was back in the pie zone, and this meat and potato bad-boy, with its trusty pea and gravy sidekicks, was making me a happy temporary Preston fan on this gorgeous Lancastrian lunchtime.

The North-West was apparently experiencing its own little micro-climate today. It was shitty in Scunthorpe last night, shitty in Leeds this morning, shitty down south according to a grumpy text from Annabel, but bloody gorgeous in Preston. The teams came out to the Elvis classic 'I Can't Help Falling in Love With You', recently reinstated as the club's unofficial anthem after former manager Paul Simpson had banned it for being 'too downbeat'.

The Preston fans were singing their variant on the ever popular 'Wash your mouth out son and fetch your father's gun' song.

"Shoot the Blackpool scum?!" said Jodie, looking a bit concerned. "That's a big extreme isn't it."

"What, encouraging murder?" I replied.

"Yeah, it's only football isn't it."

Matt looked at her with clear disappointment at the 'it's only football' statement.

Blackpool had been the better team in the first half and deservedly went ahead much to the emphatic disapproval of the home crowd. "I'm so pissed off," said Matt monosyllabically in a deep Lancastrian grunt, "I'm going to get a pie and put some more bets on."

Jodie and I basked in 15 minutes of half-time sunshine wondering where Matt had got to as the second half kicked off without him (you would have thought they could have waited out of politeness). Preston actually nearly scored a couple of times and looked sharp.

Eventually we saw Matt walk back up the stairs towards us, gritting his teeth together and noticeably pie-less.

"Pies ran out," he muttered, steam coming from both ears if he were a cartoon.

"At least you got to put a couple more bets on though mate," I reasoned.

"Ladbrokes counter had shut."

Matt's gloom was soon to be reflected in most of the home crowd as Preston faded and failed to get an equaliser. The match had started off well but ended with a bit of a whimper. It wasn't exactly Boca v River.

I said farewell to a thoroughly pissed-off Matt and a nonchalant Jodie, sneaking in one last admiring photograph of the magnificent Tom Finney water statue. Wat-er guy!

Ultimately, Preston North End are a *proper* English football club. Football League founders, the first champions, and the inhabitants of the oldest stadium in the world. If one club have all these prestigious prefixes I'm glad it's Preston. Just a shame the team were crap today! Guess you can't have everything.

PRESTON NORTH END 0
BLACKPOOL   **1** (Adam 43)
Attendance 21,273

GAME 88
DARLINGTON v Bury
League Two
Monday 13ᵗʰ April 2009, 3.00pm, Darlington Arena, Darlington

Darlington FC are a troubled club. They had played like a decent team for much of this season, lurking around the play-offs until the 10-point deduction and the subsequent selling of any half-decent player. Administration is always a stinker, but with Darlo I feel their pain even more than most. Particularly as you can specifically trace most of their problems back to their chairman from 1999-2004 George Reynolds.

Oh wow. The bizarre life and times of George Reynolds. A paragraph about our George wouldn't even touch the surface (a full book might not be sufficient either). The word 'colourful' gets floated around a lot about the man. The myth goes that from being a casual crook in the 1960s, he became a safecracker, multi-millionaire businessman, football chairman, neighbour of Spice Girls, tax evader, prisoner, pauper, he has done it all. His time as Darlington was littered with massive controversies, from allegedly fist-fighting supporters to his wife claiming to the papers that the players take bribes.

The best tale about Reynolds involves that legendary Colombian nut-job Faustino Asprilla. Reynolds claims he offered Asprilla £17,000 a week plus a cut of gate receipts to join Darlo back in 2002. Asprilla was paraded to the Darlington masses, posing with the kit and scarf at the arena, only to do a runner to the Middle East before signing the contract.

But of course Reynolds' biggest mistake was the building of the new stadium. The Darlington Arena (formerly named the 'Reynolds Arena' after himself) is a 27,000 all-seater out-of-town bowl that wouldn't be out of place in the Premier League. It's a white elephant that is FAR too big for a club like Darlington who get about 3,000 in each week if they're lucky. It's a bizarre experience watching tiny

Darlo play at this huge arena, and one which made me feel a bit uneasy.

My Darlo-supporting chum Paul and I arrived early after a traffic-free long old trek, and the ground was eerie. The vast sprawling concrete of the empty car parks made you question whether there was actually a game being played today at this Premier standard stadium. The ground had two bars attached to it, but one (naturally) had closed down. Paul and I popped into the existing bar for a drink, and I was quite taken aback with how nice it was. Modern, well designed (with the word 'Darlo' written in the Carling beer font), perfectly set out with numerous Sky Sports screens and tables, as well as historic shirts and memorabilia on the walls, it was great.

A very enjoyable pint later we went in to the ground. There were more toilets and bars than were needed, meaning no queues for either. "Mate, the toilets are top!" said Paul, "there's the Darlo badge on everything, the soap dispensers, the door handles, the toilets themselves!"

Customised Darlo soap dispensers! Necessary use of money?

The bowl-shaped arena looks the part; not dissimilar to a bigger version of Doncaster's stadium, but does not seem like it is big enough for over 25,000. Only when you sit down do you realise why this is so; the leg room is shocking, they clearly wanted to boost up the capacity by making the seats tiny! Fortunately 6 ft 2 Paul and I could stretch out next to us, what with the ground being nearly empty.

We were sat near the Darlington young offenders institute; a load of tracksuit clad 15-year-old rat-boys (one of which was bizarrely wearing a Newcastle shirt) but they definitely made for a good atmosphere. They were giving out non-stop verbal towards the Bury end, and with one of them carrying a drum the chants were constant, the kids making the best of a difficult situation by producing noise in an empty ground.

"You're just a small town in Bolton!" was countered by the Bury fans with "Stadium, you fucked it up!" quite amusingly.

"Fair play to these kids," I said to Paul, impressed by their noisy positivity.

"Yeah, they haven't yet been ground down by the harsh cold reality of lower-league football." Paul replied. "They'll be morose old men in 10 years."

"Are we morose old men yet?"

"On our way mate. On our way."

Only two of the four sides of the ground were open (it is rumoured one side will be knocked down and turned into flats to gain some money), with the message 'Come on Darlo' written in the seats behind the goal, destined to always be seen rather than sat on.

The biggest treat of the day was the surprising fact that the game was actually very good between the Quakers and the Shakers. Bury went ahead after 8 minutes but Darlo didn't drop their heads, and they managed to equalise before half-time. When Darlo equalised the kids rushed over towards the Bury fans, and began taunting them wonderfully.

"Jesus," I muttered to Paul as they were surrounding us, "deodorant hasn't reached Darlington yet has it?"

"Clearly not, but the mullet definitely has," Paul smirked, pointing at a wonderful rat-tail mulletted youth giving the Bury fans the wanker sign right in front of us.

At half-time we got a pie each, and were very pleasantly surprised. The pies are set out like at a bakers; freshly cooked and displayed at the front of the food counter. With the meat and potato pie at £1.30 it represented probably the best value for money anywhere I've been, and the pints were amongst the cheapest I've seen too.

"Do you reckon the administrators made the pies cheaper too?!" laughed Paul.

The second half was much of the same, with sloppy defending and misplaced passes making for an entertaining spectacle, and Bury's Efe Sodje put them ahead after 53 minutes. I've always had an affection for the former Nigerian World Cup star Sodje, with his bandana and seemingly endless stream of brothers littering the lower-leagues. Sodje was not to be a winner though, because Darlo again came back to equalise, the entertaining match ending 2-2.

Despite having a popular manager in Dave Penney (his face postered around with an 'every Penney counts' motto to help Darlo financially), every time Darlington look like they have a decent team or individual player they get sold immediately.

There are tiny beacons of hope around; with optimistic songs, 'Save Our Club' t-shirts and a forthcoming charity match featuring Paul Gascoigne, but one fears this may all be in vain.

The George Reynolds era is like a dirty little chapter from Darlington FC's past that has cut deep, bearing wounds today they wish they could get rid of. Apparently the executive area of the ground is ridiculous; all marble floors, escalators and laser flush urinals. The biggest scar is the stadium, which I fear will be Darlington's downfall. I pray they still exist in a couple of years, and maybe one day will at least *half* fill the ground formerly known as the George Reynolds Arena.

DARLINGTON   **2** (Kennedy 38, Abbott 74)
BURY   **2** (Hurst 8, Sodje 53)
Attendance 2,927

GAME 89
PLYMOUTH ARGYLE v Doncaster Rovers
The Championship

Saturday 18th April 2009, 3.00pm, Home Park, Plymouth

Sat on a bench at Plymouth Hoe I was playing 'spot-the-pirate'. had seen about 12 bearded and tattooed pirate-types so far, an now it was evening maybe more might emerge from their coves. had been sitting on the same bench for about an hour, munchir fish and chips and now having the obligatory *Whippy* flake. Th circling seagulls were swooping. The bastards. Once I had fende them off my dinner, two of them were fighting over a manky hotdc on the floor, violently squawking at each other and grappling unt one escaped with the edible phallus, leaving the other with bloo around his beak. Although it could have been tomato ketchup, I' not sure.

I was in Plymouth, a city about as isolated in England as you ca reach, by myself, for the sole purpose of watching Plymouth Argy v Doncaster Rovers, a mid-lower Championship end-of-seaso encounter with no relevance to either the final league table or t my life whatsoever.

Nobody had asked me to go to Plymouth to see a football team have never cared about. I was yet to have anyone read my musing on the previous 88 grounds I had been to this season, or express a interest in publishing it. I was hundreds of miles away, in a place have never been, eating an ice cream on my own.

It shouldn't have made any sense, yet I realised that I was a completely content peace with myself. The finer points of Plymoutl the Hoe, the Barbican, the park, the coastal bars and guest hous provided the backdrop for my epiphany.

It was ridiculous that I was here, it made no sense, but I was totall happy. In four more matches I would have achieved somethir really really difficult. True, watching football isn't exactly horribl but just the fact I was in Plymouth now, always the hardest of m 92, had made me realise I was actually going to do this.

My dreamy, self-congratulatory moment was cut short when a bunch of boisterous looking tracksuit-clad lads walked past me, laughing with each other merrily. Only after a few seconds I realised that it wasn't a bunch of Plymouth chavs out to steal my ice cream, but it was actually Doncaster Rovers Football Club. Towards the back of the group walking along the sleepy promenade were the only two players I recognised, Neil Sullivan (he of 'being lobbed by Beckham' fame) and Darren Byfield (he of 'being married to pop star Jamelia' fame).

"Good work this season fellas, well done on staying up." I said to Sullivan and Byfield popping out of my seat, pretty certain that I had ice cream on my chin.

"Cheers." Sullivan said, nodding appreciatively.

"Off to get some fish and chips?!" I jollily popped up with.

"No. No we're not. Manager wouldn't let us." Sullivan said, shaking his head unappreciatively as they walked off briskly.

But this weekend wasn't about Doncaster, or Neil Sullivan's longing for some chips, it was about Plymouth, the largest city in Europe never to have hosted top flight football. More so than Exeter or the Bristol teams, and possibly even more so than Yeovil, Plymouth Argyle are unmistakeably West Country. The stadium is surrounded by countryside, there is green everywhere, you half expect there to be tractors parked in the V.I.P. car park instead of Bentleys.

I think the West Country identity is mostly to do with the general attitude towards life. At Home Park the people of Plymouth were just so laid back, slow in queues and conversation, taking life easy without much razzmatazz. It's pure West Country. The team are even sponsored by *Ginsters*!

To reach Plymouth Argyle FC's Home Park you walk through the lovely vast park just north of the city, full of kids playing footy, and incorporating a fully fledged funfair (you can actually see the Ferris wheel from the stadium).

The ground has had a couple of stands rebuilt recently so I decided to buy a ticket for the only remaining old one, the splendidly creaky 'Grandstand'. Queuing up (slowly moving beyond belief, but no one seemed bothered, they were too laid-back) I observed the lovely looking club shop, the 'Argyle Retail Village' and admired the

pumping disco classics, 'Ain't No Stopping Us Now' and 'Keep O
Jumpin' providing a groove when queuing for a Plymouth
Doncaster ticket.

I entered the beautiful old turnstiles for the Grandstand and after
trip to the very primitive toilets (a black wall leading down to a rust
drain masquerading as a mass-urinal!) I noticed a Ladbrokes sign.
queued for the grimly predictable trip to the in-ground bookies wit
two sideburned old blokes in front of me.

"What you reckon Nobby? I'm going for Gallagher to score first, an
Argyle to win!"

"Sounds good to me Ken!"

"Here, apparently these bookies ran out of money last week!"

"Last week?! But it was 4-0 at half-time last week!"

"I know! Imagine that eh!"

"I guess Argyle fans are the most positive bunch in the land, a
betting on the 4-0!"

"Too bloody right mate!"

I followed the unparalleled optimism of sideburn Ken and sidebur
Nobby and bet on a thrashing! Come on Argyle!

The pre-match vibe was somewhere between stag-do and children'
birthday party. Either way, everyone was very happy at the prospec
of an approaching Plymouth match. There were kids having wate
pistol fights mixing with groups of hairy men dressed in French Mai
drag outfits (lads on tour) and the odd sideburned fisherman lik
Nobby and Ken.

I took my seat, a very crap slippery seat at a 45° angle that m
bottom kept sliding down. "Please welcome, the best in the wes'
Plymouth Argyle!!!" the announcer said as the teams emerged. ,
true crowd pleaser, he went through the line-ups, ending with "an
as ever, wearing number 12 for Plymouth.....it's you!!!!"

The Plymouth crowd (the green army as they call themselves
weren't exactly the 12th man as such, but they had good reason t
be slightly muted. Oh my. Plymouth were blooming awful. In fac
they were worse than blooming awful. They were *fucking shite*.

Doncaster went ahead through a superbly taken volleyed goal earl
on, and with Plymouth unable to pass, shoot, tackle or (mos
infuriatingly and obvious of all) BEAT THE BLOODY FIRST MAN FROM

A CROSS[1], the South Yorkshire lads looked comfortable, going in 2-0 up at half-time.

I queued in the world's slowest, but least stressful, queue at half-time for my pie, and chatted to a bloke and a girl he had his arm round. Someone they knew came up to them.

"Alright Craig! Bloody hell mate! I didn't recognise you with a white girl on your arm!" he said, pointing at the girl. "Normally go for the blacks don't you!"

Craig awkwardly laughed this off, while the girl carried on chewing her gum nonchalantly. West Country banter I guess!

Doncaster got their inevitable third leaving the Plymouth fans disappointed, but you felt they would shake it off over a cider in the pub, safe in the knowledge they would be safe in the Championship for another year.

I loved Plymouth Argyle. The warm, friendly unique folk of the West Country are probably my favourite people I've encountered across England this year. Be it Plymouth, Exeter, Yeovil or one of the Bristol teams I would love to, in my lifetime of being a football fan, see an unlikely team of farmers mix it in the top league. Because if there's one thing the Premiership needs, it's scrumpy cider, pirate sideburns, and the unmistakeable tractor-driving individuality of our beautiful South West.

PLYMOUTH ARGYLE   0
DONCASTER ROVERS 3 (Spicer 15, Hayter 33, Heffernan 70)
Attendance 11,100

---

[1] Footballers need to sort this out. Seriously! From Premier to League Two, the amount of crosses that tamely hit the first man, it drives me mad! Put a bit of boot behind it lads!

GAME 90
WEST BROMWICH ALBION v Sunderland
Premier League
Saturday 25th April 2009, 3.00pm, The Hawthorns, West Bromwich, West Midlands

Oh golly. I was about to join the '92 Club'! True, I had two more matches in 92 Pies, but I had previously been to both grounds in past seasons. I would now be a member of the only club to attract the crème de la crème of weird football nerds; bespectacled, schedule-learning geeks who can recite the Wimbledon FA Cup winning XI of 1988 without thinking.[1]

As Annabel and I approached the Hawthorns I looked at my West Brom v Sunderland ticket like Charlie did. Charlie who went to that chocolate factory. And had that golden ticket. How Charlie looked at the chocolate factory ticket, not at a West Brom v Sunderland ticket. He was probably a Wolves fan.

I held on to the ticket between my thumb and forefinger, pressing so hard I could feel my pulse in the tips. The tour of 92 football stadiums was approaching its end and I couldn't let it slip now, a gust of wind would ruin it all for me. The ticket could fly out of my vice grip! And the wind was picking up!

"Let's go in the club shop," I said, pushing Annabel towards it hurriedly.

"Okay," said Annabel, "let's guess three things each that you think will be in the shop. I go for alarm clocks, badges and boiled sweets."

"Hmmm....good call. I see your alarm clocks, badges and sweets and raise you baby clothes, reduced old 2009 calendars, and individual player portrait postcards."

Annabel took an early lead upon viewing an alarm clock in the shop window, but I quickly equalised after walking past the 'Baby Baggies' clothes section. Annabel went 3-1 up in quick succession as we

---

[1] Beasant, Goodyear, Phelan, V.Jones, Young, Thorn, Gibson, Cork, Fashanu, Sanchez, Wise. Easy.

approached the tills, leaving my player postcards as merely a consolation in a 3-2 defeat. Gutting.

"I was certain there would be out-of-date calendars."

"It's April Tom! Well I obviously know more about football than you," grinned Annabel.

"Obviously," I said, pretending to not actually be annoyed.

We took our seats surrounded by a friendly bunch including a nice looking Brummie family. When I say nice looking I don't necessarily mean attractive, the Dad had the worst teeth I've ever seen outside the Royal Family. The Sunderland fans were making some decent noise so the little girl and boy did a 'boooooo' and double thumbs-down sign at them. Thumbs-down! Now that's seriously an underused sign.

The wind had died down, the sun was out, and the match kicked off with the West Brom fans nervous about the fate of their team. Sunderland fans were in great voice for the first half hour or so, most of their songs being predictably ungracious about Newcastle's impending relegation.

"Shearer! Shearer! Shearer!" they chanted, along with "You're going down with the Geordies!" directed at the Baggies fans. A draw today would more-or-less condemn West Brom to the dreaded drop and almost ensure Sunderland's safety.

West Brom though had other ideas and produced a performance of some quality, taking the lead in the 40th minute after some lovely fluid passing football.

Toothy McGee in front of us began doing the wanker sign at the Sunderland support. His blue eyed, blonde-pigtailed daughter of about 9 or 10 watched him do this, and then stood on her chair, faced the away end and copied him exactly.

"Wankers!" he heckled.

"Yeah! WANKERS! WANKERS! WANKERS!" the tiny little girl said, doing an unnervingly well-practised wanker hand gesture at the fans. A slight progression from the innocent thumbs-down a mere half hour earlier.

Annabel by this point had tears streaming down her face she was laughing so hard. It was possibly one of the most inappropriate things I've ever seen, but brilliant nevertheless.

Sunderland's best moment came at the end of the first half, when Kieran Richardson's thunderbolt strike was masterfully tipped behind by Super Scott Carson – the England eliminator.

"You've been inCARSONated!" I said for the fifth time, nudging Annabel to see if she still found me amusing. She didn't.

The second half began after a very satisfactory pie, and immediately featured a further improved West Brom, getting another goal through the highly-rated Irishman Chris Brunt.

The noise was deafening. It might have been because they were winning, but I got such a good vibe from the home support. Even Toothy McGee in front of me had a certain rugged, unsuitable-parent charm.

"Steed Malbranque?! More like Steed MalWANK!" Toothy McGee shouted towards the pitch. Good pun Toothy!

"Yeah! Steed Malwank!" his very young pigtailed daughter said.

It was still hilarious. And there was more! West Brom won a pretty generous free kick from the ref. "The referee's a Baggie!" the home fans started singing in good humour.

"Daddy," said pigtails, "that song's normally 'the referee's a wanker' isn't it?"

I had now heard this little girl say the word 'wank' in three different contexts.

Carnival time truly arrived when Menseguez sealed the victory for the Baggies with a beautifully taken third goal in the 88th minute. The cloud of gloom I had experienced over much of the Midlands this season had been lifted. The fans were singing Tony Mowbray's name, and he looked genuinely touched, his wrinkled face gurning into a smile.

"Did it before, we'll do it again!" was the chant as the crowd began to leave, referring to their great escape of 2005.

"Not impossible now!" I said to Toothy and his sweary children, patting him on his back while his daughter continued to give the wanker sign to Sunderland fans. He gave a wide optimistic smile, showing off his yellow and black keyboard teeth, and left me feeling an odd sense of warmth inside on my induction into the 92 club.

WEST BROMWICH ALBION 3 (Olsson 40, Brunt 58, Menseguez 88)
SUNDERLAND   **0**
Attendance 26,256

GAME 91
BRENTFORD v Luton Town
League Two
Saturday 3rd May 2009, 3.00pm, Griffin Park, Brentford, West London

The early May sun was beaming down on platform 2 of Brentford station. John looked excited. His wide smile was infectious.

"It doesn't get better than this T!"

"Last day of the Football League!"

"Brentford to be presented with the League Two trophy!"

"Beautiful sunny day!"

"Just got my £400 bonus from the ski season!" John laughed. "It's going to be a long day."

Yes, it was the final weekend of the Football League. I had thankfully managed to get hold of a couple of tickets for the match I simply *needed* to be at, Brentford v Luton. It was top versus bottom, a final day match up of zero-importance but of maximum excitement.

Brentford had won the league the previous week with a game to spare, and West London was braced for a day jam-packed with glorious celebration. The contrast couldn't be any greater with Luton; sadly relegated a few weeks ago with the 30-point deduction proving too difficult to come back from.

John was back from his ski-season with longer hair, a scruffier beard, and a dry thirst for some lower-league footy. And an even drier thirst for sampling some drinks in each of the four pubs on the corners of Brentford's Griffin Park.

"So what were the highlights of the skiing then?" I asked John, and received an onslaught of tales of debauchery, some funny, some gruesome, some both.

".....and I hope I'll never see *her* again!" finished John. "So, it's come to this then! You've actually nearly finished the whole thing!"

"Yeah, it's an odd one to take in."

"Do you think there will be a pitch invasion?"

"I hope so!" I grinned. Wow, a pitch invasion! That would be something to remember.

I had been to Griffin Park once before, and it was just as lovely as I had remembered it. Popping up as if from nowhere in a nice residential area, it is a beautiful old ground absolutely oozing character, both inside and outside. Indeed I had heard the legend of a pub on every corner, so obviously it was our responsibility, nay, *duty* to check them all out.

(pub #1 – The Griffin)

"This is a nice place!" John said, sipping his Kronenbourg, glorying in a pint in the capital that was less than half the price of a pint in Val D'Isere. We flipped between watching the Man United v Middlesbrough match inside the pub and chopping outside for some power-sunbathing.

The atmosphere was building up tremendously, the crowd of 95% red and white-shirt wearing supporters were increasing by the minute. I don't think I've ever seen a group of football fans more relaxed and content than this. Kids were allowed in the pub which added to the friendly feel of the little place.

(pub #2 – Princess Royal)

"This is a nice place!" John said, sipping his London Pride, glorying in a pint of good English bitter. "So have Brentford been that brilliant this season?" he asked.

"Yeah I think they have. League Two's a competitive division," I said, greeted with a look of 'no it isn't' from John. "Okay, League Two's *quite* competitive. They've gone from strength to strength though. The manager Andy Scott's done a first class job." I said, talking like a bloody lower-league expert.

(pub #3 – The New Inn)

"This is a nice place!" John said, sipping on his double whisky and coke. "Not exactly a summer drink that is it?" I said, sipping my macho fruity cider. Kick-off was approaching. We had been in the pubs for about 3 hours and barely noticed that thousands of fans had descended the area. It was time to enter....

Situated in the Ealing Road Terrace I can honestly say that everything about watching Brentford was an absolute pleasure. True, it was a very good day to see them, but out of the 91 grounds I have been to this season I can't think of a place with a more comfortable atmosphere than today's at Griffin Park. The mixture of the edgier earthier football fan with the families, lone football nerds and drunken neutrals (like me and John) was seamless.

Everything about the club was family friendly, but not in a sanitised 21st Century football club MK-Dons type of way. There were even 1950s-style rattles going off throughout the match, the noise (perhaps just in my mind) resembling a bee.

The game itself was pretty forgettable. Half-time came and John and I realised that we hadn't really been watching it; instead soaking up the atmosphere, the songs, and the funny company. The subs were signing autographs and posing for photos when they were warming up. It was a day for celebration.

We sacrificed the last 5 minutes of the first half to get some more beers, and of course what would be my final *Pukka* pie of the season. Thank the Lord. With greatest respect to the reliable *Pukka* pie, if I never saw another one I would die a happy pie-muncher.

Drinking our beers from behind the terrace I noticed the adverts on top of the opposite stand. Fosters! John Smith's!! Kronenbourg!!! Strongbow!!!! Bulmers!!!!! the row of adverts proudly pronounced (not actually with increasing exclamation marks, that was merely an editorial amendment to exaggerate the drama of the statement).

Brentford are seemingly a club founded on alcohol. The land on which Griffin Park was built was originally owned by Fuller's brewery, and the Griffin in the Fuller's logo is how the ground got its name. Dynamite trivia for a pub-quiz that.

The players were showboating, getting around the beleaguered looking Luton back four with some head tennis. "That's why we're champions! That's why we're champions!" sang the support, right on cue. People were barely watching the game, but rather waiting for the glory of the final whistle. Although saying that, there was an almighty cheer when Brentford took the lead in the 73rd minute.

The terrace was completely rammed. We were right next to the base of the floodlight, so we could actually sit on this big concrete base amongst the supporters packed around us and still see the action well. Full-time was approaching, but there was one last bit of glory in a tremendous season for the bees. In the 89th minute Newton scored an absolute peach; a curling shot from outside the box that was the final nail in the coffin of Luton's season of misery and Brentford's season of joy.

The ref had re-started the game, and the 4th official had put up the board for injury time, but the injury time never came. As soon as the clock hit the 90th minute the fans began the pitch invasion. And what a pitch invasion it was!

Fans were running past John and I towards the pitch. We looked at each other.

"Ready?"

"Ready!"

We sprinted onto the pitch with the other hundreds and hundreds of Brentford fans. The feeling was one of slightly naughty childish glee, running around celebrating, but also one of tremendous football ecstasy (despite neither of us actually being Bees fans of course).

"Championeees championeeesss! Ole Ole Ole!"

We were running up to random fans and hugging them, taking pictures to mark the occasion and glorying in our first ever pitch invasion.

The pitch was eventually vacated as the players and staff went off behind the scenes for what seemed like an age. We had jumped back into a seating stand on the other side of the pitch, as the curved archway-shaped champions podium emerged, along with the players. As a suited gent from the FA handed over the League Two title to Andy Scott, the fireworks went off, and red and white streamers exploded into the air.

"Well J, it might not be the Premier League title, but this is a historic championship winning moment..." I said, patting John's back as the fans began storming the pitch again for the second pitch invasion.

All the right boxes were being ticked now. Shower of confetti? Check. Players wearing silly red afro wigs? Check. Champagne poured over the staff's heads? Check. Players walking around the pitch with their kids on their shoulders, mingling with the fans? Check.

John began chatting to a player who could have been the star man or could have been a reserve team member, as is our lack of knowledge of the Brentford team. But it didn't matter, for during this final pitch invasion, these men were *stars*. I managed to find Andy Scott, looking dapper in a tight grey shirt and trousers, and congratulate him on his achievements.

"Cheers mate, see you next season," he said warmly. I sincerely hope so Andy. Everything about the club and the ground represent what is good about lower-league football in the UK. More than 10,000 people were in to see the 11th biggest club in London today. The beautiful old ground mixes terraces and seating perfectly, has a great charismatic club shop and is in a warm and tight community. I loved Brentford. And long may their rise continue.

"How about that then?" I laughed to John as we walked off the pitch for the final time.

"Haha! Unforgettable! I just can't belief how calm the police and stewards have been with it all today."

The Luton fans were watching the celebrations come to an end, I caught the eyes of some looking forlorn and desperate at their last sight of the Football League. The contrast of the two seasons, Brentford's and Luton's, show why football is the best sport in the world. How can two such different emotions be caused by the same game?

"Look at that sign," laughed John, looking at the scoreboard with 'Keep off the grass' written on it.

With silver streamers in my hair and some stolen Griffin Park grass in my pocket I was in a state of slightly drunken wonder. The 10,000 people were packing the small side streets of the stadium all heading towards the same train station. There was only one logical place to go next.

(pub #4 – the Royal Oak)
The final pub was packed with both Brentford and Luton fans in good spirits.

"I always knew you'd end up doing it." John said, patting me on the back as we sat down on the concrete beer garden outside.

"You liar! Your exact words were 'it's impossible'!"

"Nah I secretly had faith. I remember that once we went to that Dagenham and Redbridge game on the Friday night you were going to end up completing it. Otherwise you would just be some loser going to Dagenham on a Friday night for no reason."

"Well technically that's what you did then isn't it?! Going to Dagenham on a Friday night for no reason?"

"I was giving you moral support."

"Oh I see. Well thanks. But don't get ahead of yourself, I've still got one game left. The car could break down, or I could catch leprosy and be under house arrest."

"We'll see. Seriously though, I'm proud of you mate, well done." John said, putting his sweaty arms around my neck and holding me in a hug.

"QUEERS!" shouted a handful of Luton fans, laughing away.

We broke out of our rare moment of tenderness and awkwardly moved into a manly handshake.

"Another pint you twat?" said John, heading up to the bar.

BRENTFORD   2 (Osborne 73, Newton 90)
LUTON TOWN 0
Attendance 10,223

GAME 92
BOLTON WANDERERS v Hull City
Premier League
Saturday 16th May 2009, 3.00pm, Reebok Stadium, Horwich

It was 3pm Saturday afternoon. *Match-day*. My favourite time of the week.

Across the country hundreds of thousands of people will turn out with friends, families, lovers, drinking buddies, fighting buddies, or by themselves to watch 22 grown men kick a ball around for the sake of entertainment.

For the 75,000 people at Old Trafford today, watching Man United pick up their third successive Premier League trophy against Arsenal it would be an afternoon to never forget. The Football League clubs were dealing with every emotion in the football canon; either coming to terms with relegation, promotion, the impending play-off finals, financial meltdown or mid table mediocrity.

But I was watching *my team*. For the first and final time this season I was sitting with *my* fans. In a match which meant absolutely nothing for the team other than the difference in pride between a 12th and 14th finish in the table. And as Kevin Davies and Johan Elmander kicked off for Bolton Wanderers, I couldn't be happier.

Five hours earlier I was nervous. Why on earth was I nervous? What was I nervous about? I was among family, more specifically my brother Greg and cousin Bri. On a nice scenic train between Manchester and Bolton. Nothing to be nervous about.

"You look terrified," said Greg, munching on his early morning Cheesy Wotsits.

"I know! Why? Why am I nervous?" I asked, chomping on my nails, as if they were Cheesy Wotsits.

"Is it the tickets? All the people coming with us today? The prospect of Bolton v Hull boring everyone in the crowd to slashing their wrists?"

"I don't know, maybe I'm nervous about not making it!"

"T, we're two train stops from the Reebok. And it's 5 hours until kick-off."

"Anything could happen!" I said, paranoid and looking around for a rogue assassin on the train, perhaps another person who had completed the 92 in one season and wanted to get rid of the competition.

"Anyway, we have the pie factory first so chill out. Have a pie."

Oh yes. The pie factory! That was the reason we were heading to the Reebok 5 hours before kick-off. Greenhalgh's Craft bakery, Bolton's match-day pie suppliers, had been in touch with me earlier in the week asking if I would like a tour of their factory before kick-off! To which I said, 'Yes please!'

The train arrived in Horwich Parkway, the station in the Middlebrook retail complex where the Reebok proudly lies. It's not exactly actually *in* Bolton, which was naturally met with often angry scepticism back in 1997 when the ground replaced the wonderful Burnden Park as Bolton's home.

The Reebok is one of the few new stadiums that justifies itself though. Yes it is out of town, yes it is named after an absolute giant of a sporting conglomerate, yes it lacks any of the history that made Burnden Park one of England's most famous grounds. But the design of the stadium is truly spectacular, and one that as a Bolton fan I am proud of.

The curved semi-circle West stand came into view, with the magnificent white poles arching the floodlights towards the pitch. I hadn't been here for over a year, but after visiting 91 strange new places, the Reebok felt like I had returned home.

We got off the train and met David, the bloke from Greenhalgh's Craft bakery; a very large man wearing all white.

"I'm Tom," I said, putting out my hand and receiving a shake that could crush a small child to death. The next couple of hours were probably the most surreal of my life. David drove us to the factory and took us for a guided tour, watching the workers make their bread, cookies and of course pies. We had to wear full white mad-scientist baker's coats and hair nets which was rather amusing. The whole thing was a bit like Willie Wonka's chocolate factory if Roald Dahl's imagination was slightly more realistic and Lancastrian.

With a parting gift of several free-pie tokens for the match (and 3 bags of piping hot pies too) we headed back to the Reebok.

"Well that's something to tick off the to-do-list! Go for a V.I.P. tour of a pie factory!" I laughed, as Greg Bri and I headed to the ground to collect the tickets. I tucked into a very tasty balti pie, when a massive blob of orange balti gloop slopped straight onto my spanking white new shoes that I had *finally* treated myself to.

"You haven't learnt then? After 92 of them I would have thought you'd have mastered the art of eating a pie by now!" said Greg sarcastically. "You did exactly the same in your first game at Charlton you moron."

No I hadn't learnt. They're still impossible to eat. And now my shoe looked stupid with a splodgey orange birthmark on it.

The very kind powers-that-be at Bolton had sorted me out 40 tickets in a block together for the various friends and family I had coming today.

"Hello, I have some tickets put aside for Tom Dickinson please," I asked the lady at the ticket counter.

"Ooooh! Pie man!" she shrieked with star-struck excitement, handing over the tickets, "here you go!"

I should probably explain.

Something odd happened about two weeks earlier.

The bundle of complimentary tickets, the tour of the pie factory, the odd star-struck pie-hungry female...

I had oddly become sort-of mini famous all of a sudden.

In the space of a week I was in most of the national newspapers, Radio 5 Live, Richard and Judy show (where I ate Morecambe's pies with Tito Jackson and Joan Collins – beyond bizarre), BBC website and various local radio and papers. Gosh! I was even being discussed in a gay chatroom. One thought I looked like a 'butch Alan Carr' and another said 'I'd give him a meaty one' (did he mean a pie?).

The best of the lot though was a live interview on BBC One with Bill Turnbull and Kate Silverton on BBC Breakfast. The media did tend to focus on the pies rather than the tremendously difficult and (arguably) fascinating football adventure. But never mind!

My first interview was a phone chat with the Metro, I was on a busy train without preparing for the answers. The reporter asked me the best and worst pie, and off the top of my head I said that Morecambe had the best pie, and Walsall had the worst pie. Mainly because I didn't like Walsall as a club.

For some reason though what I say about pies is now the gospel truth. I was main news on the official Morecambe FC website; *The Shrimpers have won at least one award this season, the best pie award!* And as for Walsall, well they have declared a fatwa against me. I had to explain my comments to the local paper, with the Walsall South MP Bruce George making an official statement about me and defending the pies at Walsall.

This was my favourite thing that has ever happened in my life.

Greg, Bri and I headed to the pub next to the Reebok and grabbed a large table for the incoming masses. It was a fantastic mix of people coming today; mainly those that had been gracious enough to support me in my stupid adventure by coming to games with me along the way.

The first people to arrive, rather brilliantly, were my grandparents, at the same time as some old uni lads including Collo and his hard-as-nails boxer mate Kingy.

"Come this far then la!" said Collo, giving me his signature bear hug.

"Just got to make sure you don't die in the next 2 hours."

"Hahaha," I laughed nervously, keeping an eye out for those rogue assassins.

Familiar faces kept arriving, much to my delight.

"I'm wearing my Chelsea socks today to make me feel better about being here," said Liam, flashing some disgusting blue footwear at me.

Jamie and Duffy arrived over from Liverpool. "Can't believe the only other game we managed to get to was Chester!" said Duffy.

"Oh Chester. That was a poor one wasn't it? They've been relegated now!" I said.

"I won't shed a tear," muttered Jamie.

Every time new people arrived I had to go out and show the man on the gate the match tickets to allow them in, which was becoming a bit of a pain in the arse.

"Anyone who comes up and says they're with Tom Dickinson, just let them through, I've got 40 tickets," I said to the bloke, flashing my tickets.

"Oh are you the pie man?" he asked.

"Yes. I am the pie man."

"Okay, sure."

The Harpenden contingent arrived; 3 cars worth of people including Annabel, my parents and John, who had been drinking in the car since 10am. They arrived and told the bloke on the gate they were with Tom Dickinson, and were swiftly allowed through.

This was my new favourite thing that's ever happened to me. I felt like a rock star.

Annabel greeted me with a kiss, and a fairly sincere "I'm proud of you." And a very sincere "Thank God it's bloody well over now."

Almost everyone was here now.

"Thanks so much for coming folks. I think we've got enough Bolton shirts, scarves and hats from over the years for everyone," I said, distributing my old Bolton stuff between my Man United, Spurs and Chelsea supporting mates.

One more person arrived at this point though. One who certainly didn't need any Bolton gear, as he was already fitted in his 1985/86 home shirt, with the LDV Vans 1989 winners scarf around his neck. It was my Godfather Chris.

The man who got me into football, who pretty much inspired me to do 92 Pies.

The man who was meant to be working in Abu Dhabi!

"You're meant to be in bloody Abu Dhabi!!!" I said, hugging Chris as he came in, and immediately feeling bad for using a mild curse word when describing a strict Muslim city.

"Yeah well I couldn't miss this could I?" said Chris in his thick Bolton accent.

This literally made my day. He had been in cahoots with Dad about meeting at the pub. The sly old bugger. We had a large catch up over double espresso (Chris had left his house in Bournemouth at 6am to get here. That's commitment.) before I rounded up the troops to head into the Reebok.

We all went in and took our 40 seats together, but I had to quickly shoot off to meet a photographer from *The Sun.* He wanted a picture of me with a pie, so we went up to the food counter and I produced one of my Greenhalgh's tokens. The girl looked at me blankly.

"Sorry we don't accept tokens."

"I don't think you understand, I was personally given these by the man that is in charge of making the pies! They're *his* pies!" I protested.

"We don't accept tokens."

"Bollocks to this, I'm in a hurry," Dan the photographer said, handing over a couple of quid for a chicken and mushroom one. We headed out into the arena and he plonked the pie in my hand.

"Can you take the foil off? It'll look better," he asked. I took the foil off and had the piping hot, just cooked pie in my palm.

"Now smile!" he said, snapping away. The pie was literally burning my hand. All my group were laughing and cheering!

"Wheeey pie man, give us a wave!" Ali heckled.

"I think the skin on my hand is burning!" I said through smiling teeth. As soon as he had finished the photos I chucked the boiling pie on the floor.

"I never really liked chicken and mushroom much anyway." I said.

With my fingerprints possibly no longer existing, I took my place next to Chris.

"You didn't tell me you were going to be in the programme T!" he said with a hint of pride in his voice. I had done an interview with the Bolton programme, and they had put me in with a double page spread. There I was, grinning away with pictures of me at Burnley, Newcastle, Arsenal, Accrington and Darlington! Looking a bit like a butch Alan Carr in most of them.

There was enough excitement going on to last me a lifetime, but in the midst of it all there was a football match kicking off. Yep! Bolton v Hull. Hull needed some kind of result; it was looking like being between them and Newcastle for the final relegation spot.

Bolton kicked off to rapturous applause. Lofty the Lion was running around the pitch like a lion possessed. The fans were in good voice; I was leading the chants, as my loved ones joined in the 'We're the one and only Wanderers' song. Jamie Duffy and John were amusing themselves with the Bolton clappers handed out, mainly smacking each other with them. Even more exciting than this, Bolton took the lead in the 26th minute through the hard-arse Icelandic right-back Gretar Steinsson. Get in!

Many funny chants, laughs and jokes later it was the second half, and Hull immediately equalised through Fagan after a horrible slip by Danny Shittu. This didn't stop the fans singing his special 'Mary Poppins' song though;

"Shit Shitty Shit Shitty Shit Shit Sheroo! Who needs Cahill, we've got Danny Shittu!"

Bolton weren't very good today; most of the squad aren't up to the job. How I long for an Okocha or Djorkaeff type figure back at the Reebok!

Enough boo-hooing though. I know my place as a Bolton fan. Lower mid-table is OK for the moment. Looking at the likes of Leeds, Southampton, Norwich and Charlton I'll take mediocrity over a complete collapse any day.

The match finished 1-1, not a classic but not awful either. The former Bolton favourite Phil Brown came over to clap the Hull fans, who were pretty magnificent today.

I thanked the folk who came along, as they slowly frittered back to their corners of the country, most of whom would probably not go to another football game with me for a very long time.

It dawned on me.

I had been to every one of the 92 Football League grounds in one season.

I watched the Bolton fans pour back into their cars and to the train station. They wouldn't go back to the Reebok until August. The football season was nearly over. I felt an amazing sense of satisfaction, but also a little bit lost.

John and I got in the car with my Dad driving us back to sunny Harpenden.

"It's time John," I said to my loyal friend who had supported me throughout the journey.

"Time for what?"

"Time for you to admit that Sam Allardyce is a misunderstood tactical genius."

John looked devastated. He had thought I had forgotten the bet. I hadn't. He took a deep inhalation. The Reebok Stadium was still in the backdrop of my vision.

"Sam Allardyce is a misunderstood tactical genius." John said, swallowing his pride. I felt magnificent.

"So next year," continued John, changing the subject, "how about we do every national stadium in the world?"

"That's about 200 grounds John."

"Okay, every league champion in every European country?"

"That's a lot too. Would that include Monaco? And Vatican City? Does Vatican City have a football team?"

"I'd like to think they do. Okay, how about we try and track down every member of the Croatian 1998 World Cup squad and see what they're up to?"

"No."

"Every non-league ground in England?"

"No."

"Drink a *pint of beer* at every pub in England?"

"I think you have an alcohol problem."

"I think you have a football problem." John laughed.

I do indeed have a football problem. I'm absolutely 100% addicted. But I don't want to be cured.
Ever.

Just don't show me a bloody pie for the next couple of years.

92 Clubs
92 Grounds
92 Games
92 Pies
1 Season
1 Satisfied football fan ☺

BOLTON WANDERERS 1 (Steinsson 26)
HULL CITY **1** (Fagan 47)
Attendance 25,085

MY LISTS

MY TOP 5 PIES

1. MORECOMBE The daddy of all pie-makers, Pott's Pies, provide the perfect mix of piping-hot meaty goodness and crisp pastry.

2. DARLINGTON A bakery-style set-up that defies the club's financial woes. And some of the cheapest food in the football league.

3. NORWICH CITY Delia Smith inspired grub baked with love. Keep your eye peeled for the legendry 'pie of the week'.

4. WIGAN ATHLETIC Thick and generous Pooles Pies, a true chunk of Wigan in pastry form.

5. HARTLEPOOL The suffix of 'award winning' is plastered in front of the steak pies, and you can see why.

MY WORST PIE

WALSALL Cold and stodgy, a lame effort from the 'pie pioneers'.

BEST MATCH

1. Huddersfield Town 3-4 Port Vale
2. Burnley 3-2 Tottenham Hotspur
3. Hartlepool United 5-3 Huddersfield Town
4. Peterborough United 5-4 Bristol Rovers
5. Derby County 2-1 Sheffield United

BEST FANS

1. Derby County
2. Bristol City
3. Burnley
4. Swansea City
5. Brentford

BEST MASCOT

By a county mile Chaddy the Owl at Oldham;a mooning, brawling, cheeky, interfering hero.

WORST MASCOT

Tied 1st place: Wycombe's creepy ginger weirdo and Macclesfield's pathetic lazy lion.

BEST CHANTS

1. 'We only sing when we're fishing'- Grimsby's fishy elite
2. 'We're all swearing in the family stand...Bollocks' - Bury fans in the family stand.
3. 'You're going down with the Hereford' - Hereford fans towards the Brighton end.
4. 'Oh I'd rather be a farmer than a chav' - Yeovil fans.
5. 'We like fluffy sheep oh we like fluffy sleep' - Swansea's patriotic support.

LEAST CHARMING STADIUM

1. Kenilworth Road - LUTON TOWN
2. Bescott Stadium - WALSALL
3. The Diva Stadium - CHESTER CITY
4. The New Meadow - SHREWSBURY TOWN & The Weston Homes Community Stadium - COLCHESTER UNITED (they merge into one for me!)
5. The DW Stadium - WIGAN ATHLETIC

MY FAVOURITE CLUBS - Go and see them!

1. Brentford
2. Exeter City
3. Aldershot Town
4. Bury
5. Yeovil Town
6. Fulham
7. Bradford City
8. Grimsby Town
9. Everton
10. AFC Bournemouth

ACKNOWLEDGEMENTS

This ludicrous project wouldn't have come close to existing without the continued love and support of Annabel Burrows and my parents, Fiona and Matt Dickinson. Thanks gang.

Many thanks to all those who sorted me tickets, gave me a bed for the night, helped boost my publicity and kindly accompanied me to some (often rubbish) football matches.
Ali Dickinson, Greg Dickinson, Steph and Rupert Hunter, my Grandparents, Paul Collins, John Barker, Paul Stairmand, Liam Klimek, Robbie Redway, Adam Duffy, Jamie Clayton, Lizzie Burch, Faye Blaisdale, Nicola Thompson, Tim Crutchley, Mark Klimek, Patricia Burrows, Amber Burrows, Stuart Fuller, Russ Walsh (buy Potts Pies!), and most importantly Chris Bradley, without whom I would probably be writing a book about train-spotting or tiddlywinks.

And finally a gracious thank you to Matt Smith and Blackline Press for making 92 Pies come to life.

Visit www.92pies.co.uk for more pictures, stats, fun and frolics, including my '93rd' pie at Wembley.

ABOUT THE AUTHOR

Tom Dickinson was born in 1986 in Hertfordshire, but pressured into supporting Bolton Wanderers from a young age. He went to the University of Liverpool and studied Politics, but still doesn't really know the difference between the voting systems. He can however name you every FA Cup final goal-scorer in reverse order back to 1990.

He lives in Clapham, South London with his flatmates and the uninvited house mouse Algernon.

ALSO AVAILABLE FROM BLACKLINE PRESS

CHANGING ENDS
A Season in Non League Football
By Mike Bayly

Over the course of the 2009-10 season the author embarks on a journey around the country taking in various non league games, in an attempt to document the thoughts and motivations of those who aren't part of football's financial revolution. Taking a light hearted yet informative 'diary of a season' approach, the book aims to review the trials and tribulations of non league football and its role in a sport dominated by an elite few. Woven into this is a study of wider contemporary issues, such as London APSA - the country's leading semi-professional Asian team - through to AFC Liverpool - the fan owned club started as an alternative for supporters priced out of top flight football.

Is football still the people's game? This book delves beneath the surface to find out.

"Compellingly and cleverly crafted" *NORTHERN VENTURES NORTHERN GAINS*

THE REAL TRACTOR BOYS PLAYING AWAY
On tour with Suffolk's non-league football clubs
By Matt Smith

In 2008 I started out on a journey to watch a game at every senior non-league football ground in Suffolk. I kept a diary and in early 2009 THE REAL TRACTOR BOYS was published. I enjoyed the experience so much, I decided to get on the road and watch every Suffolk club again, but this time playing away from home - outside of the county.

Nine months and almost 2500 miles later I completed my tour. I watched a pre-season friendly in Kent, an FA Cup replay in Bedfordshire, a penalty shoot-out in Essex, a 9-0 thrashing in Norfolk and a penalty-taking goalkeeper in Cambridgeshire. This is my diary.

"You won't want to put this fine book down quickly" *EAST ANGLIAN DAILY TIMES*

ORDER NOW @ www.blacklinepress.com